D1567339

Building Craft Equipment

Building Craft Equipment

An Illustrated Manual

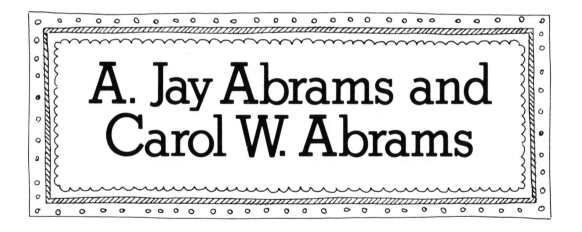

A. Jay Abrams and Carol W. Abrams

Praeger Publishers   New York

Published in the United States of America in 1976
by Praeger Publishers, Inc.
111 Fourth Avenue, New York, N.Y. 10003

Library of Congress Cataloging in Publication Data

Abrams, A   Jay.
        Building craft equipment.

        Bibliography: p.
        1. Handicraft—Equipment and supplies.
2. Woodwork.   I. Abrams, Carol W., joint
author.   II. Title.
TT153.7.A27   745.5′028   74-30992
ISBN 0-275-51950-3
ISBN 0-275-89600-5 pbk.

Printed in the United States of America

1-20-11 Baker 8.22

Dedicated
to Jean and Jim Young
for whom thanks is not enough

CONTENTS

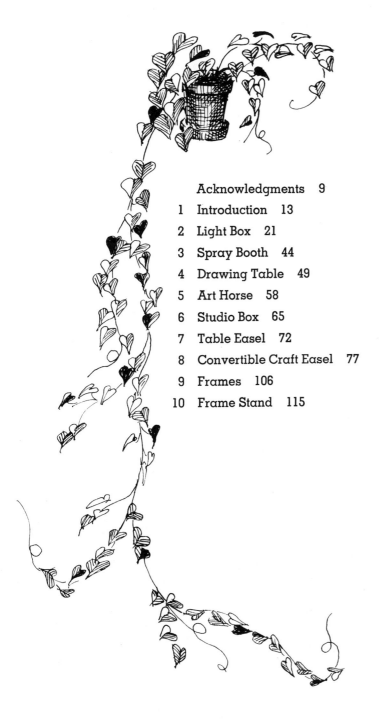

ACKNOWLEDGMENTS

In preparing this book we have had the benefit of knowing and working with persons whose contributions, guidance, and inspiration have made the experience of doing it joyful and the task rewarding. We are particularly grateful to our editor, Allan Edmands, whose spirited and conscientious participation provided inestimable help in the preparation of the final manuscript. We are also indebted to Mel Pickhardt for providing technical know-how on a number of projects—notably the electric table kiln and potter's wheel—to John Walker for his studio-box design, to editors Ellyn Childs Allison and Cherene Holland, to designer Gilda Kuhlman, and to John H. Gilchrist for reading the manuscript and providing constructive criticism, to Lee Anne and Fred for consultation, to Ken Russell for checking the figures, and to Belle Abrams whose typing at four o'clock in the morning can still be heard on quiet autumn nights in Woodstock. To each, our thanks. And to others unmentioned, much appreciation.

We would also like to acknowledge the courtesy extended us by Woodstock Building Supply and Fowler and Keith Hardware during repeated inquiries about tools and materials.

Building
Craft
Equipment

1·INTRODUCTION

I never built anything until I was twenty-two, mostly because I never thought to build anything. This coupled with the fact that, whenever I sought to begin any kind of project, my father would come along, in bow tie and plaid sports shirt, and supervise until I lost all interest in completing the job. The follow-up was always the same: "You never finish anything" and "Remember to pick up all the tools and put them back where you found them." From the outset I was raised to feel that, if I were to enter a trade that required the skilled use of my hands, I would starve.

But at the age of twenty-two I finally began to lose faith in the credibility of these observations. As is the case of many, my first successes in building things were scored making bookshelves. And so I made a lot of them (figure 1-1). Whole walls of bookshelves spread throughout our not-really-large-enough-to-support-so-many home in Rockland County, New York.

fig.1-1

And I looked at the shelves, and I saw they were good. But, my God, had I made that many? Alas, there was room for no more. But what else could I build? Now that I had come that far, I knew I couldn't just stop. Of course, my experience was still rather limited. Until that point, everything that I had constructed was made of plywood and pine shelving boards, tacked together with finishing nails. Knowing I could get that far, however, gave me the faith that I might go farther and build things with other, more complicated structures, using different materials. About that time Carol was getting really involved with crafts, but, sadly, our budget didn't match her enthusiasm. Needless to say, the cost of materials was high, and equipment was completely out of sight. At first the idea of building craft tools didn't even cross my mind. But then I began to look around, and what I saw triggered my imagination. Craft tools, by and large, were made of wood just like my bookshelves. And although some tools, such as floor looms, appeared to be quite complicated, I realized, when I looked at them carefully, that breaking them down into their simpler elements made it easier to understand just how they had been put together. All tools after all are people-made; therefore it's quite logical to think that, with some effort, a person could understand even their most subtle aspects.

I started with simple things, which matched—at least to some extent—the level of my achievement. And quickly I found myself becoming involved with increasingly difficult things. Though my errors were by no means infrequent, the feedback that I got from seeing myself doing this kind of work, coupled with the sheer pleasure of using a piece of equipment that I alone had built to my own specifications, provided the staying power. In fact, when it came to the convertible craft easel, it took three bad starts to finally come up with a workable unit. And of course, there was the vast array of minor annoyances that I kept confusing with major stumbling blocks. Every time I split a piece of lumber with a wood screw that was just a bit too large, I would wonder if the whole project was realistic. But persevere, persevere, persevere. Mistakes are part of what it's all about, and a lot of learning goes on when they happen. Fortunately for you, you've got this book to help you out. While having it is by no means a guarantee that you won't run into problems, the fact that I've gotten to at least some of them first means that you will be able to avoid making the mistakes that I did.

What we've done is collected together all the designs and building procedures for all of the tools that we've made for ourselves and others, and we've added a few that friends of ours have put together so that we can provide you, the reader, with a selection of things to make that have already been tried out. It is by no means necessary that you follow all of the instructions that we give without variation. In fact, as you read through, you may well find steps that you will choose to omit or substitute with a different procedure you feel will result in a superior product. I'm sure it's that very process that is responsible for much of the variation in design that already exists on the craft-equipment market. And, of course, tailoring what you make to you is one of the big pluses in making it yourself. If some of the commercially available products are unsuitable for the way you work, you can always take that into account when you're putting your own together and avoid the perennial battle that would otherwise have ensued. After all, a tool that's marketed commercially is designed to appeal to the majority, and you may well not fit that description (figure 1-2).

We've found that making and using our own things add a new kind of dimension to what we do. We feel an overall connectedness with the

fig 1-2

components in our studio that is difficult to put into words. And the basic familiarity that we have with all the working parts takes most of the guess-work out of making adjustments and repairs.

One good way to use this book is as a kind of catalogue of ideas. Just sit down in your favorite chair, open it up, and look around. It just may be that the experience of doing this over a period of time will lead you to the workshop with an idea of your own that you'd like to play with, or perhaps with a variation of one of ours. We've tried to make browsing simple. In fact, we'd recommend it even if you already have a specific project in mind. Get to know how we've broken things down. For instance, scan the notes in the margin. They can give you a good idea of what's involved in building a project from the beginning. Also study the illustrations. Much effort has gone into making these clear so that you needn't rely upon your powers of visuali-zation to get you through. Maybe you've never thought of building a spool rack, or a table hoop stand, or a potter's wheel. But maybe, once you've looked those chapters over, you'll give it some thought. It's amazing what you can do with basic materials, a little time, and some guidance. Take it from us, it really does work. There's no doubt that if we hadn't made the things ourselves, we would have only a fragment of the resources that are currently at ready access to us (figure 1-3).

fig.1-3

For your convenience when you're actually in the process of building along with us, use the marginal notations to help you find your place on the page and to aid you in identifying the steps you don't feel that you have to read. Some of what's included may be familiar enough to you that you will feel competent to do the work from the illustration(s) alone or even com-pletely unaided.

To avoid being too repetitious, we've decided to cover some of the basic issues and details of techniques, tools, and materials in this chapter. This way if you have any questions about what you'll need or how to do something that is not fully described in the chapter you're working from, then you'll know that you'll probably find it right here.

As far as tools for making tools go, we've made a real effort to minimize the necessity for using the electric-powered variety. This is not to say that we think that using them isn't a good idea. Quite to the contrary, if you have them, of course use them. They can save both effort and time. However, because so many people, particularly those who haven't done much in the way of woodworking, may only have access to the hand variety, we wanted to be certain to account for this. In putting together a good working tool kit you'll need a number of basics (figure 1-4):

hammer
nail set (punch)
handsaw
coping saw (for internal cutting)
hacksaw
hand drill and bits (primarily for smaller holes)
brace and bits (for holes of larger diameter)
screwdrivers (assorted sizes for different-size screws)
pliers
long-nosed pliers (for reaching hard-to-get-at places)
plane
right angle (carpenter's square)
try square
straight edge (a metal ruler can be most useful)

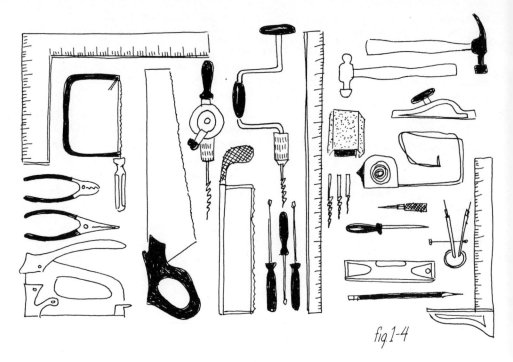

fig. 1-4

level
awl
pencil
flex tape
compass
sandpaper block
staple gun

By and large, they're the kinds of things that would ordinarily be found in a household tool kit, and with the complete set you'll be ready to build any project that we've described.

When choosing the specific materials that you want to use, we definitely advise flexibility. Many times you can find just what you need in a pile of otherwise scrap wood. In fact, that's one of our favorite sources. Usually with just a bit of trimming and a few dimensional adjustments we can find almost all that we need right behind our shed (figure 1-5). Of course, if you don't have a shed or, for that matter, a pile of scrap wood, then you may have to go to the lumber yard. But here, too, be flexible. Wood comes in several grades, and, depending on the kind of finishing off that you're planning on doing, you should select one that's suitable. If, for example, the plan calls for 1×3's, you have at least two options. Assuming that you're not going to be bothered by the presence of a few knots or some rough edges, furring strips would be the most economical solution. If, on the other hand, you have a satiny furniture finish in mind, a decent grade of pine board might well be in order. Plywood, too, offers a number of options. The least expensive form of this material is construction grade (CDX) or plyscore. It's rough on both sides but comes in a choice of thicknesses—most commonly ⅜ and ⅝ inch. Here again, if you're not interested in aesthetics, this stuff will most certainly do the job. However, where appearance does matter, you can save by buying plywood that's finished on only one side. Take some time before going to the lumber yard and decide on just what it is that you want and how much you need. That way, you will tend to neither overbuy nor underbuy.

fig 1-5

In our instructions we have made a point of giving the actual size of the material that's needed. This means that, if you want, you can save time and effort by having the lumber yard cut things to size. Typically this involves some additional expense, but unless you're equipped to do the cutting at home—this can be particularly bothersome with 4- by 8-foot sheets—it's well worth the investment (if you've got the money to invest).

One thing that you really should keep in mind when you're at the lumber yard, list in hand and ready to buy, is that in the building-materials business not all things are as they appear. Lumber in particular is a most noteworthy example. When a 1×1 is what you ask for, you'll get a piece of wood with actual measurements more like $\frac{3}{4} \times \frac{3}{4}$, and that's the way it is for all of them: 2×2 is really $1\frac{1}{2} \times 1\frac{1}{2}$, $\frac{5}{4} \times 3$ is $1\frac{1}{8} \times 2\frac{1}{2}$, and 4×4 is actually $3\frac{5}{8} \times 3\frac{5}{8}$. Fortunately, we've taken all this into account when giving you dimensions to follow. But keep it in mind if you intend to strike out on your own.

In some chapters we've made reference to a material called *particle board*. Like plywood it can be found in 4- by 8-foot sheets, in thicknesses that are in the same kind of range. Unlike plywood it is not composed of several thin layers of wood all glued together but is, rather, made up of numerous wood shavings or particles—therein its name. It, too, is a rather strong material good for use as a plywood substitute and at a somewhat lower cost. If you're going to be using it, plan on doing your cutting with a sharp saw blade, and take care not to bang the corners (they do tend to break off).

Another item that we mention a number of times is T nuts, and it's good to know something more about them. Physically they are metal cylinders threaded on the inside and joined at one end with a flat surface from which long points are extended (figure 1-6). Their purpose is to provide threads in holes through which bolts are to be passed, thereby eliminating the need for conventional nuts. Installation is an easy matter of tapping the cylindrical part of the T into the hole so that the pointed extensions from the flat surface penetrate the wood, giving the nut a firm grip.

fig 1-6

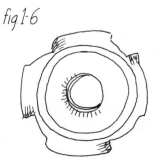

As you read through our materials lists, you will observe that bolts and screws are used with far greater frequency than nails. This is because they give more rigidity to the structure while at the same time allowing you to

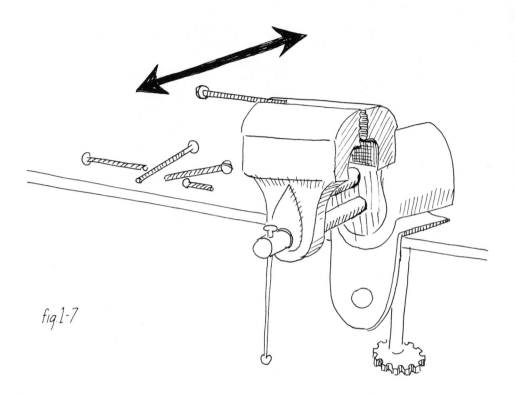

fig. 1-7

disassemble if necessary. However, bolts in particular are rather expensive. If you're at all like us, you already have several in assorted sizes, no two being the same length and most of which tend to be too long (figure 1-7). Well, if you're also in possession of a hacksaw—and we've already suggested that you should be—you might consider cutting them down to size. Actually a vise would be a big help in doing this, but a clamp can be used as a not perfect, but better than nothing, substitute. With long, easy strokes most bolts can be shortened with relative ease.

Be careful, especially when sawing, not to get things in your eyes. Get into the habit of wearing goggles or safety glasses. This is not an easy thing to get used to doing; however, saving your eyes is important enough to make going to the trouble worthwhile.

Work gloves are another good idea, particularly whenever materials like glass or potentially irritating chemicals are involved. Here again the habit of wearing them takes time to acquire—and it may be that you feel such precautions are unnecessary—but once you've gotten the habit, you won't regret it (figure 1-8).

One procedure that is basic to several of the projects is that of starting wood screws. For the longest time I thought that the only way to do it was to mark my spot with a pencil, locate the point of the screw on it, bear down on the screwdriver, and drive it in. Well, that's the hard way. Not only will you be working unnecessarily, but chances are that you'll wind up destroying the heads of most of your screws. The easy way is to make a pilot hole, that is, a hole smaller in diameter than the shank of the screw you're using. If you're working with soft wood, you'll be able to make one that's adequate using your awl. If you can't get your awl in, then the wood you're using is hard, and drilling is the best way to do the job. Just be sure that the hole

fig. 1-8

you make isn't too large. To help you in selecting the proper bit for the purpose, we've included charts, one matching screw sizes with appropriate bit sizes, and the other (a British variation) matching gauge sizes with hole sizes—given as fractions and decimal equivalents.

Screw size	Bit size
0	1/64
1	1/32
2	1/32
3	3/64
4	3/64
5	1/16
6	1/16
7	1/16
8	5/64
9	5/64
10	3/32
11	3/32
12	7/64
14	7/64
16	9/64
18	9/64
20	11/64
24	3/16

Use a slightly larger bit for hard wood.

	Hole	
Gauge	Inch decimal size	Inch fractions
0	0.060	1/16
1	0.075	5/64
2	0.095	5/64
3	0.095	3/32
4	0.110	7/64
5	0.125	1/8
6	0.140	9/64
7	0.155	5/32
8	0.175	11/64
9	0.185	3/16
10	0.200	13/64
12	0.220	7/32

Exact drill sizes need not be followed closely, and in any case are variable in accordance with the kind of wood being screwed. Hard woods generally need a larger thread hole than soft woods.

Also, to facilitate the finding of the right sizes in screws, as well as nails and bolts, we've included figure 1-9 to show you what they look like.

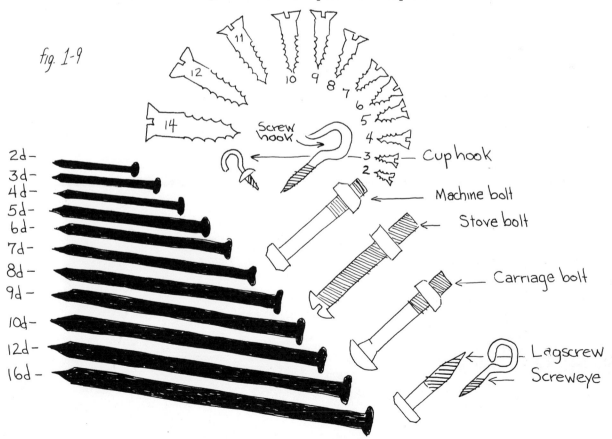

fig. 1-9

This way, if you happen to have some nails, screws, and bolts lying around in a mayonnaise jar or coffee can somewhere, you will be able to tell just how many you already have and what you'll need to buy.

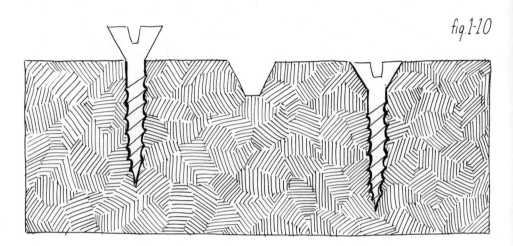

fig. 1-10

Another good thing to know about is countersinking. This is a way of making the heads of flatheaded wood screws disappear. When you look carefully at flatheads, you'll find that the heads themselves are tapered to the screw shank, thereby forming a kind of cone. Countersinking involves nothing more than making a basin for that cone to rest in so that the screw when tightened will not stick above the surface of the wood. While there are countersinking tools specifically intended for this purpose (usually fitted into a drill chuck), the same effect can be achieved by simply enlarging the opening of the hole with a knife and smoothing it with sandpaper (figure 1-10). While the results may not be as clean, they are nevertheless adequate for the purpose.

And lastly, develop a good working relationship with the person in your local hardware store. Usually he's the kind of person who's been raised with such expressions as "ten-penny nail" and "screw-tipped auger," and will willingly share what he knows—which is typically a great deal more than anyone else in the neighborhood—in exchange for an audience for his favorite fishing story. And of course, if you've got such a hardware store man, treat him with extra care because he's a member of an endangered species (figure 1-11). With the growing popularity of the discount-grocery approach to the hardware business, it may be just a matter of time before the last favorite fishing story is spun.

fig. 1-11

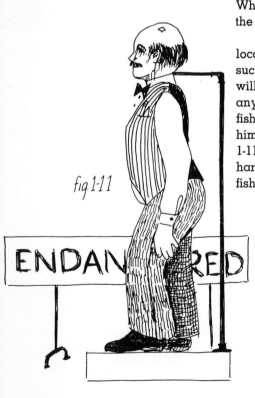

ENDAN ~~GE~~ RED

2·LIGHT BOX

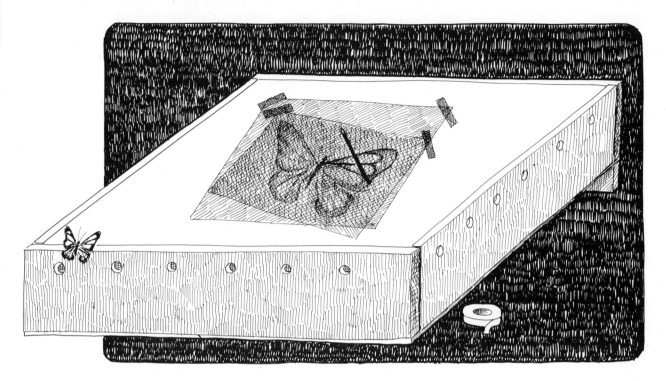

Once upon a time, in the days when we had not yet discovered the light box, pattern transfer was a tedious bore. Regardless of what we used or where we did it, there were always accompanying annoyances. Certain techniques were definitely more acceptable than others, but the various and sundry discomforts that these methods involved made them less than a delight to anticipate. Somehow the thought of standing at the drafty studio window in the middle of one of those picture-book January snowstorms trying to get masking-tape rings to hold a precious original to the frosty glass just wasn't appealing. One day a close friend of ours, a painter by trade, happened along and witnessed our dilemma. She was most sympathetic, having undergone a similar experience, and suggested that we try using a light box. Realizing that we had none available to us, she volunteered one of her own. We accepted gratefully, and, in short order, the unit was in our studio. Its drawing surface couldn't have been any more than 9 by 12 inches, and it was made entirely of plastic. It was lit by a single incandescent bulb that had to be turned off intermittently during use to permit the unit to cool. It was the kind of thing that you would probably get if you answered one of those "be an artist instantly" advertisements found in the backs of most popular magazines, among such other items as Dr. Simeon's False Moustache Paste and Foot Deodorizing Salve and Mother Burdette's International Correspondence Institute for Rainmaking Arts and Sciences. Well, we tried it, and we were delighted with what it could do.

The light box is a wonderful craft tool. Its uses are many and varied. With it all kinds of pattern-transfer and layout problems can be greatly simplified. Whether you're going to cut a stencil, convert the subject of an old photograph into a pattern for an unusual piece of mosaic, needlepoint, or stained glass, or compose a design for some other application, like making a quilt or decorating a ceramic pot, you'll find that a light box can not only save you time but actually stimulate creative energy. With it you can borrow from what has already been done, either as a whole or in part, and combine it and recombine it with anything else that feels right to open up scores of exciting new possibilities. You'll be able to better visualize the potential product of your efforts as you're designing it, adding and subtracting elements at will without wasting valuable materials.

The principle of the light box is a simple one to experience. Find a piece of paper with something on it—your telephone bill, a cherished family recipe for down-home dark bread, or a quick sketch of someone you saw reading *Crime and Punishment* on the Lexington Avenue subway. Place a blank piece of paper over it and hold both up to a sunny window. You will be able to see through the empty sheet to the marked one beneath. The effect is the same as if you were using a sheet of tracing paper as the top piece. By simply following the contours of the marks with a pencil, you can transfer the pattern onto the blank surface. With a sufficiently bright light source you can make accurate transfers from extra-heavyweight papers to extra-heavyweight papers or other materials. A light box provides the evenly illuminated drawing surface for just this kind of work, and it is certainly far more convenient than your typical window in terms of portability, availability of light on a twenty-four-hour-a-day basis, and angle of work surface.

There are several ways to build a light box. The features that you should include in yours depend both on the way you work and the kind of work that you do. Being able to fashion a tool that meets your own personal specifications is part of the advantage of making it yourself. If you would like to work on a flat surface, then make it that way. If, instead, you prefer working on a slightly tilted surface, the opportunity is here to make it that way. You can also choose the size of the work surface and, in fact, the size of the whole unit. It's up to you to determine whether your light source will be fluorescent or incandescent, how much light you'll have to work with, and how much control you'll have over it. These decisions are very important, so choose carefully. After all, it's your tool and you have to live with it.

The dimensions given are based on the size of our own light box, which has proven to be an extremely fine, flexible tool. If you think it's too big or too small, simply adjust the dimensions to suit your needs, remembering to make appropriate proportional adjustments throughout.

The working surface of the basic light box described here is flat. This is particularly useful in situations where you will be arranging several items into compositions and it would be impractical to have to tape the parts down to the surface. Also, if you are working with particularly runny liquids or small tools that would inevitably tend to roll or slide off a tilted surface, then this design would probably be best for you. Of course, many people do prefer working on a tilt. The principal advantage here is accessibility. You don't have to bend or stretch quite so much as with a flat box to get to the far end of the work surface. And this can be awkward, particularly when your box is large. Also, if you find it difficult to visualize things when they are flat, a tilt can be a definite asset. We have, therefore, included a technique for tilting the unit so that you can decide for yourself what will best accommodate your work situation.

The four sides of the box are made of wood. We used ½-inch, construction-grade plywood for our first light box, and it's still in good shape. But construction grade is pretty rough stuff, neither face being finished. If you decide to use it, be certain to watch for splinters. Most lumberyards will insist on selling you no less than a full 4- by 8-foot section, and you will, no doubt, wind up with more than you need for this project. Therefore, if you anticipate building a few things, each calling for some plywood, plan ahead and bring all of the dimensions with you. For a small charge, you can have the whole piece cut up at once. This will not only reduce the amount of heavy work you'll have to do later but also make the ride home in your small foreign sports car an easier matter. And another thing, in joining the ½-inch plywood sections, we found it absolutely necessary to strengthen all corners with metal braces. If splinters, leftover wood, and braces don't appeal to you, there are a number of other options; ¾-inch plywood finished on one side or pine shelving board will certainly do the job. In fact, we will be describing the construction of a box using ¾-inch plywood, based on our experience building what we consider to be our finest light box.

Plan on using double-strength glass as the work surface of your light box to provide the needed durability. Or—if you're always dropping things like scissors, brayers, spray cans, or hand-painted Japanese teacups—consider using Plexiglas instead. For the bottom of the box, we're suggesting a piece of Masonite if you're using incandescent lighting, or ¾-inch ply if you've decided on fluorescents.

Remember, before going shopping, check and see what you already have. If it seems to fit the specifications, don't hesitate to use it. After all, isn't that what you've been saving it for?

If you're like us, you will learn what your specific requirements are through trial-and-error experience. And you'll discover solutions to insurmountable problems quite by accident. One example from our experience will suffice:

Typically, one of the most bothersome things about homemade light boxes is the presence of a molding lip around the perimeter of the glass surface. We installed one on our first light box. The glass on the box was really secure, except for some slipping back and forth when the box was tilted up. The disadvantage was that it was impossible to comfortably use paper, straight edges, or anything else that exceeded the dimensions of the glass itself. For example, we were unable to use our metal yardstick on that box because the glass surface only measured 24 inches. There was just no way to lay it flat over the work. Instead, it would rest on the elevated molding. Also, that ridge of molding was physically uncomfortable to work with since it engraved reddened linear depressions on our arms soon after either of us would sit down to work. When you design any craft tool, it's always important to consider how comfortable the tool is going to be to work with when you've completed it.

There are various ways to install glass onto light boxes. Because of the potential discomforts just described, the molding method is not among our favorites. Some of our friends have chosen not to make use of any fastening technique whatever. They insist that it is as practical for their purposes to simply lay the glass in place and let gravity keep it down. The advantage over moldings is one of comfort while working. Also, you can get to the bulbs by removing the glass. However, one big problem is that you will have to be mindful of the glass's rather tentative mounting whenever you move the box from one place to another. If you won't be using it for extended periods and you want to get it out of the way by storing it on its side, you have to remove the glass and accommodate it separately for its safe storage.

Therefore, we heartily recommend that to permanently affix the glass to your box you use aquarium cement. It's perfect. It adheres well to glass, forming a strong bond. It can be purchased at any pet-supply shop, and its cost is low enough to make it practical to use. A friend of ours, an aquarium builder with several elaborate aquariums to his credit, is responsible for our discovery of this great stuff. One evening last spring, he invited us over to see his then most recent piece of work. This proud, tank-building craftsperson anxiously led us downstairs into his darkened cellar workshop. With the clicking sound of a switch, the wall was filled with light. And there it stood —a mammoth tank filled with silver dollars and a hefty *Corydoras hastatus* catfish. As we looked, we noticed that only one face of the tank was actually glass. The others were plywood coated with resin. We noticed also that the huge piece of glass did not appear to be held in place by any molding whatever. We craft-tool makers sensed that something about this was to be of great importance to us—*aquarium cement!* Why hadn't we thought of that before?

The following day we spent behind the shed looking for the raw materials for a new light box. There was little doubt in either of our minds that the time had come to build an improved model, based upon our revelation of the night before. Since we had already constructed one, this new box went faster. But the greatest time-saver of all proved to be the aquarium cement.

ASSEMBLY

INCANDESCENT BOX

Wood

Quantity	Material	Cut to	Description
2 sections	¾-inch plywood	4 by 24 inches	front and back walls
2 sections	¾-inch plywood	4 by 22½ inches	side walls
1 length	½-inch quarter-round molding	8 feet [a]	supporting ledge
1 section	⅛-inch Masonite	24 inches square	bottom
1 length	2 × 2	24 inches	riser [b]

Hardware and Other Stuff

Quantity	Material
1 panel	double-strength glass [c]
1 section	old window screen
1	single-pole–single-throw switch [d] (with accompanying wood screws and mounting nut)
8	corner braces [e] (with accompanying wood screws)
4	flush-mounted plastic standard light sockets (with accompanying wood screws [f])
4	25-watt incandescent bulbs
1 length	lamp cord (with plug), approximately 12 feet long
1 [g]	wire nut
4 pieces	aluminum foil, cut to 2½ inches square
3	No.7 roundheaded wood screws, 1½ inches long [b]
8	No.5 roundheaded wood screws, 1½ inches long
4	No.5 roundheaded wood screws, 1 inch long
16	No.18 finishing nails, 1 inch long

4 pieces   sponge, cut to very small squares [e]
            white glue
            white paint [h]
            glass frosting
            aquarium cement [i]

FLUORESCENT BOX

Wood

Quantity	Material	Cut to	Description
2 sections	¾-inch plywood	4 by 24 inches	front and back walls
2 sections	¾-inch plywood	4 by 22½ inches	side walls
1 section	¾-inch plywood	24 inches square	bottom
1 length	½-inch quarter-round molding	8 feet [a]	supporting ledge

Hardware and Other Stuff

Quantity	Material
1 panel	double-strength glass [c]
1 section	old window screen
1	single-pole–single-throw switch [d] (with accompanying wood screws and mounting nut)
8	corner braces [e] (with accompanying wood screws)
2	1-bulb fluorescent light fixtures (with accompanying cords and wood screws)
1 length	lamp cord (with plug), approximately 7 feet long [j]
3 [g]	wire nuts
2	screw-on rubber legs [b]
8	No.7 flatheaded wood screws, 1½ inches long
8	No.5 roundheaded wood screws, 1½ inches long
16	No.18 finishing nails, 1 inch long
	white glue
	white paint [h]
	glass frosting
	aquarium cement [i]

[a] Will be cut into smaller pieces during assembly.
[b] If you want your light box to tilt.
[c] Do not purchase until walls are assembled and measured (see text). Get an extra scrap at the same time.
[d] Toggle or push-button.
[e] Optional.
[f] Or use 1-inch-long roundheaded wood screws. The diameter of the shank will depend on the mounting holes in the sockets.
[g] One is unnecessary if switch has screw or solder terminals.
[h] One pint will be more than adequate.
[i] One tube should be enough.
[j] If grounding is necessary, use a grounded power cord with a three-pronged plug.

The Frame

The best way to begin assembling the light box is to label the four rectangular sections of plywood that will be the walls. Labels will provide you with an orientation to these parts that will be particularly helpful during the actual construction procedures. Using letter symbols, mark top and bottom edges

Label the walls

as well as the inside and outside faces of each of them. Also indicate which of the 24-inch sections will be positioned at the front and which will be used at the rear. This is particularly important for hole drilling. And that's what you'll be doing next.

Regardless of what light source you have decided to use, it will be important to provide ample ventilation in the box to permit the cooling of the air inside. If the air in the box doesn't circulate, you will have to continually turn the lights off during use to keep the temperature down. That, of course, is impractical. Then again, drawing on hot glass can be very awkward. (If you continue to have doubts as to the importance of ventilating your light box, let us put your mind at ease. We've recently seen a toy that is modeled after a kitchen oven. It works; you can actually cook certain foods on it. We've tried it, although we still prefer our real one. Upon close inspection we found that the only source of heat used in that toy was a standard incandescent bulb.) The easiest way to ventilate is to drill a series of holes, at least ½ inch in diameter, on each wall of the box, about 1½ inches from the top (figure 2-1).

Drill the ventilation holes

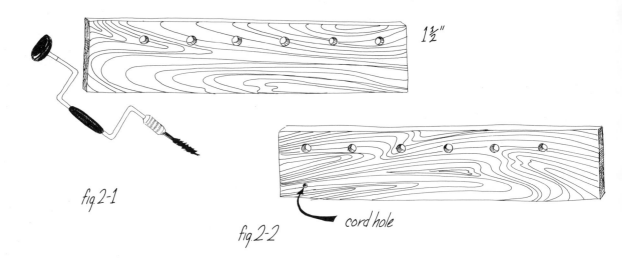

1½"

fig 2-1

fig. 2-2

cord hole

Drill the hole for the cord

When you're done with the vents, don't bother putting your drill down. This is the perfect time to drill a hole for the power cord. Do this in the back wall, about 1 inch up from the bottom and near one corner (figure 2-2).

Drill the switch mounting hole

If you plan on having an on/off switch mounted right on the unit, you'll need another hole. This time, however, you may have to change bits. (Of course, you can avoid this hole if you want to. On/off type switches are made that can be mounted on the power cord itself. They're relatively easy to put on, but they're a little inconvenient to use since they're not always around when you need them.) If you're willing to go along with another hole, measure the diameter of your drill bit against the threaded shank of your switch; it should be approximately the same diameter as the shank. Drill the switch mounting hole through one of the 22½-inch side walls at a location that you'll find convenient for use (figure 2-2). In our incandescent box that location was on the right wall near the front. With ¾-inch plywood the shank of your switch probably won't go all the way through the hole. If you find this to be the case, insert a somewhat larger bit into your drill. From the outside face of the board, drill over the hole you've just made, about halfway down into the wood. This will leave a countersunk basin around the original hole. Check with your switch to be sure that you've gone far enough to permit some of the threaded shank to show through. Later, this will enable you to thread the switch mounting nut onto the exposed shank.

With your holes drilled you are ready to assemble the box. The way that we suggest joining the wall sections of the unit is to glue, butt, and screw them together. It's best to assemble two at a time forming right angles. Begin by standing one of the 22½-inch plywood sections on end, supporting it between your legs. Lay a 24-inch section flat in your lap, with one end over the edge of the vertical piece and aligned with it. It is in this position that they should be joined. Mark two points about 3 inches apart at the overlapping end of the flat piece in your lap (figure 2-3). These points are where you'll be putting the screws, so don't make them too close to the edge of the wood. Depress the marks with your awl. Coat the surfaces to be joined with white glue and drive the 1½-inch roundheaded wood screws into place. Check to be certain that the joint is tight. Assemble the other set in the same manner. Now connect both sets to form the complete 24-inch-square frame (figure 2-4). (One 22½-inch board plus the thicknesses of two 24-inch boards makes a 24-inch length.) Make sure that it's solid. Keep in mind that this is a light box and that it's going to hold part of you up. We don't know anyone who doesn't lean on his box to some extent while using it. Also, if you're going to move it around at all, you certainly don't want the action of carrying it to weaken it. Then again, you probably won't be using it to hold up the rear axle of your Microbus. However, if, after joining the four sides of the box, you feel that you would like to reinforce them with a little something extra, use corner braces. Two of them installed at each corner, inside or out, will be more than adequate.

Join the walls

Install corner braces (optional)

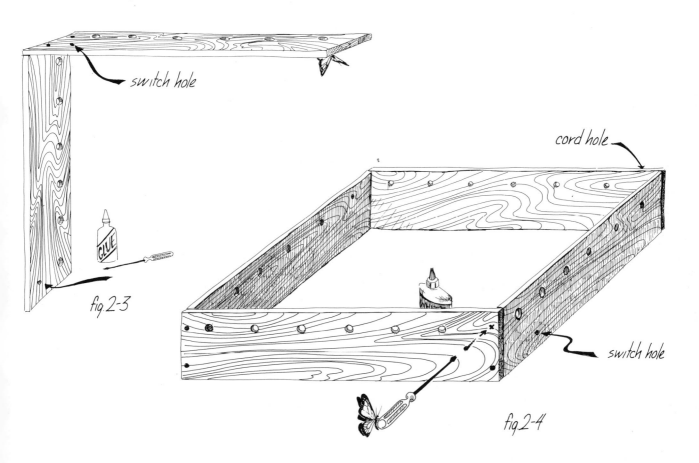

switch hole

fig 2-3

cord hole

switch hole

fig 2-4

Once the wall assembly has been completed, you can accurately determine the size of the glass that you'll need. Measure the interior dimensions carefully and purchase a piece of glass to fit them. The glass work surface will be seated on a ledge that runs around the interior of the box. Because it is important that this surface not be recessed below the top edges of the walls, it is desirable to mount the supporting ledge down from these edges at a distance equal to the thickness of the glass. When you're having your glass cut, ask for one of the small sections that has fallen into the scrap barrel. This will be your gauge, enabling you to get the ledge indented just enough. Invert the box assembly on a flat surface, such as a desk top. Place the glass fragment inside the box against one wall, and mark the wall where the glass meets it (figure 2-5). It is here that the top face of the molding should be located. Repeat on the other walls.

Measure and mark for the supporting ledge

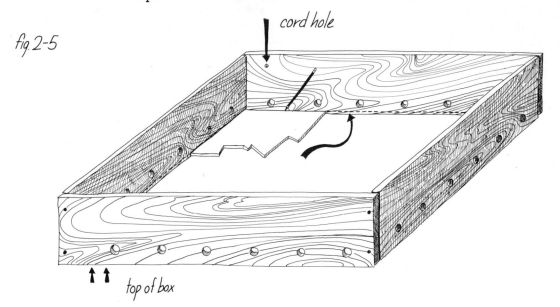

fig. 2-5

cord hole

top of box

For the ledge we used ½-inch quarter-round molding, glued and tacked in place with finishing nails. The best way to install it is two sections at a time. This will enable you to cut the pieces more accurately for a better fit. Measure the interior length of any two opposite sides, allowing for the molding already in place. Cut and mount two sections of molding at this length (figure 2-6).

Install the supporting ledge

fig. 2-6

switch hole

To check your work, gently lower the glass into position. If the ledges have been mounted correctly, there should be no places where the walls protrude above the surface of the glass. If there are a few, mark the wall by drawing your pencil along the edge of the glass, underscoring these high spots (figure 2-7). Remove the glass and, with a plane or a coping saw, carefully shave off the excess wood, down to the pencil line. Check your work by replacing the glass on the box. If you've shaved off enough, remove the glass and put it aside.

Shave off any high spots on the walls

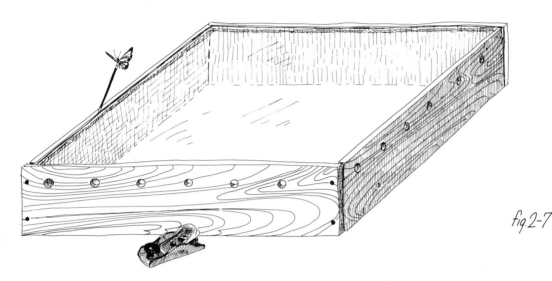

fig. 2-7

Because the edges of plywood are usually kind of rough, we suggest that you spend some time smoothing them off with sandpaper (figure 2-8).

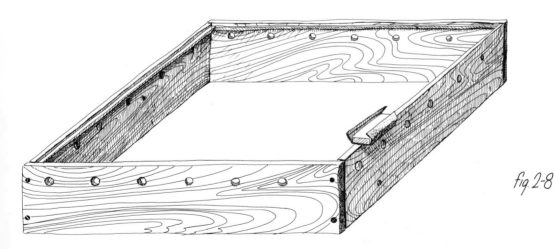

fig. 2-8

When you've done this to your satisfaction, you're ready to paint the unit (figure 2-9). We found that by doing this we further reduced the splinter hazard and noticeably increased the total amount of light on the drawing surface. And, of course, the more light you have available to you, the more penetration power you'll have when working with heavy materials. You can use almost any white paint that you may already have, so long as it's not flammable when it's dry.

Sand and paint the walls

When the paint is dry and before you go on to the electrical work, consider the value of screening off those holes that you've drilled for ventilation. Inasmuch as they may well be large enough to be penetrated by small fingers, it's a good safety procedure to cover them. After all, the bulbs are going to get hot, and there will be wires running along the inside walls,

fig. 2-9

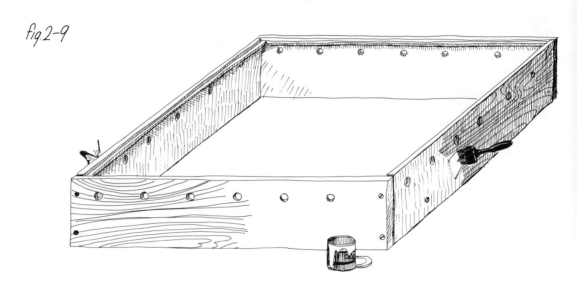

both of which can present some hazard to probing little hands. In building any tool, it always makes good sense to consider and protect those around you in both the design and construction. We stapled a narrow strip of window screening inside (figure 2-10), but small scraps are just as useable.

Install safety screening over the ventilation holes

fig. 2-10

The Wiring

And now for the electrical work. Before you can begin to wire your light box, you have to decide whether you want incandescent or fluorescent lighting. Perhaps the largest single advantage of incandescent lights is that of initial cost. If you're going to be buying the electrical supplies needed for your light box, using incandescent lights will save you money. The greatest disadvantage in using them is the heat they give off; they tend to warm up the work surface. However, if your studio is insulated like ours, you may welcome the soothing warmth on your hands. Fluorescent lighting is cool blue-white, and spreads somewhat more evenly over the drawing surface. And although the cost of fixtures and replacement bulbs is higher, item for item, than for incandescents, the fixtures are a one-time investment, and bulbs will need to be replaced less frequently. Also, fluorescent lighting uses less power. It's up to you.

But, whichever lighting you choose, you will need a switch. The switch we recommend that you install on your light box is a single-pole–single-throw (spst) toggle or push-button type. All this means is that the switch will have only two positions, on and off, and that there's only one terminal, or connection point, on each side of the switch. When buying one, be sure that it's rated to handle the current that's coming out of your wall. To install the switch, you'll have to use a long-nose pliers to hold the nut over the threaded shank (figure 2-11). Unless the drill bit that you used in countersinking the switch mounting hole was pretty large, you'll find that turning the nut is difficult. No need for concern, however—just turn the body of the switch, keeping the nut from turning with the pliers. Twist it until it's snug.

Install the switch

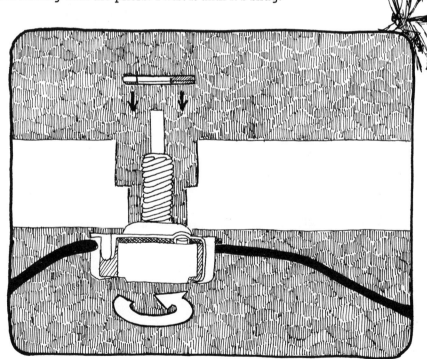

fig 2-11

INCANDESCENT

For all interior wiring in the incandescent box we suggest using lamp cord. It's the same stuff that we use for the power line. If you've bought the length we suggested, you'll have more than enough for the power line, and you can split the balance for wiring up the socket fixtures. If for any reason you plan not to use lamp cord, it's important to keep in mind that *all* wiring in the box must be able to handle household current. If you were raised with a Christmas tree, then you probably know something about wiring. For example, you may know that series wiring is less desirable for rigging lights than parallel wiring. In fact, a series-wired string of lights can present an absolutely knotty problem when just one small bulb burns out. For the same reason, it is not a very good idea to wire the lights in your light box in series—if one goes, they all go. We're certain there are applications where this particular feature is a practical advantage, but your light box isn't one of them. Thus, the circuit we are describing is wired in parallel.

Mount the sockets

We used sockets that can be flush-mounted, that is, mounted directly on the surface. These are usually molded plastic, frequently icky brown, with two metal screw terminals—one brass and one silver. They are easily mounted with screws. If none came with the sockets you bought, 1-inch roundheaded wood screws will do it. The procedure is as simple as marking the location of the mounting holes that are built into the socket and driving in the screws. (If the screws don't easily penetrate the wood, start the holes with your awl.) For the size box that we have described you'll need four sockets to provide adequate, even illumination. They can be positioned in different ways. You can center one on each of the four interior sides (figure 2-12), or you can locate them near the corners. The important thing is that you distribute the light evenly under the drawing surface. Be certain that you mount your sockets so that the bulbs that will be installed in them will clear the undersurface of the glass by at least an inch and any other interior surfaces of the box by about the same amount. This is to avoid the scorching of wood surfaces and hot spots on the drawing surface, neither of which condition is desirable.

fig. 2-12

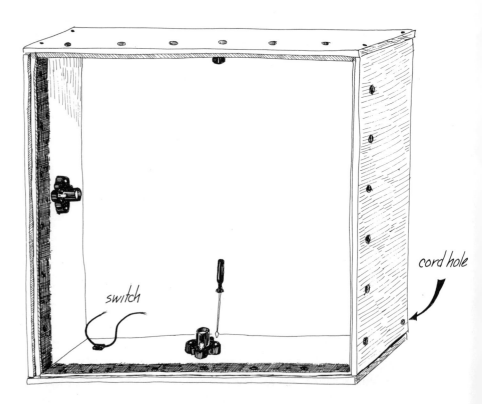

switch

cord hole

With your screwdriver, loosen the screw terminals on all the light sockets and on the switch if it's the kind that has them. Number the sockets with pencil, starting with the one closest to the switch and going counterclockwise around the box.

Loosen all screw terminals and number the sockets

To begin the wiring, cut a length of lamp cord to be used as a power line. We used a 7-foot section. Pull enough of it to reach the switch in through the hole you've drilled for this purpose. Knot off the cord on the inside (figure 2-13). When the light box is in operation, this knot will keep the cord from pulling out through the hole. And it will prevent the breaking of connections inside the box when any unexpected stress is applied to the power line—like someone tripping over it or pulling it to see if it's attached to something.

Pull in the power cord and knot it off

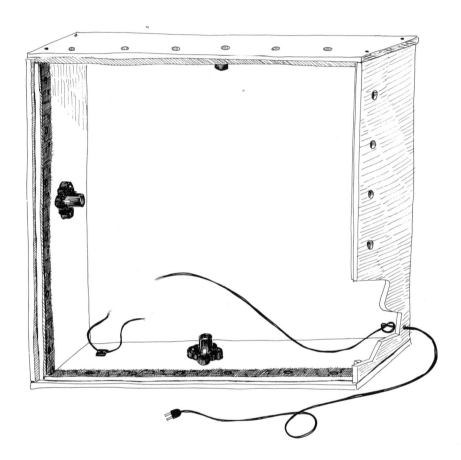

fig. 2-13

Then split the cord from the inside down to the knot. Any sharp blade will be sufficient to start the split. Just make a small cut on the end of the cord at the indented center channel of the insulation, and pull both wires apart (figure 2-14).

Split the cord

Take one of the two wires and bring it to the brass terminal on socket number one. You'll probably find that you have some surplus. To determine how much you'll actually need, pull the wire straight to the terminal without slack. Then slacken sufficiently to provide for stapling it along the side of the box after it's been connected. Cut it about an inch beyond the terminal. About ½ inch short of the end draw a sharpened blade around the plastic casing, applying enough pressure to cut the plastic. But try not to damage the copper fibers inside. With a pair of pliers, your fingers, or your teeth, firmly grasp

Connect socket one

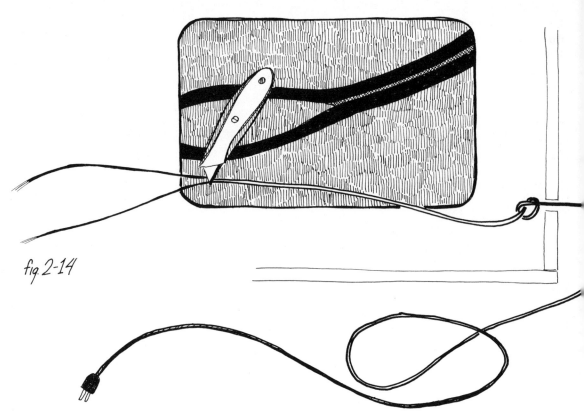

fig. 2-14

the end piece of casing and draw it off the end of the wire. This process of baring ends is called, appropriately enough, stripping. With the insulation removed and the copper bared, twist the metal fibers together and bend them into a hook. Place it around the shank of the brass screw on the socket. It's always best to have the hook point in the same direction that you turn the screws in to tighten them (figure 2-15). But don't tighten the screw yet.

fig. 2-15

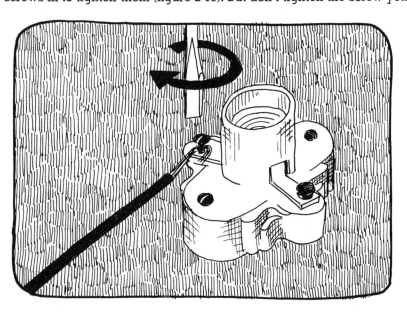

Connect the switch

Now strip the other wire from the power line. If there are wires built into your switch, strip them and hold the bare end of one of them adjacent to the bare end of the wire from the power line. Twist the two together and cap them off with a wire nut. Wire nuts are plastic insulating caps with threaded interiors. You just screw them over the wires being joined until snug (figure 2-16). The other line from the switch should be connected to the silver terminal on socket one. Hook the bare end of the wire around the screw, but do not tighten yet.

fig. 2-16

If the switch you've got has screw terminals, attach the wire from the power line directly to one of them and tighten the screw. With a switch having solder terminals, use rosin-core solder to make the connection. If your switch has either screw or solder terminals, you'll have to add a length of wire to make the connection. Measure off the distance between the switch and socket with a piece of wire, allowing enough slack for tacking the wire comfortably against the side. Cut what you need and strip both ends. Attach one end to the switch and the other to the silver terminal of the socket. You can tighten the switch screw, but don't tighten that screw on the socket.

Measure the distance between the first and second sockets, again allowing enough extra to permit effortless tacking. Cut two pieces of insulated wire at this length and prepare the ends. With one of them attach the brass terminal of socket one (figure 2-17) to the brass terminal of socket two. Con-

Complete the circuit

fig. 2-17

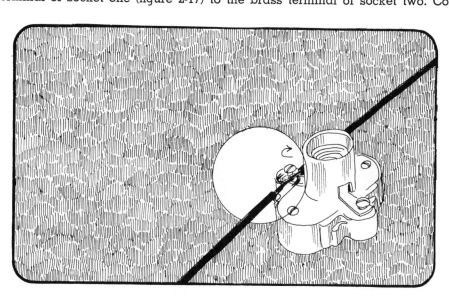

nect the silver terminals with the other. Once this has been done, the screw terminals on socket one can be permanently tightened. Connect sockets two and three in the same manner, tightening the terminals on socket two. Now repeat the whole thing once more, connecting sockets three and four. Your circuit is now complete (figure 2-18). Test the terminal connections by gently pulling the lines to be sure that all wires are secure.

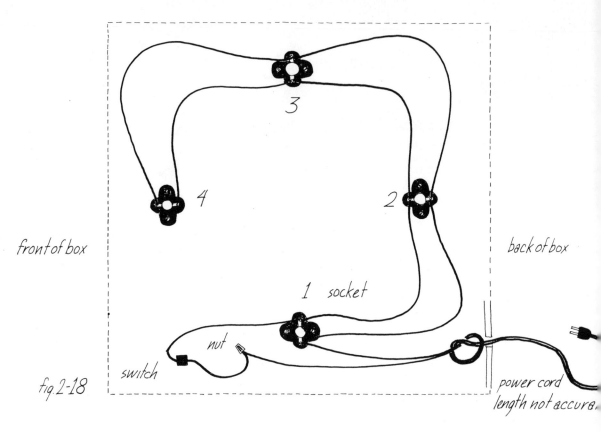

front of box

back of box

3

4

2

1   socket

nut

switch

fig. 2-18

power cord
length not accura.

Organize and staple the wires to the walls

Now, if you haven't been doing it right along, staple the wires neatly along the side walls (figure 2-19). While you may not feel that this is really necessary, it will reduce the possibility of wires touching hot interior parts, such as incandescent bulbs, and having their insulation burned off. This smelly occurrence increases the likelihood of shorts caused by the contact

fig. 2-19

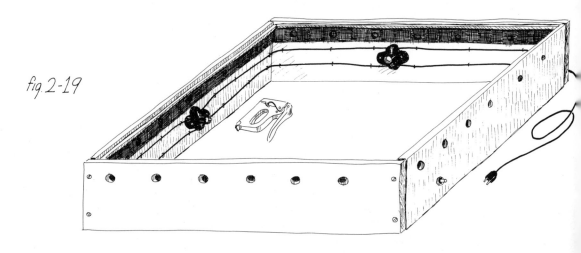

of two such damaged lines. With wires that have been carefully organized and attached to the surfaces they travel over, this kind of problem is nonexistent.

As a bottom for the incandescent light box we used ⅛-inch Masonite. A piece measuring 24 inches square should cover the area. Coat what will be the inside surface of the board with white paint (figure 2-20). When it's dry, cut out four squares of aluminum foil. These will act as reflectors, amplifying the light output of your box, and will also protect the bottom from scorching. Determine about where the light bulbs will be located relative to the bottom by screwing bulbs into the sockets and slipping the bottom into position under the side walls. Staple the foil onto the Masonite at these points (figure 2-21).

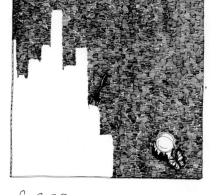

fig. 2-20
Paint the inside surface of the bottom

Attach foil squares to the bottom

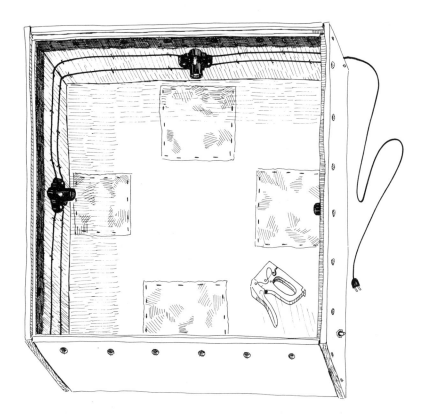

fig. 2-21

Install the riser (optional)

If you want your work surface to tilt, the easiest way is to elevate the back end of the box. For this you'll need the 24-inch length of 2 × 2 and 3 1½-inch roundheaded wood screws. Mark two points near the rear edge of the masonite no more than 1 inch in, with about a 20-inch spread between them. Position the 2 × 2 beneath, and align it with the edges. For your convenience in driving the screws, support the other side of the bottom piece with a hunk of scrap wood. Depress the points with an awl and drive the screws through the masonite, into the 2 × 2 below. A third screw can be added between them for additional strength (figure 2-22). When you mount the bottom onto the box, your work surface will gently slope. We didn't recommend gluing here only because you may decide that you prefer the flat box for some applications and the tilted one for others. This way you can still have both. You might consider using a pad under the box to prevent it from sliding on and/or marring the surface that you use to support it. Or you can use sponge cushions, as described in the next paragraph.

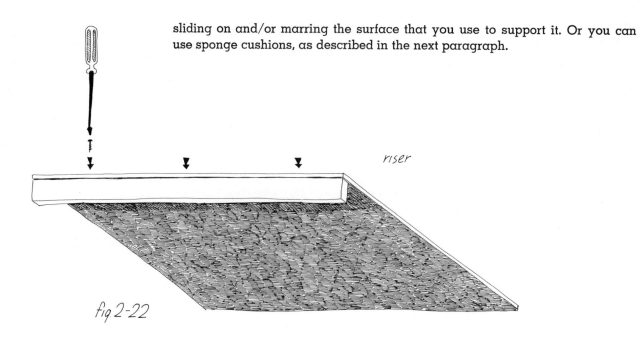

riser

fig. 2-22

Attach the bottom to the walls

To attach the bottom, you need only the four 1-inch roundheads. Drive them in at the corners so that they will pass through the Masonite and into the edges of the side walls (figure 2-23). Glue small squares of sponge over the screw heads. These cushions will function as legs, and they will prevent the surface beneath the box from being scratched.

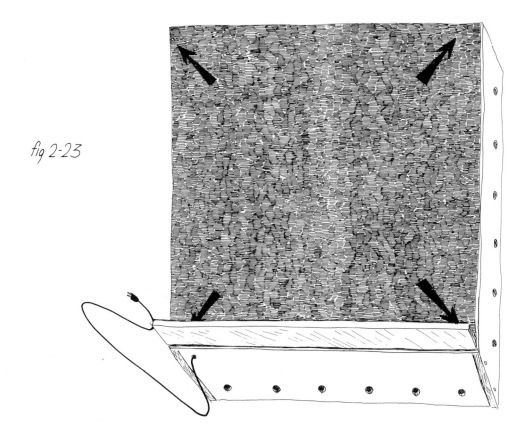

fig 2-23

FLUORESCENT

The easiest way to install fluorescent lighting in a light box is to purchase preassembled units, like the kind that are made for under-the-counter applications. Two of these should give you plenty of light. These fixtures typically come complete with their own cords and plugs, as well as on/off switches. These plugs should be cut off. Also, after you've measured what you'll need, you should cut off the excess cord. It just isn't a good idea to leave excess wire inside the unit, even if it's neatly coiled. Any switches that are built into the fixtures will be of little value to you because they won't be accessible from the outside of the light box. Before installing the fixtures, make certain these switches are in the on position. They should remain that way permanently.

One thing to look for, before you get down to work, is the number of individual wires coming out of each fixture. You will find either two or three. If there are only two wires coming out, you can use lamp cord and a standard plug for the power line. But if there is a third lead, the ground, you'll need to use a grounded power cord with a three-pronged plug. Either way, though, the wiring isn't very difficult.

Both fixtures are mounted directly to the bottom of the light box. In the fluorescent unit, where the bottom must be of sufficient thickness and strength to hold the fixtures securely, it's best to use ¾-inch plywood. Different fixtures will mount best in different ways. Most, however, use some kind of mounting-screw system. That ¾-inch plywood should provide plenty of substance for the screws to cling to. If you've bought your fixtures new, check the directions for mounting that came with them. Hopefully, they will be understandable and easy to follow, but this usually has not been our experience. Read them over carefully. If they still don't seem to make sense, check any diagrams that are provided and inspect your fixture for mounting holes. Chances are, you'll be able to find them easily. When you've deciphered the mounting procedure, proceed with the mounting. Place the fixtures parallel with the front and rear edges of the bottom board, indenting each of them a short way from its adjacent edge. Make certain that the wires from each extend out the same side (figure 2-24).

When the fixtures are mounted in place, you can determine how much of the cord to cut. Hold the two cords together and cut them so that about 2 inches of the remaining cords can still be held together. Split the cords back part way to the fixtures and strip the ends. Take one wire from each cord and twist them together. Do the same with the remaining pair of wires (figure 2-24).

Mount the fixtures to the bottom

Cut off the excess cord

Connect the fixtures to each other

fig. 2-24

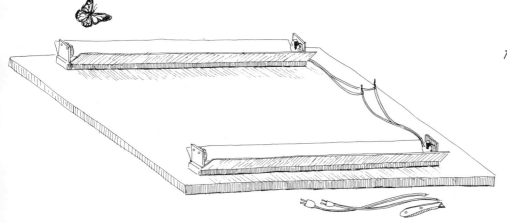

Pull in the power cord and knot it off

Align the walls of the box on top of the bottom piece so that the switch is on the same side as the fixture wires. Insert the power line in through the cord hole in the rear of the box. Pull enough through so that you can easily reach the two twisted wire connections, leaving slack enough for tacking. Knot off the cord.

Split the line back enough to enable you to twist-connect one of its wires to one of the two junctions. It doesn't matter which. Install a wire nut on this set of three (figure 2-25). The other power-line wire is connected to the

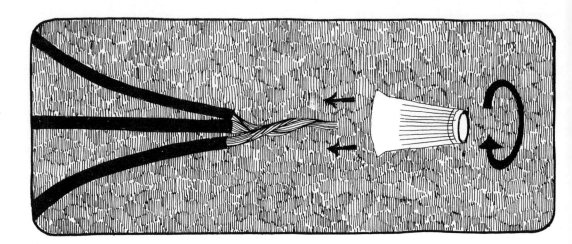

fig. 2-25

Complete the circuit

switch, either at the screw or solder terminal on its body or to one of the lines extending from the body. The other side of the switch is then connected to the remaining set of fixture wires. If the switch has screw or solder terminals, you will need an extra length of wire. Install the needed wire nut or nuts (figure 2-26). If your fixtures are the three-wire type, then the third, or ground, wires are joined directly with the third lead (ground) on the power line (figure 2-27). Test to be certain that all wire nuts and terminal connections are good by pulling the lines gently. Organize and tack down the wires.

Attach the bottom to the walls

To attach the bottom to the side walls, eight 1½-inch flatheaded wood screws are used, two along each side (figure 2-28). Be sure to countersink. If you want the work surface to tilt, install two screw-on rubber legs to the bottom near the rear. The higher you raise the rear, of course, the more the box will tilt.

Finishing Touches

In order to distribute light evenly on the work surface, it will be necessary to frost the glass. There are a number of products currently on the market that can handle this job. The one we used comes in an aerosol can and is applied in several layers to the underside of the work surface. Begin by spraying a thin film over the glass—heavy applications will produce a patchy frosting. Allow time for drying; then spray it lightly again. Be patient— a good job will take time. To achieve the effect that we wanted, several coats

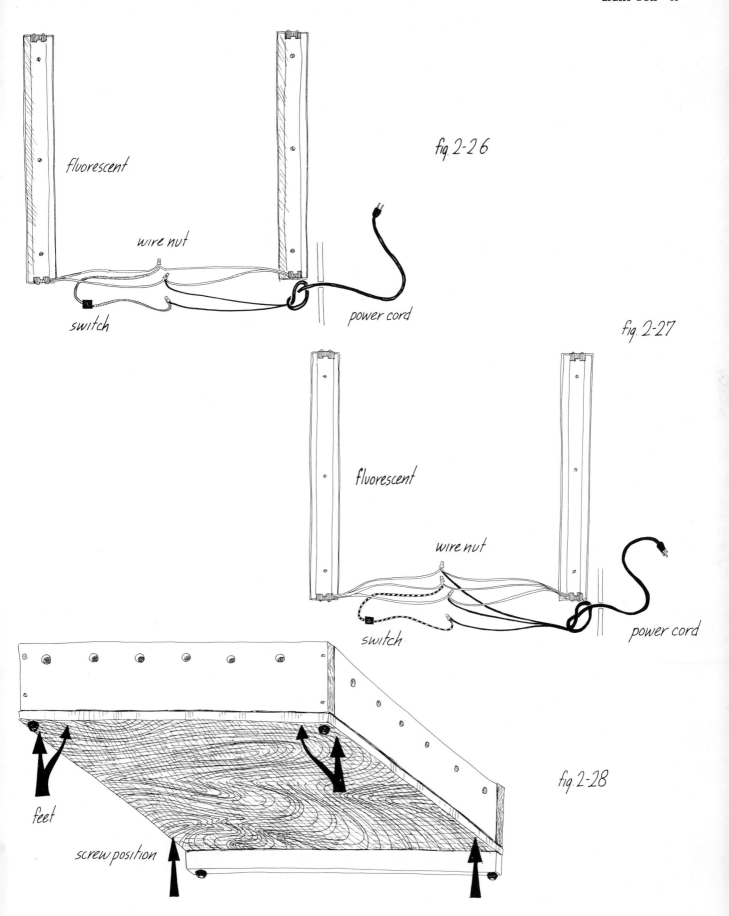

fig. 2-26

fluorescent

wire nut

switch

power cord

fig. 2-27

fluorescent

wire nut

switch

power cord

fig. 2-28

feet

screw position

were necessary. There's really no formula for the number of times you'll have to recoat before it becomes translucent enough for the purpose. You'll have to use your own judgment. Intermittently test the surface by laying the glass in position on the box and turning the lights on to see whether or not the light is sufficiently diffused. You'll know that you're getting close when you can no longer distinguish the bulbs and sockets beneath. In general, when using aerosol sprays, don't place the spray nozzle too close to the surface being sprayed. This will cause a formation of extra-heavy deposits on the surface that can run in long annoying drips if the glass is raised during the spraying procedure. And again, heavy deposits and runs will make the frosting uneven. Unless otherwise specified on the label, hold the can from six to twelve inches away while spraying. If the can is held back too far, however, you will be releasing more of the stuff into the atmosphere than onto the glass. If you move the can in short, even, back-and-forth strokes, the material lays out really well. Stop spraying and shake the can every so often to help keep the frosting smooth. Because this method of frosting does not chemically alter the glass (it just covers it), the coated surface can be scraped away. Keep this in mind when moving the glass about. If you scratch some of it off, you'll have to try to patch it, and that is no easy matter.

Next, permanently secure the glass to the box with aquarium cement. Run a bead of the adhesive along the supporting ledge inside the walls of your box. You push against the bead rather than pulling from it. This procedure appears universally in the directions given with the products we've seen. Do it slowly and evenly, and be certain to get it into the corners (figure 2-29). When you've done this, carefully place the glass, frosting side down, in position (figure 2-30), applying slight pressure around the edges. And that's it. Give the cement time to set up before testing to be sure that the glass is secure.

Enjoy it.

fig. 2-29

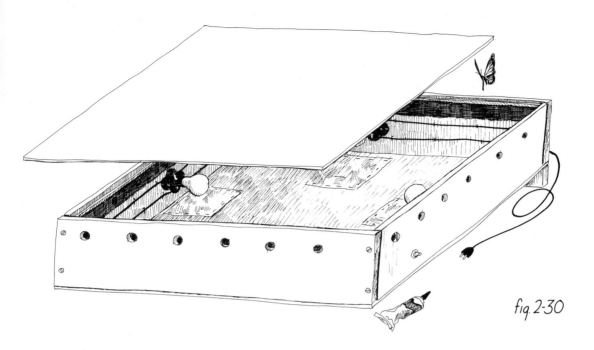

fig. 2-30

3·SPRAY BOOTH

This is a short project that pays big dividends. If you have ever had the occasion to use aerosol sprays for any purpose—whether for fixative, varnish, paint, or glaze—then you probably know well all the annoyances and discomforts that can be created by this kind of work. Little colored flecks lie all over the furnishings of your studio, and the air is thick with assorted noxious and volatile substances. Even when carefully applied, sprays will always release some material into the air; it's in the nature of the process. Having unfortunately undergone these experiences, we can say without reservation that building a spray booth is a really wise move. If you haven't as yet had much occasion to use spray materials but anticipate needing to use them, well—just trust us. A spray booth is an effective means of reducing both the hazards and annoyances of this process. It will enable you to confine the spray to the area that you're working on, trapping most of the material that would otherwise become a part of the air you breathe.

A spray booth is actually nothing more than a freestanding set of panels—a back piece, two winged sides, and a top. It can be made of any of several materials, including masonite, plywood, or even cardboard. Personally, we prefer masonite because it's lightweight yet quite durable. In deciding what size to make your spray booth, you should consider a couple of things. One is where you're going to use it. If, for example, you have a counter top in mind, then you certainly don't want to construct something that will overhang it by several inches. The other and perhaps most important factor is the size of the work that you'll be spraying. If the spray booth is too small to comfortably accommodate your pieces, then it's virtually useless. Plan accordingly, allowing just enough space beyond the size needed for your projects to encompass the spray itself.

The panels are joined with hinges that can be flush-mounted. Almost any flat cabinet hinges will do the job. If, like us, you decide to use masonite, however, you will have to make one adjustment. The wood screws that are usually provided with the hinges will not be appropriate for mounting them on masonite or any other thin material. It is therefore necessary to substitute bolts and nuts. For ¼-inch masonite, bolts ½ to ⅝ inches long will be fine. Anything longer would be awkward. Of course, if the spray booth you're building is intended to stand permanently in your studio, you won't need hinges at all. But for most uses we don't recommend this. In fact, although the spray booth is structurally sound, one of its nicest features is its collapsibility; it is portable and generally easy to get out of the way when not in use.

The two side pieces and the top piece are all hinged to the back piece and can flap down when not in use. The entire unit can be stored flat.

ASSEMBLY

Wood

Quantity	Material	Cut to	Description
1 section	¼-inch masonite	24 by 24 inches	back
2 sections	¼-inch masonite	18 by 24 inches	sides
1 section	¼-inch masonite	17¾ by 32 inches [a]	top
2 lengths	½-inch quarter-round molding	17 inches	stops

Hardware and Other Stuff

Quantity	Material
6	flat cabinet hinges
18	bolts to fit hinge holes, ½ to ⅝ inch long
18	washers for bolts
18	nuts for bolts
	wood glue
	wide cloth tape
	paint or varnish [b]

[a] Will be cut further during assembly (see text).
[b] Optional.

First, trim the top piece so that it is a trapezoid. Make a mark 3 inches in from the end of one 32-inch edge. Draw a line from the mark to the closest corner of the other 32-inch edge (figure 3-1). Repeat at the other end. Cut along these lines. You should (hopefully) end up with a trapezoid, having a 32-inch base, a 26-inch top, and, if Pythagoras was right, two sides that are approximately 18 inches long. Lay this piece aside for the time being.

Place the two side pieces at either side of the back piece and adjacent to the edges to which they'll be attached (figure 3-2). Lay the hinges at the joints, spine side up, and position them in from the bottom and top edges about 1½ to 2 inches. Mark the mounting holes through the hinge plates onto the masonite (figure 3-3). Drill at these marks, using a bit large enough to produce holes

Trim the top piece into a trapezoidal form

Join the sides to the back

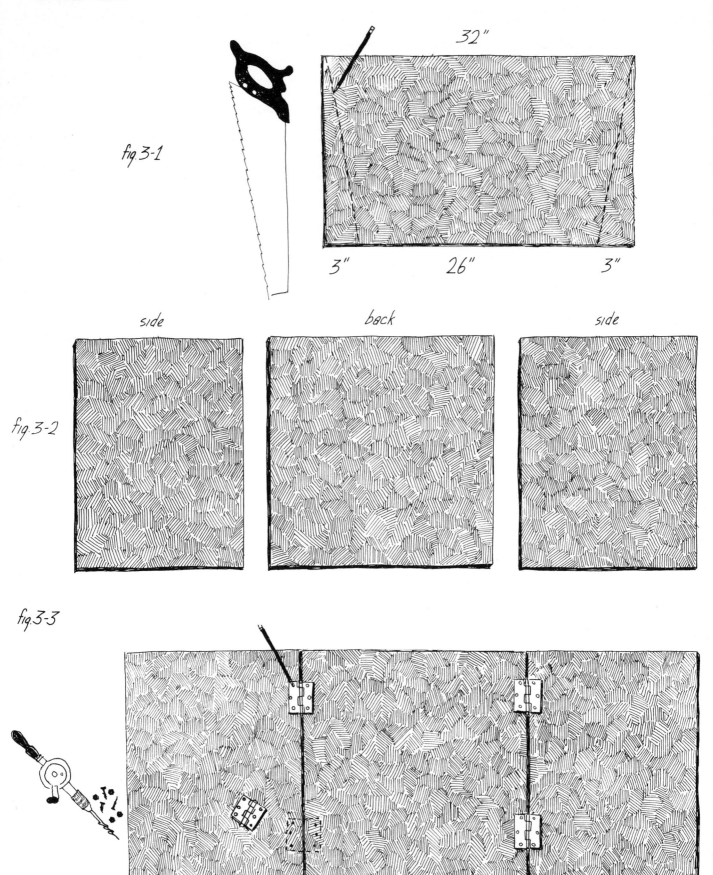

fig 3-1

32"

3"   26"   3"

side   back   side

fig. 3-2

fig. 3-3

through which the bolts can pass but not much larger. Using a washer and nut on each bolt, secure the hinges in place.

Now flip the whole thing over. Place the 26-inch edge of the top piece adjacent to what will be the top edge of the back piece. There should be 1 inch of overhang at either end (figure 3-4). Position the hinges and drill the holes. Mount the hinges spine side up.

Join the top to the back

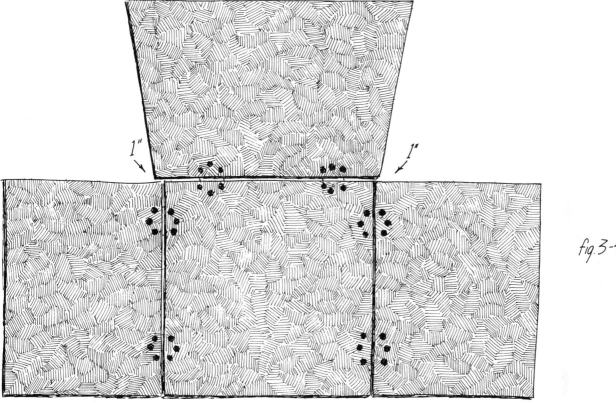

fig. 3-4

Place the strips of molding along each of the two 18-inch tapered sides of the top piece, about an inch away from the hinged seam (figure 3-5). Glue them down. These will serve as stops for the side pieces when you stand the booth.

Glue the molding to the top

With all of the parts unfolded, you have a perfect opportunity to cover the three seams with wide cloth tape. This will prevent any of the spray from escaping through them. First, tape the two side seams. Then, turn the unit back over and tape the top seam (figure 3-6).

Tape the seams

With hinges mounted and tape in place, you can raise your spray booth. Stand it by spreading the side pieces and dropping the top down so it becomes interlocked with them.

Raise the booth

As a finishing touch, you can cover the edges of the masonite with cloth tape and coat the whole unit with paint or varnish. In fact, such a coating would make it a little easier to wipe the surface clean, but then again, we don't know anyone that actually does that. To use your spray booth, just stand or prop your piece inside and spray down into the booth. Have a (cough) good time.

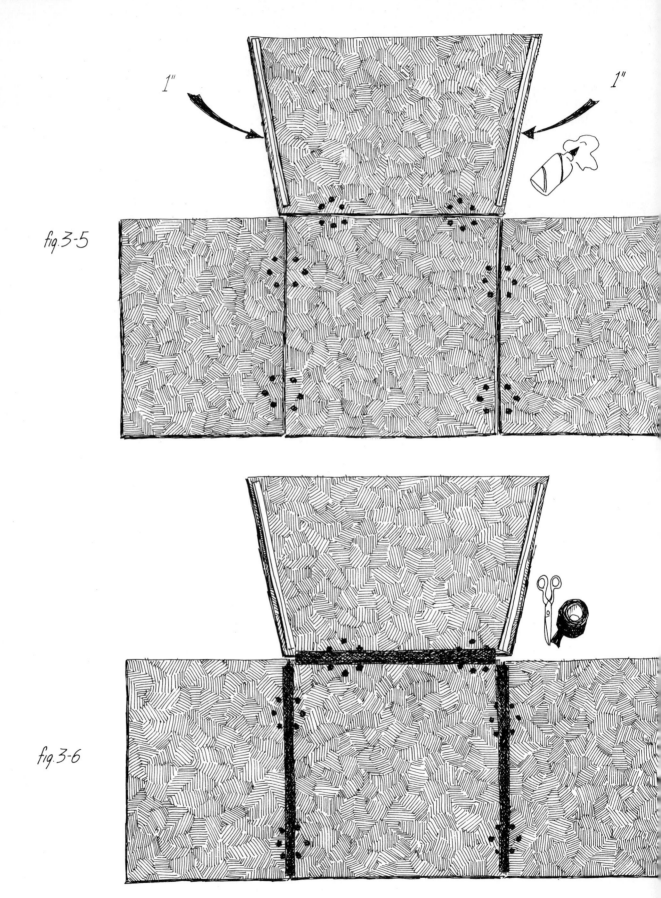

fig.3-5

fig.3-6

4·DRAWING TABLE

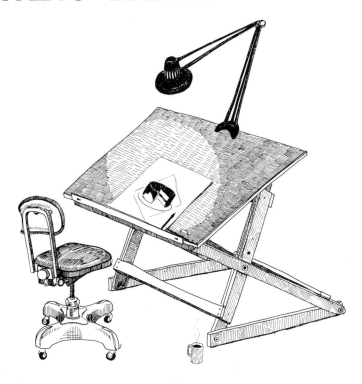

It wasn't until after we put our drawing table together that we realized just how much we needed it. Until then, slumping over a resurfaced wooden kitchen table, which we had bought for a dollar from a friend's "usable junk" store on the other side of the river, was just a matter of accepted practice whenever either of us needed a stationary surface to work on. It's not that the old table didn't have a lot of personality. Maybe even a little too much. For one thing, it just wouldn't stay still. Regardless of how many nails we drove into those legs, or how many braces we ran between them, that table insisted on swaying at some of the damnedest times. And with every move, it would creak, and when it creaked, we'd hammer in more nails. And so it went.

Until we finally decided to do something about it. Both of us knew there was a better way, but neither of us had thought much about it. Surely a box of nails was not regarded as standard equipment in all drawing studios. We began our search with catalogues. We sat on the floor in front of the fireplace with a stack of rather well-worn catalogues between us. As the early-December fire warmed us after a day of cutting and splitting green poplar, we reviewed them; and, discouraged, we tossed them, one by one, into the blaze. A few of those catalogue tables might do, but certainly none at those prices.

We needed to take another approach. Perhaps we could find a used one. If we were especially fortunate, we might even find one that had been used solely on Sundays by a little old retired economics professor in Port Jervis to hold up the business supplement of the Sunday paper. Alas, there were none—that is, no tables—none anywhere we thought to look. If, indeed, there was such a man in Port Jervis and he did own such a table, he just wasn't selling. Actually, we did see one or two of them in a secondhand furniture shop, but, at the prices the proprietor wanted, it would have paid us to resubscribe to those catalogues.

Well, what if we were to build our own? What would really be involved? We began to sketch out some ideas. And an interesting table slowly began to take shape. We wanted one that would offer the basic features of those we had looked at but without the needless and occasionally bothersome frills and the inflationary price. We consulted a good friend with a head for technical details. What came out of all of this is what this chapter is all about—a project for the artist who's decided to find an alternative to what he's using now that will give him what he needs at a manageable price. With the added satisfaction that can come from making something really useful from scratch.

ASSEMBLY

Wood

Quantity	Material	Cut to	Description
1 section	¾-inch particle board	36 by 48 inches	table top
2 lengths	5/4 × 3	43½ inches	front and rear frame pieces
2 lengths	5/4 × 3	31½ inches	side frame pieces
2 lengths	5/4 × 3	41 inches	table braces
4 lengths	5/4 × 3	52 inches	legs
2 lengths	5/4 × 3	40 inches	spacers
2 lengths	5/4 × 3	38 inches	feet
2 lengths	1 × 3	46 inches	outside leg braces
2 lengths	1 × 3	41 inches	inside leg braces
1 length	lath [a]	36 inches	lip

Hardware and Other Stuff

Quantity	Material
22	No.16 flatheaded wood screws, 1¼ inches long
16	No.16 roundheaded wood screws, 2¼ inches long
2	No.12 roundheaded wood screws, ¾ inch long [a]
8	¼-inch roundheaded stove bolts, 3 inches long
16	washers for ¼-inch bolts
8	wing nuts for ¼-inch bolts
2	⅜-inch roundheaded stove bolts, 4¼ inches long
4	washers for ⅜-inch bolts
2	wing nuts for ⅜-inch bolts
¼ pound	6d finishing nails
2	C-clamps [b]
1 sheet	linoleum,[c] cut to 26 by 48 inches
	contact cement [d]
	wood glue
	paint or varnish [a]

[a] Optional.

[b] Or a friend with a strong grip.

[c] As used for linoleum blocks.

[d] One quart should be sufficient.

Once all the pieces are cut, they should be marked and arranged for easy identification. Your first step should be to drill mounting holes for the legs into the two side frame pieces. Using a ¼-inch bit, drill a hole 2 inches from each end of each piece, along the midline of the piece (figure 4-1).

Drill mounting holes in the side frame pieces

fig. 4-1

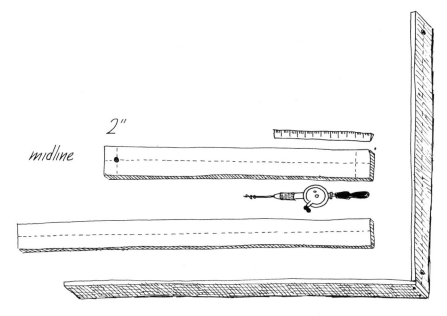

Now all the frame pieces should be attached to the table top. To make certain that they will all be properly set back around the underside of the table top, measure in at two points on the top side 2¼ inches from the edge of each 36-inch side. Draw a line through them. Do the same, measuring 1 inch in from each of the 48-inch sides. The result should be a 34- by 43½-inch rectangle (figure 4-2), which will serve as a guide when positioning the frame.

Draw a frame guide on the underside of the table top

fig. 4-2

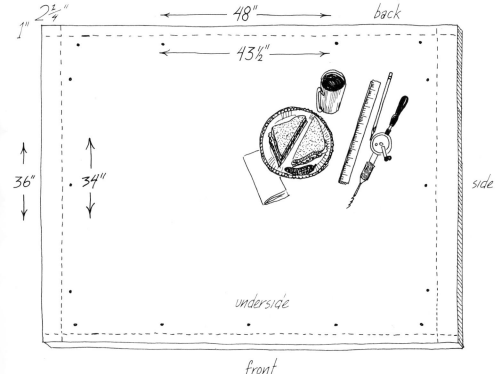

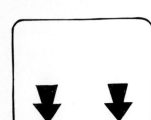

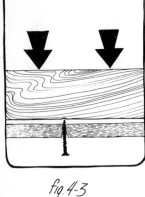

fig. 4-3

Mark the screw positions
on the frame pieces

fig. 4-4

Predrill and countersink the
screw holes and start the
screws

Join the frame to the table top

Mount the table braces

Now you'll need your drill and a bit that's smaller in diameter than a No. 16 screw. Drill a series of holes—five on each of the long sides and three on the short sides. Evenly distribute them and position them all about ⅝ inch in from the lines (figure 4-2). Now countersink the holes. Drive the 1¼-inch flatheads in partway, until the tips just barely protrude through to the other side.

Turn the board over again. Stand the front frame piece on edge, inside the rectangular outline along one of the 43½-inch sides. Mark the positions of the screws onto it by pressing the piece firmly against the points that extend through the top (figure 4-3). Do this next with the back frame piece, using right and left pieces to space it. Positioned correctly, front and back frame pieces will abut snugly against opposing ends of the side pieces. Depress all marks with an awl.

Brace the table top between your legs, hold the front frame piece in mounting position, and drive the screws until they grab it. Now you can lay the thing down and twist them tight. Repeat with the remaining pieces to complete the frame.

The 41-inch table braces should fit comfortably into the frame. While their exact location needn't be determined by precise measurements, it's practical to mount them about 10 inches in from the front and rear of the frame. We found it best to draw two lines marking their locations and then to drill three holes along each of them, using the same bit as before. Again countersink and screw the flatheads part way into the table top, and then mark their positions onto the braces. Depress these marks with your awl. Hold one of the braces up for mounting. Here again you may find it useful to support the table on edge until the screws take hold of the brace. When all the screws have been tightened, put a couple of 6d finishing nails into each joint (figure 4-4).

The legs should be assembled as two units of two. However, before we get to that, there's a little trimming that ought to be done. Because each leg will be connected to both table frame and foot with rotating joints, enabling adjustment of the tilt of the drawing surface, the ends of each should be rounded to facilitate the turning. An easy way to mark the curve is with a compass. Rule off a square at each end of one of the legs and locate its center by drawing diagonals across it (figure 4-5a). Place the point of your compass where the diagonals meet. Adjust it so that its pencil will reach the edges of the wood at only three points and thereby describe a circle with a diameter equal to the width of the wood. Draw the arc for cutting and trim along it with either a saber or coping saw (figure 4-5b). Do this with the other legs. Now, using your drill with a ¼-inch bit, make holes at the two compass-point marks on each leg. These will be the mounting holes.

To complete the preparation of the legs, attach the spacers to two of them. Center these, 6 inches in from each end of the legs, and, once positioned, affix them with a combination of a good wood glue and the 6d finishing nails (figure 4-6).

Before joining the legs to the table top, it's advantageous to connect them to the right and left feet. This will be done with the ¼-inch stove bolts. But first you'll have to drill some ¼-inch holes into those feet. Position them, one on each foot, following the same procedure used in positioning the holes in the legs—squaring off the ends and drawing diagonals. When you've finished this, bolt a leg with a spacer attached to each foot, using washers under bolt heads and with nuts. Be certain that the spacers are on the same side of the legs as are the feet. Then attach the remaining legs, remembering to mount them on the opposite faces of the feet (figure 4-7). For neatness and saftey both, all bolts should be attached from the outside.

Round the ends of the legs

Drill mounting holes in the legs

Attach the spacers to two of the legs

Drill mounting holes in the feet

Bolt the legs to the feet

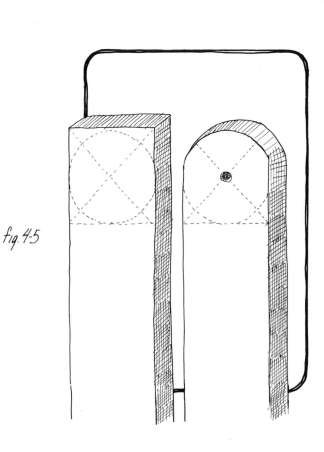

fig. 4-5

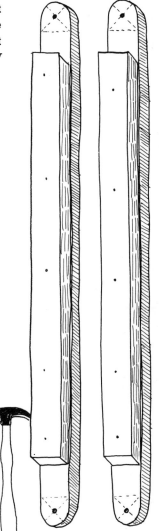

fig. 4-6

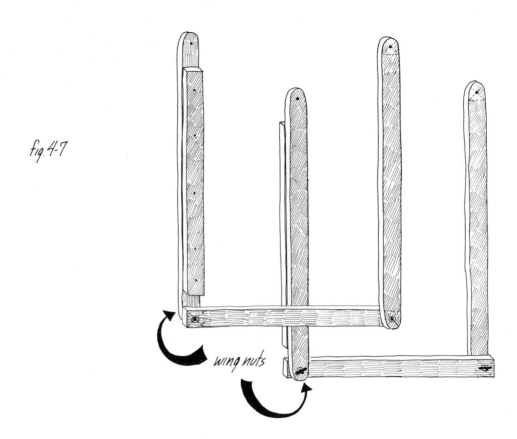

fig. 4-7

wing nuts

Bolt the legs to the table top

With both sets of legs completed, you're ready to join them to the table top. Each leg should be attached in a location corresponding to its location on the foot. This means that if the leg is mounted from what is to be the inside face of the foot, then it should be mounted on the inside surface of the table frame piece (figure 4-8). And remember to cross the legs when you put them on, as shown in the illustration. Again, insert the bolts from the outside.

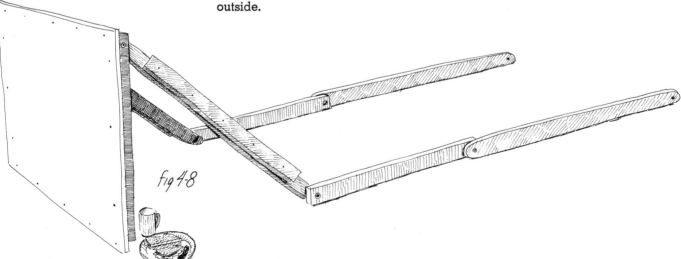

fig 4-8

Mount the leg braces

The leg braces should be positioned horizontally across the legs, about 6 inches in from the ends (figure 4-9). Drive two No.16 2¼-inch wood screws at each joint. The screws are mounted one above the other to prevent rotation, which would result in wobbling. Leave a space of 1¼ to 1½ inches between them.

leg braces

fig.4-9

Drill the intersection
mounting holes
for each table position

Stand the unit carefully—possibly with the aid of a friend—and tighten all the bolted joints until it can more or less support itself. Now the objective is to determine what angles you will probably find most comfortable for use, given the nature of your work and your personal style. Once this has been decided, get set to drill a couple more holes. But this time you'll have to change drill bits to accommodate the ⅜-inch bolts we recommend, necessary for added strength at two important joints. Where you actually drill the holes will depend upon where the legs cross once the table has been tilted to suit you. What you have to do is drill through the paired legs at a central point on the intersection. When you do the drilling, it's still a good idea to have someone around to help unless you happen to have a pair of C-clamps (they look like their names). If you do, we suggest that you use them to hold the legs together at both intersections, particularly while you're trying to drill the hole (figure 4-10). If not, your friend can help to achieve almost the same effect. The better his or her grip, the better the results. After the first hole is drilled, be careful not to change the position of the table top as you move to the other side to repeat the same procedure.

Now for the next work position. The assumption is that you have more than one favorite angle for your work surface. If this is the case, find the next position you want your table to allow. Again clamp the legs together, and again drill through the central place in the intersections. Actually, you can make your table adjust to as many positions as you want. All that you need is time, tools, and patience.

When you've finished drilling holes, pick the least tilted position and install the ⅜-inch bolts, with washers for each, from the outside. Tighten them up and you're ready for the big finish—that is, putting on the drawing surface. We've advised you to use the linoleum that's typically used for making linoleum blocks. It'll make a smooth, cleanable surface that has fairly good

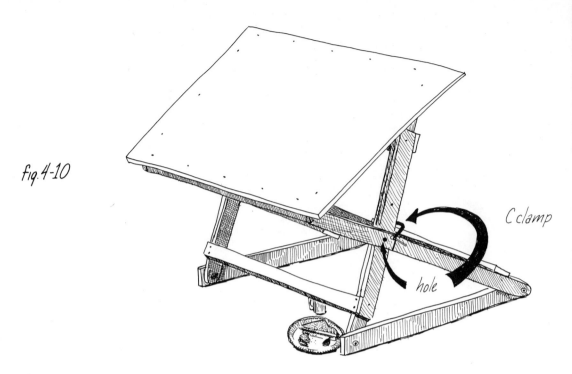

fig. 4-10

C clamp

hole

Glue on the drawing surface

recovery, and it's not too hard to install. If you didn't have the piece cut to the size of the table top when you bought it, you can do it yourself with a utility knife and a metal straight edge. After that it's just a matter of gluing it on (figure 4-11). For this kind of job, you'll be most satisfied with contact cement. To find out what to do with the stuff, read the package directions. But there's one thing to watch for that is true for all of the contact cements we're familiar with: Align the linoleum carefully before trying to cement it

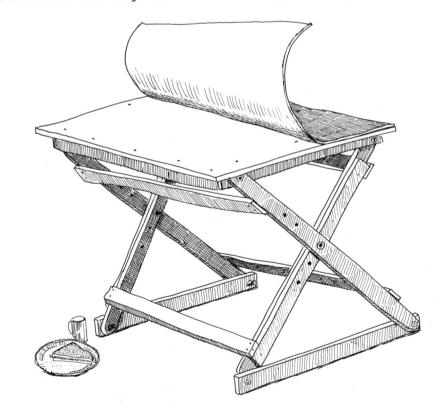

fig. 4-11

down. Typically, this kind of adhesive bonds on contact, leaving no opportunity for making adjustments. So just be careful.

Once you've gotten this far, you might think of yourself as being finished. And you might well be—that is, if you don't plan to go any further. You may, however, decide that you want to go one or two steps further in the interest of greater flexibility and general craftsmanship. With regard to the latter category, we're thinking in terms of putting a good finish on all of those wooden parts—varnish, paint, or whatever else appeals to you.

In terms of flexibility, we're thinking of a lip, a removable strip of lath that can be added to the front of the table top to keep your pencils from rolling off the work surface. A 3-footer will do this job really well. And to attach it, use two No.12 roundheaded wood screws about ¾ inch in length. Measure in about 2 inches from each side of the strip and at each of these points drill a hole having the same diameter as the heads of the screws. Adjacent to these holes on the right side, drill two somewhat smaller holes, about the diameter of the screw shanks. Drill these so that they open up into the first holes (figure 4-12). When this strip is mounted on the front edge of the table top (by driving the screws through the smaller holes, but not too tightly), you'll find that it can be easily removed and resecured simply by sliding it to the right or left respectively.

Put on a coat of finish

Mount the removable lip

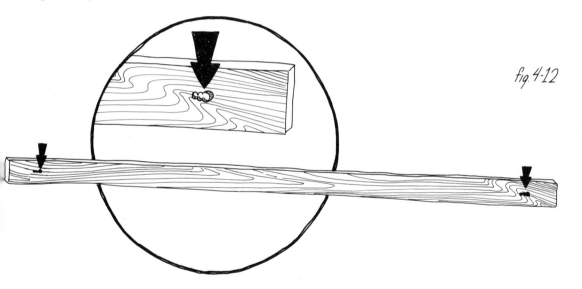

fig. 4-12

Well that's it. The only major thing to remember is that when you want to change the tilt of the table, just loosen up the bolts on the feet and the frame, remove the ones where the legs cross, adjust the drawing surface, reinsert the bolts that you removed, and tighten all of them up.

5·ART HORSE

If you've enjoyed the flexibility of a drawing board but can never seem to find a good place to lean it when sketching in a studio situation, then we suggest that you consider using an art horse. You've probably seen them before. In fact, you may remember having used one in art school—that is, if you went to art school. They're really quite simple to construct, certainly less complicated than building a drawing table or a studio easel. Yet they can be really practical, particularly when the only alternative is using a window ledge, which invariably faces you away from the very subject you intend to draw. Well, perhaps that's not the only option open to you, but we would be willing to venture that none of your options would be quite as convenient as an art horse. We can still recall the discomforting sight of twenty-seven art students crowded into a small studio sketch class with their drawing boards propped against walls, occupied stools, and anything else that could be seen around. Maybe you can personally remember those dreadful leg cramps that would inevitably come from trying to support your board on your knees, with your legs entwined in such a manner as to remain motionless, at least until they had begun to turn a marvelous shade of blue.

Basically, the art horse offers a place to work comfortably, providing both a structure against which to lean a drawing board and a seat for you. With it you can use your drawing board like a drawing table and yet have it available when you're working on location. The key word in construction is rigidity. An art horse that sways and creaks with every stroke you make will undoubtedly prove frustrating. For this reason, we've suggested that you use ¾-inch plywood or particle board for this project. This is the minimum standard that's necessary to easily support the weight of both you and your materials. Shelving board is another possibility worth considering, particularly if you do your own sawing. Although more expensive per square foot than either plywood or particle board, the difference in cost for the amount that you need would be offset—at least, somewhat—by the time you would save in cutting out the sections required for construction. Of course, the final choice is yours. Additionally, you'll need 5 feet of 1×3 or 1×2, which will be used to reinforce the joints for added rigidity. The only other wood that's required is 4 feet of ½- to ⅝-inch lath stripping. But lath is not the only option. All that it will be used for is to provide ridges against which the drawing board can be held securely. And if you've got something in the old scrap barrel that you think can do this job, just forget the lath. The dimensions we give here are necessary for an art horse capable of holding drawing boards up to 24 by 30 inches.

ASSEMBLY

Wood

Quantity	Material	Cut to	Description
1 section	¾-inch plywood [a]	12 by 33 inches	seat
1 section	¾-inch plywood [a]	12 by 34 inches	front
1 section	¾-inch plywood [a]	12 by 17 inches	back
1 section	¾-inch plywood [a]	12 by 31 [b] inches	shelf
5 lengths	furring strip [c]	12 inches	reinforcers
4 lengths	½- to ⅝-inch lath	12 inches	ridges

Hardware and Other Stuff

Quantity	Material
25	No.7 flatheaded wood screws, 1⅜ inches long
	wood glue
	plastic wood
	paint

[a] Or particle board (or even shelving board). Be sure to save a small scrap.
[b] Will be trimmed further during assembly.
[c] 1×3 or 1×2.

After you've cut all the pieces to size, label each of the plywood sections so you will know where it will be located on the finished art horse. This will make following the assembly instructions an easier matter.

On both the front and back pieces mark one end with a capital B, signifying "bottom." Lay the back piece over the front piece, making certain that the B edges are flush. At the top of the back piece, draw a line onto the front piece (figure 5-1a), dividing it in half (figure 5-1b). On the B side of that line mount one of the blocks of furring strip onto the front piece. Coat both surfaces to be joined with a good strong wood glue and press the block firmly into position (figure 5-1c). Turn the piece over and predrill and countersink three screw holes. Don't make these holes too close to the edge of the furring-strip block or the wood will split. Drive the screws into place deeply

Label the plywood sections

Mount the seat reinforcer on the front piece

(figure 5-2). Patch over the screw heads with plastic wood. Set the piece aside, allowing the glue to dry.

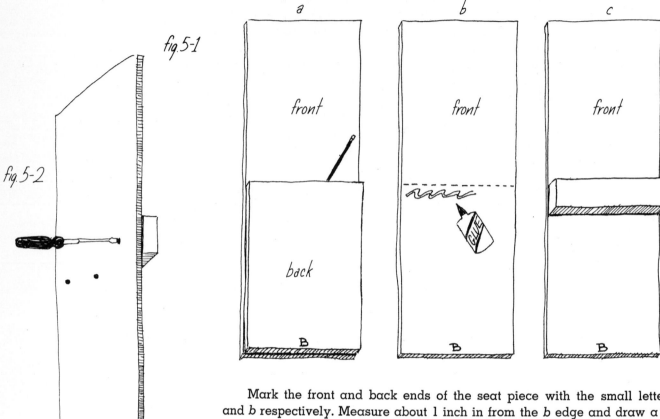

fig.5-1

fig.5-2

Mark the front and back ends of the seat piece with the small letters *f* and *b* respectively. Measure about 1 inch in from the *b* edge and draw a line at that distance across the wood (figure 5-3a). In the same way as with the front piece, mount a block of furring strip along the *f* side of this line. Be

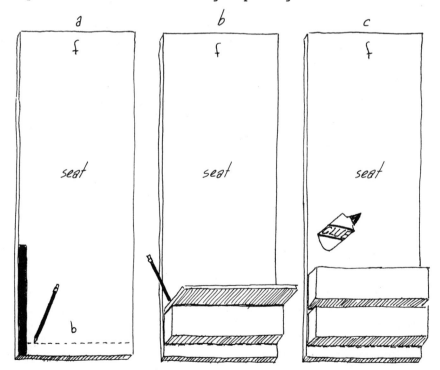

Mount the slot
on the seat piece

fig.5-3

certain that all screws are in tight. And now see if you can find a scrap of material you're using for the back piece. Stand it adjacent to the furring strip that you've just installed, along the f side (figure 5-3b). Run a pencil on the outside of this scrap piece. The distance between this line and the furring-strip block will be equivalent to the thickness of the scrap and, therefore, the back piece. On the f side of this line mount another furring-strip block (figure 5-3c). Together these two strips produce a slot into which the back piece will be inserted.

   Lay the front and back pieces side by side, with B edges aligned. Measure up 12 inches from the B edge of the front piece. At this distance draw a line across both pieces. This can be done quite easily with a T square or a metal right angle (figures 5-4a and b). Mount a furring-strip block along the B side of the line on each piece (figure 5-4c).

Mount the shelf reinforcers

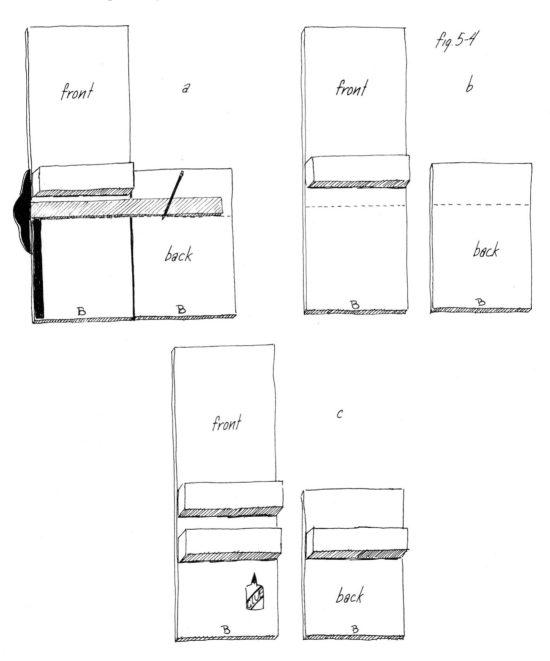

fig. 5-4

With this done, all parts are ready for final assembly. That is, unless you'd like a handle on your art horse. This is definitely optional, but it can be kind of practical for moving about. If you want the handle, sketch a 2- by 4-inch rectangle near what will be the upper end of the front piece, about 2 inches down from the top edge and set in 4 inches from either side (figure 5-5a). Drill at each of the four corners with a ½-inch drill bit (figure 5-5b) and saw along the lines with a coping saw, the kind with a thin little blade and a frame built in a high arch. Just remove the saw blade, poke it through one of the corner holes, reattach it to the frame, and begin to cut. At each corner hole turn the blade in the direction appropriate for following the rectangular form (figure 5-5c). When you've gone around all the way and the piece has dropped out, separate the blade from the frame and withdraw it from the hole (figure 5-5d).

Cut out the handle

fig. 5-5

a   b   c   d

To assemble the parts into a whole, screws in the company of a strong adhesive are recommended. Start by joining the back piece to the seat piece. You'll need either a friend or a chair to help you. If a chair is the more readily accessible, position it in front of you, or, if you prefer, you in front of it. Turn the seat piece so the slot faces down. Lay the end without the slot on the chair seat and slide the back piece into the slot (figure 5-6). Balanced in this manner, the unit should stand. Mark two points at which screws are to be driven, being certain that they are in line with the butt end of the back piece. Spread glue on the upper edge of the back piece and in the slot on the seat piece. Begin the holes with awl and screw starter and drive the

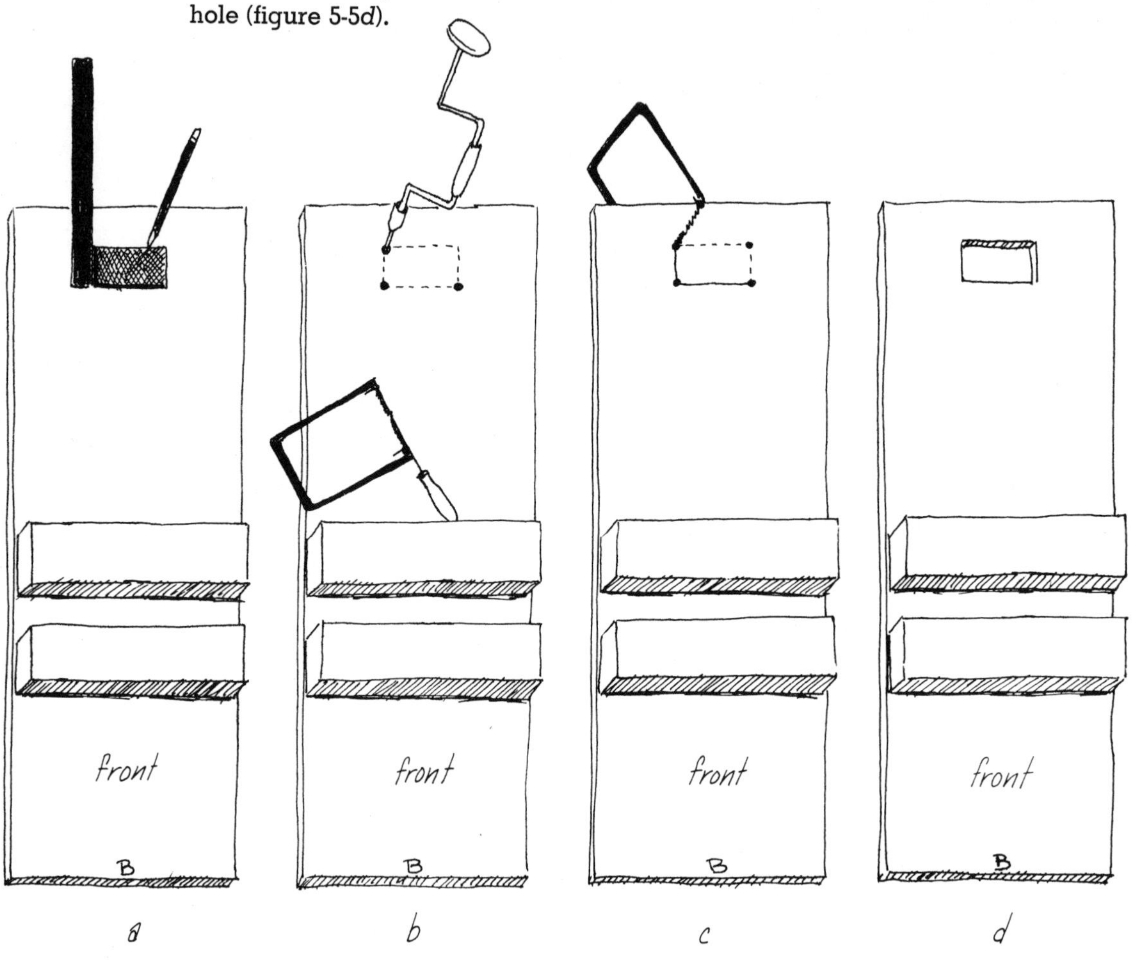

Join the back piece to the seat piece

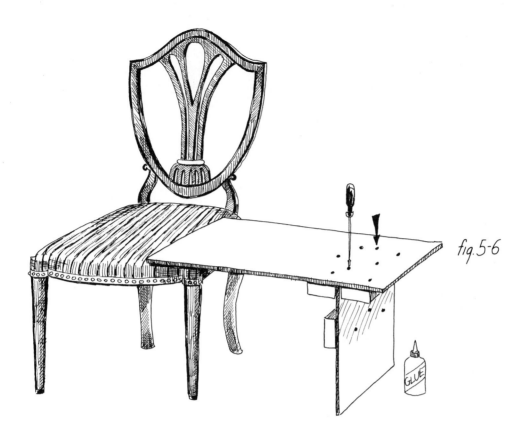

fig. 5-6

screws in securely. Allow some time here for the glue to set up before continuing. Consult the label of the product you're using for specific information about drying time.

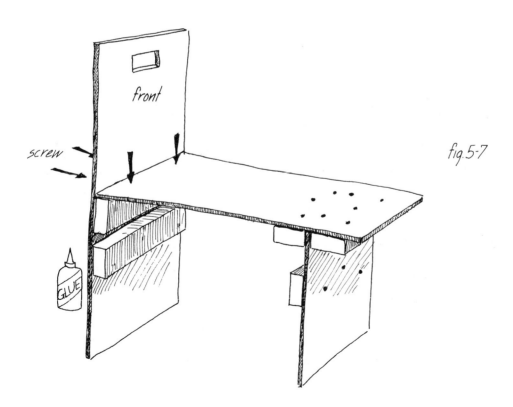

front

screw

fig. 5-7

Join the front piece to the seat piece

When you feel that you've waited long enough, replace the chair with the front piece. Apply glue to the upper edge of the top furring-strip ledge as well as along the undersurface of the seat piece that will be rested upon it. Lay the seat piece in position on the ledge. Here, in particular, a friend would be a real value in helping you hold the thing together while you drive the four screws into place. At this joint they should be driven from two directions, one pair through the seat and into the furring-strip support below and the other pair through the front piece and into the edge of the seat (figure 5-7). If no friend is in sight, you can abut the front piece against a wall that has no baseboard while you drive the first (vertical) pair of screws. Check your alignment carefully before starting the holes to be certain that the screws will go where you want them to.

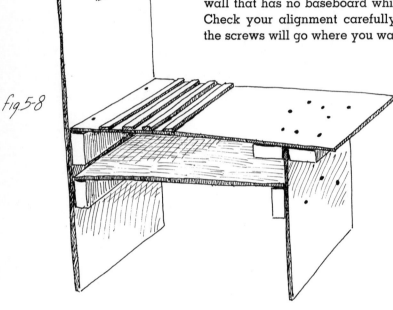

fig 5-8

Install the shelf

With front and rear pieces tightly in place, you have reached the last big step in construction, the addition of the shelf. Measure the inside distance between the front and rear pieces and cut the remaining section of plywood to that length. Invert the unit and coat the bottoms of the two remaining furring-strip ledges with glue and slide the piece into position over them. Screw the piece solidly into place. This small effort will provide you with a useful shelf beneath your art horse on which to keep pencils, pastels, erasers, carrots, martinis, and the like.

Glue on the ridges

Finally, with all of the heavy work behind you, glue the four 12-inch lath strips into position on the top surface of the seat, the first one 4 inches from the front piece and continuing with each piece at a distance of 2 inches thereafter (figure 5-8). These will enable you to lean your work surface in any of several positions with the bottom edge held securely.

You might also consider painting your completed art horse, especially if you don't want to see the word *front* on the front piece every time you remove your drawing board.

6·STUDIO BOX

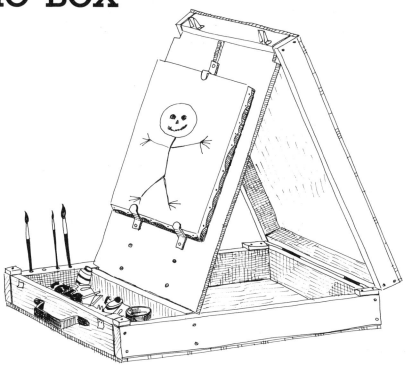

So often we hear artists who take particular delight in wandering into the beautiful hills that surround the village of Woodstock, New York, tell stories of sketching trips to private places—the woods are full of them—that wound up in dismal failure with the realization that the needed box of vine charcoals was back four miles on the shelf under the art horse. Well, here's a studio that comes with a handle on it. That's right, a studio, complete with an adjustable easel, canvas storage space, and bins for brushes, paints, and accessories. It just might be the perfect answer for you if you like working on location and have difficulty keeping everything together.

This studio box is durable and handleable, and it requires only the few materials described here. Our dimensions will result in a box measuring 18 by 23 by slightly less than 4 inches, a size we find convenient. But feel free to alter the specifications to fit your requirements. Also, while we have referred to painting materials only, please be advised that this tool can house almost anything. A sketch pad or two can surely replace the canvas and pallet—that's with room to spare—and pens might well replace brushes. Although it really doesn't matter what part you assemble first, to make it easier for us to tell you how to do it, let's agree to start with the base. You'll need both the long and short sides. On each end of the long side pieces mark two screw positions (figure 6-1). Also mark two positions about 8 inches in from one end of each piece. These will be for the stop piece—the actual distance from the end depends on the angle you will want for your easel. Predrill and countersink all twelve holes.

Take one of the short pieces and, holding it vertically, overlap its end with one of the longer pieces, forming a right angle. To help you hold it in this position, prop up the other end of the long side with the remaining short

Mark screw positions in the long sides of the base

ASSEMBLY

Wood

Quantity	Material	Cut to	Description
2 lengths	1 × 4 [a]	2 by 23 inches	long sides of base
3 lengths	1 × 4 [a]	2 by 16½ inches	short sides of base and stop piece
2 lengths	1 × 4 [a]	1⅛ by 23 inches	long sides of cover
2 lengths	1 × 4 [a]	1⅛ by 16½ inches	short sides of cover
3 sections	¼-inch plywood	18 by 23 inches [b]	cover and base surfaces and easel board

Hardware and Other Stuff

Quantity	Material
2	removable-pin hinges (with accompanying wood screws)
2	latches (with accompanying wood screws)
1	handle (with accompanying wood screws)
3	No.10 roundheaded machine bolts, ¾ inch long
3	wing nuts for No.10 bolts
20	No.8 flatheaded wood screws, 1½ inches long
38	2d wire brads
3	bendable hunks of metal
	white glue

[a] Have the lumber yard rip one 8-foot length of nominal 1 × 4 into 2- and 1⅛-inch widths. One long ½-inch-wide piece of scrap will be left over. Make certain your crosscuts are precise, however, especially for the 2-inch-wide pieces. The only scrap after crosscutting will be one 1⅛-inch-wide piece, 16½ inches long.

[b] Will be cut further during assembly.

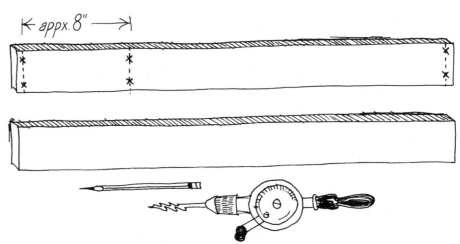

fig. 6-1

Assemble the frame for the base

side piece (figure 6-2). The pilot holes should be aligned with the butted end of the short side piece. Push an awl through each of the pilot holes and into the wood below. Remove the awl and drive two of the wood screws at these points. Repeat this procedure to join the other short side piece and the stop piece as well. Now invert the unit and position the remaining long piece. Drive the screws to tie it down.

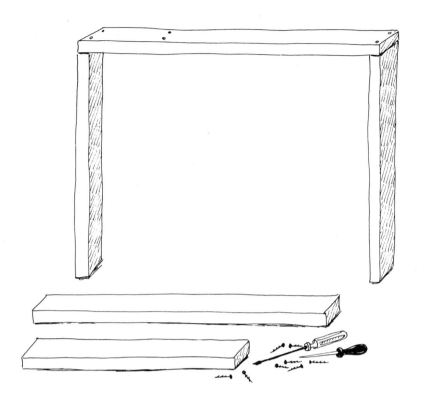

fig. 6-2

At this point all you have to do is tack on the base surface. Run glue around all the edges of the side pieces that are facing up and seat the base (figure 6-3). Use sixteen brads, more or less evenly distributed, to complete the job.

Attach the base surface

base

fig. 6-3

←glue

Assemble the cover

The cover is made in essentially the same way. The basic differences are the absence of a stop piece and the height of the side pieces.

When you've completed the cover, you're ready for the last major step—the preparation of the easel board. Start by drawing some lines on the surface. To locate them correctly, measure in at two points 5¾ inches from each long side. Connect the points by drawing two lines running lengthwise down the board. Measure in 10½ inches from one short side and mark the spot on each of the lines. Now mark off a series of points, each at a distance of 2 inches from the point preceding it, so that each line will have a total of seven such marks on it (figure 6-4). Drill at each of these, using a bit slightly larger in diameter than one of the machine bolts. After drilling measure in 2 inches from the center of the same short side, and at that point drill an additional hole (figure 6-5).

Drill holes in the easel board

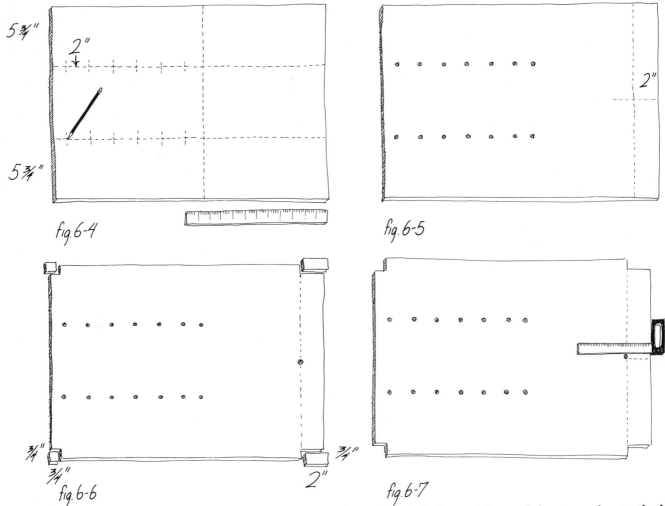

fig. 6-4

fig. 6-5

fig. 6-6

fig. 6-7

Cut off the corners of the easel board

Now you can put down the drill for awhile, and locate a fine-toothed saw. All four corners of the easel board must be removed. On the side that you've been measuring from, the chunks to cut out are ¾ by 2 inches, with the 2 inches measured lengthwise on the board. On the other end, ¾- by ¾-inch squares are all that need be eliminated (figure 6-6). (However, don't throw the pieces away! Just put them aside.) There's one more thing that saw has to do. That last hole that you drilled 2 inches in from the center of one side has to be converted into a slit. You can accomplish this by running lines from each side of the hole parallel to the long sides all the way to the edge of the wood. To guide them use a try square (figure 6-7). Cut along each with your saw.

Now, regarding those corner pieces, mount them on the top corners of the base sides as shown in figure 6-8. Use one brad in each of the smaller pieces and two in the others. When these are in place, the easel board can be positioned securely between them. Do this and place the cover over the top.

Cut a slit in the far end of the easel board

Mount the corner pieces

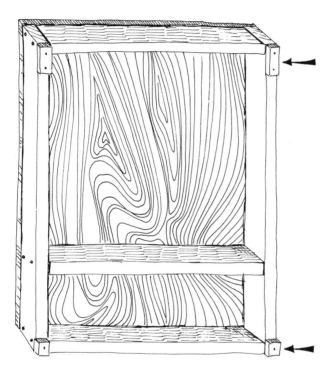

fig. 6-8

Position the pair of hinges on the short side furthest from the stop so that their spines are aligned with the edge of the easel board (figure 6-9). Use an awl to mark the mounting holes and drive the screws to secure the hinges.

Mount the hinges

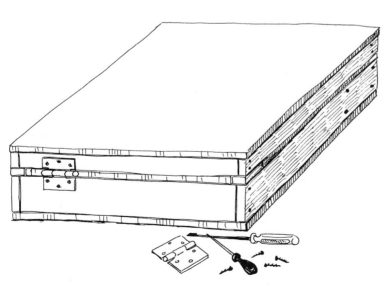

fig. 6-9

On the other short side mount the latches. Because of the variety of styles, you'll have to rely upon the instructions given with the kind of latch you've purchased. If perchance there are none, then the hardware dealer is the person to consult. Your handle can also be mounted on the same side. Typically this is accomplished with two screws that are provided in the package. Notice in figure 6-10 that the handle appears on the base rather than the cover. This is primarily because there is a little more surface to work with.

Mount the latches and the handle

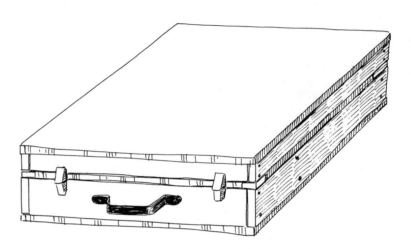

fig. 6-10

Now open the box and remove the easel board. Between the short side with the handle on it and the stop piece drill about four holes into the edge of the left long side piece with a 5⁄16-inch bit. Make them 2 inches deep (figure 6-11). Their purpose? To hold brushes when the unit's set up for work.

Drill the brush holder holes

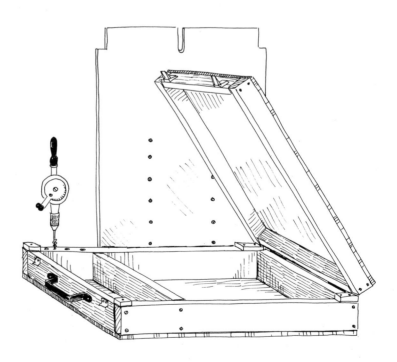

fig. 6-11

However, before you can mount your canvas in place, you'll need some clips. Bend the three small hunks of metal into shape (figure 6-12) and drill holes in each of them to accomodate a No.10 bolt. As you've probably guessed, two of the clips are fitted into the holes in the easel board and one is positioned in the slot. All are tightened with wing nuts.

To set the studio box up you just raise the cover, position the easel board as shown in the figure at the beginning of the chapter, remove your pallet and canvas from the large storage compartment and your brushes from the smaller one. Place the brushes in the holder holes and open up the paint tubes (also contained in the small compartment).

Prepare the easel clips

fig. 6-12

7·TABLE EASEL

If you happen to find yourself in a situation where you're cramped for space, then chances are you're finding your floor easel, if you have one, a constant menace. Even if it's one of the less cumbersome, portable kind, avoiding it can be a real problem. Unless you fold it up after every use—and who does that?—knocking into it at some time during the day is no doubt inevitable. One possible solution for you is to construct a table easel. While it would necessarily limit the size of what you can work on, it does represent a remarkable economy of space. In fact, a number of our friends, particularly those having little room to work in, use it as a second easel. And, like the collapsible floor-stand model, it's portable—even a little more so. It can be a great value if you're teaching painting to groups of adults or children. Here again, the substantial savings in space will enable you to accommodate more people then you might otherwise consider feasible. And, of course— even if you do have room to spread out (although if you're like us, you've never really witnessed this situation)—any space that you can keep open will enable you to accommodate something else later.

The table easel we're suggesting is very compact, yet it's substantial enough to work at fairly comfortably. If you should decide to make one (or more) of them, you'll find that it's really quite easy to put together. The dimensions that we have included are only a suggestion, based upon the size of those that are most commonly available commercially. But feel free to make the unit larger. Adding a few inches all around shouldn't create any problems at all.

ASSEMBLY

Wood

Quantity	Material	Cut to	Description
2 lengths	1 × 2	18 inches	top and bottom of frame
2 lengths	1 × 2	20 inches	sides of frame
1 length	1 × 2	20 inches	support leg
2 lengths	1¾-inch lath	20 inches	track
1 length	1¾-inch lath	18 inches	bottom-ledge lip
1 length	1 × 1	3¾ inches	clamp
1 length	1¾-inch lath	3¾ inches	clamp lip

Hardware

Quantity	Material
4	No.7 roundheaded wood screws, 1½ inches long
4	No.7 roundheaded wood screws, 2 inches long
8	No.4 flatheaded wood screws, ⅞ inch long
1	2-inch T hinge (with accompanying wood screws)
5	No.4 roundheaded wood screws, ⅞ inch long
1	³⁄₁₆-inch roundheaded stove bolt, 2½ inches long
2	large washers for ³⁄₁₆-inch bolt
1	wing nut for ³⁄₁₆-inch bolt
2	cup hooks
1	lightweight chain, 24 inches long

Begin by building the basic frame structure. The top of the frame should be bound to both side frame members with four well-placed wood screws. To position them correctly, measure the width of a 1 × 2 in from each end of the 18-inch-long top piece. Draw lines at these points, thereby forming squares at both ends. Within them draw two diagonal lines from corner to corner. Measure in about ½ inch from each end of one diagonal, marking two points along it (figure 7-1). Lay the marked top piece over the end of each side piece and position the sides so that they are parallel to one another and perpendicular to the top. Drive in the four 1½-inch roundheaded wood screws.

As indicated in figure 7-2, the bottom of the frame is not attached in the same way. This is because of the piece's dual function. Not only is it a component of the basic structural unit, but it serves as the bottom ledge of the easel as well; for this reason it's mounted on edge. Also in variance with the top piece, the screws that hold the bottom piece should be driven from the back—that is, through the side pieces. Therefore, turn the unit over so that the top piece faces down. Mark the side pieces at their bottom ends by measuring the thickness of a 1 × 2 (a little under an inch) in from the ends. Within each of the two rectangles that you've drawn mark two points, being sure to position them a safe distance in from all edges. Now stand the bottom piece in position beneath the side pieces and, holding it that way, install the four 2-inch roundheads.

The frame should now be pretty sturdy. If you really want to insure your unit against weakness, consider coating the faces being joined with some white glue before screwing. Personally, we haven't done so, and our little easel is quite steady.

Attach the sides to the top

Attach the bottom

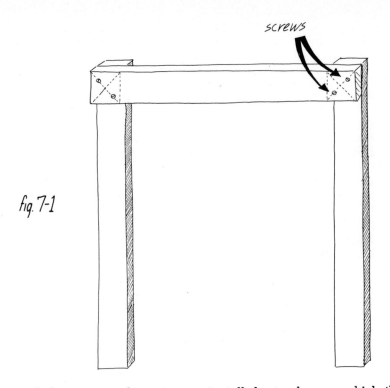

fig. 7-1

Install the track

Before turning the unit over, install the track upon which the clamp will slide. The most important thing to do first is to center it. You do this by locating the centers of the top and bottom frame pieces and marking them with a pencil. Then lay the two 20-inch-long lath strips across the top and bottom frame pieces, on both sides of center and adjacent to each other (figure 7-3). Place the ³⁄₁₆-inch bolt between them. Now slowly and carefully slide the bolt from top to bottom, thereby separating the two pieces of wood

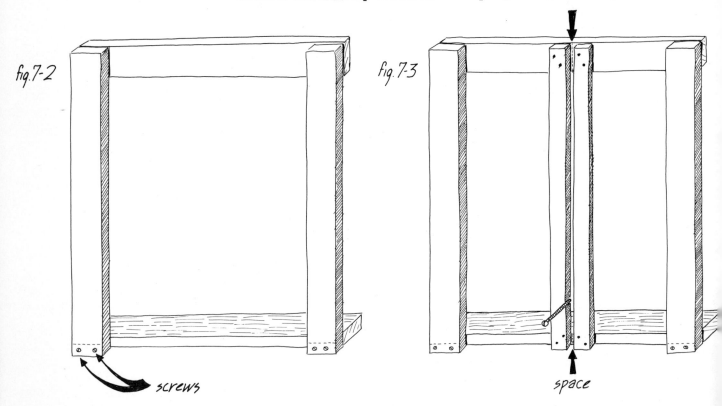

fig. 7-2

fig. 7-3

the thickness of the bolt. Mark their locations on the top and bottom frame so that in case you should accidently knock them off you can easily reposition them. Now decide where you want the ⅞-inch No.4 flatheads necessary to secure the track. Be certain that you wind up with two on each end of each piece. Because lath strips are typically rather soft, you shouldn't have to worry about countersinking the heads. Chances are that, as you tighten them, they will slowly be pulled in.

Once the track has been secured, you can mount the T hinge. This should be centered too. In fact, the rectangular plate, or pad, of the hinge mounts directly on the track, at the upper end. Make certain the spine of the hinge is up. These pads usually have three mounting holes; however, if the center hole is over the space between the two lath strips—as it probably will be— then only use two to attach it. In doing so, be certain that the hinge has been properly aligned. This is done relative to the top edge of the frame as shown in figure 7-4.

Mount the hinge

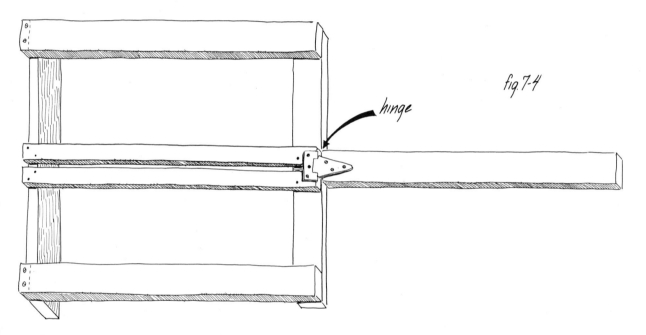

hinge

fig. 7-4

Lay the support leg out above the unit so that it is perpendicular to the top frame and in line with the triangular plate, or strap of the T hinge. When it has been correctly placed, you should be able to attach the strap to the leg, enabling it to swing down over the track.

Attach the support leg

Turn the whole unit over. This is as good a time as any to attach the lip to the bottom ledge. We felt that three ⅞-inch No.4 roundheads would do this job adequately inasmuch as there probably won't be much stress applied to this piece. One at each end, but not too close, and one in the middle should comfortably distribute the load (figure 7-5).

Attach a lip to the bottom ledge

The counterpart to the bottom ledge is the clamp. However, unlike the bottom ledge, the clamp is movable. But before you mount it onto the track, you've got to attach its lip. This is done with two screws rather than three.

Attach a lip to the clamp

When the clamp and lip have been joined, you'll have to drill a hole through them. Use a drill bit that's about equal in diameter to the ³⁄₁₆-inch stove bolt. To locate the point to bore, draw diagonals across the face of the lip and mark a spot about halfway between the point of intersection and

Drill the hole for the bolt

Secure the bolt

Attach the chain

the top edge, the edge where the 1 × 1 and the lath strip are flush (figure 7-6). Drill all the way through. Pass the bolt, with a washer under its head, through the hole and then through the center of the track. Place another washer over its end and secure it with the wing nut.

When you balance the easel in a standing position, you'll notice that it's necessary to take some precautions to prevent the leg from collapsing. This problem is solved with cup hooks and chain. One of the hooks is screwed into the inside face of the leg, near the bottom, and the other into the bottom ledge, near the track (figure 7-7). The length of chain that you draw between them will determine the tilt of your easel.

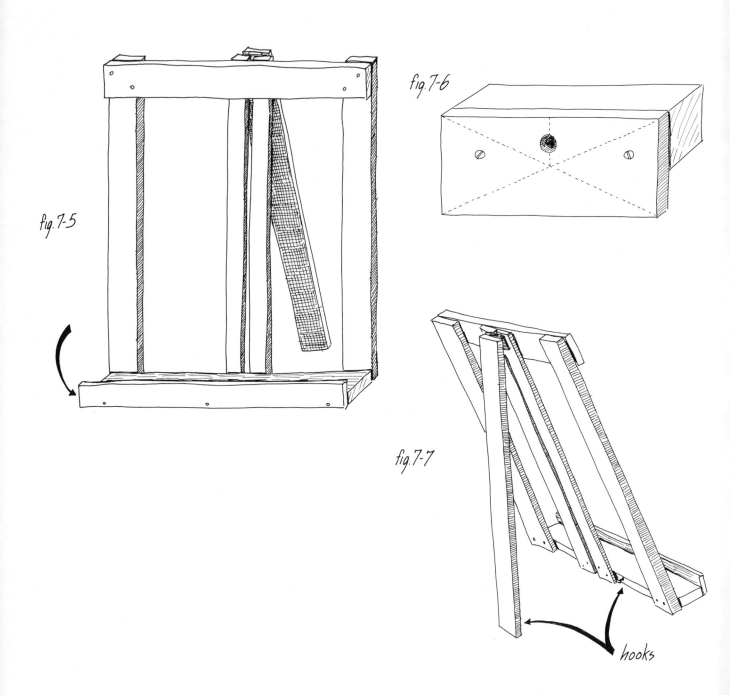

fig. 7-5

fig. 7-6

fig. 7-7

hooks

8·CONVERTIBLE CRAFT EASEL

We spent a long and discouraging summer trying to find an easel that would truly meet our needs. We had thumbed through pages of art- and craft-supplies catalogues and walked miles through shops to spend hours waiting at counters to discuss our requirements with clerks who could provide little more than a sympathetic nod. Somehow nothing that we saw seemed quite appropriate, and everything was too expensive for the limited budget that we had allocated for the purchase. Perhaps the one largest problem was trying to accommodate the needs of two artists working in totally different media, one in mosaics and the other in weaving and rug hooking. After some time we felt certain that compromise was inevitable. It was obvious that our wish for an inexpensive easel, capable of handling both of us, occasionally at the same time, doing entirely separate things, was not to be fulfilled through the usual commercial channels.

However, one day in late August, while strolling down Tinker Street, we came upon a studio painting easel standing on the sidewalk in front of a small book and art-supply shop. We stood and looked at it, wearied by the sight of another inflexible tool with an unacceptable price dangling from a string. And we paused. No words passed between us as we raced to the pile of wood and assorted oddities behind our tool shed. The sounds of saw and hammer mingled with the songs of birds, insects, and tree toads, and with a burst of new energy we worked for days until we had what we wanted—an easel of our own design and, better yet, our own making. It was huge, clumsy, unstorable, and, in general, ugly. But in late August of that summer that easel was a beautiful thing.

The convertible craft easel that we will show you how to build is several generations away from that old tool. This easel does all that we wished for back then and quite a bit more. It is easy to build, comfortable to use, and extremely versatile. Because it can accommodate two projects or two people, it's particularly efficient for craftspersons working together in tight quarters, and it can be set up to handle entirely different kinds of projects. It's great when there are children around. Offer to share it and get them involved with crafts. Of course, if you don't care to share your work space, you will have the advantage of keeping two of your own projects going at once. If you're a dabbler, you will no doubt find this easel to be a flexible and usable, if not a loveable tool. The easel is designed with three sets of attachments described in designs one, two, and three so that it can be used for many different craft processes.

The workboard described in design one is particularly fine for doing macrame. You will easily be able to handle large, typically cumbersome pieces on it anywhere you choose to set up. Just fasten the project to the surface, let the cords hang loose, and knot, knot, knot. By using another design-one workboard on the other side of the easel, you can work two pieces without spinning webs around the furniture.

If you have an interest in weaving, design one makes a comfortable board loom. Push in some T pins, wrap your warp, and your loom is ready for a shuttle full of yarn. Craftspeople we know who do rug hooking enjoy working their rugs when they are vertical so that it's possible to really see the whole piece as it grows. By fastening the rug canvas to the craft easel equipped with a design-one board, vertical hooking can be done easily.

When you use the design-two workboard with easel clips, combining it with the materials tray accessory, the convertible craft easel becomes a great place for drawing, painting, or doing collages on paper, fabric, or anything else you can find to hang on it. The materials tray has a removable insert to hold up paint and glue containers.

If yours is a compulsion for designing with broken bits of ceramic tile, nearly discarded chunks of wood, or colorful pieces of fractured glass, then you will find design three of particular value. With the set of design-three adaptors your easel will firmly support relatively large mosaic projects. As with hooking, it can be a great advantage to be able to work mosaics while they are in a hanging position. This is especially true for the craftsperson working at spontaneous designs. Where the project is held vertically, a fast adhesive like mastic is best in order to avoid slippage. The fact that the adaptors used in design three are completely adjustable will enable you to mount the project low enough to work at while sitting or high enough for you to be comfortable standing.

Design three is also a good tool for weavers doing frame weaving, particularly if your frame is large. Sometimes finding a way to support the frame while working with it can be a real problem. By mounting your frame on the convertible craft easel, you will be able to work your piece without holding it in your lap. The easel will keep it stationary, and you won't have to worry about a place to set up every time you feel like adding a few wefts. Because using the easel to hold your work makes it easy for you to stand back and see the weaving evolve, you can have greater control over the evolution of the total design.

Anything mounted on stretcher strips can be worked at using the craft easel with the design-three adaptors. This includes primed canvas. Almost all the painters we know do a number of paintings at the same time. By using convertible craft easels, they manage to reduce the problem of finding work space in a busy studio where at least one variety of media is being worked, since the basic easel can be fitted with any combination of design adaptors.

Because the easel is lightweight and folds almost completely flat, it needn't be a studio-bound tool. If you have a special place, whether under the ancient sugar maple behind grandfather's barn or on the roof of your apartment building, just bring your easel and your materials and set up. Your craft belongs wherever you're comfortable. Enjoy yourself.

The Basic Easel

Regardless of which attachments from designs one, two, and three you'll want for your craft(s), you'll have to make the basic easel. Building it is no problem. It's an inexpensive project requiring few tools and a minimum of experience in woodworking. While power tools are in no way necessary to complete this project, if you own or have access to some, they can save you time. The list of materials you'll need follows.

ASSEMBLY

Wood

Quantity	Material	Cut to	Description
4 lengths	furring strip	72 inches	legs
1 length	furring strip	36 inches	top crossbar
2 lengths	furring strip	34 inches	bottom crossbars

Hardware

Quantity	Material
4	2-inch T hinges (with accompanying wood screws)
8	No.8 wood screws, 1¼ inches long
4	½-inch cup hooks [a]
2 lengths	lightweight chain, 4 feet long [b]

[a] This is the smallest size you should consider.

[b] The longer the chain, the more you'll be able to adjust the tilt of your work surface.

The first step in building the easel is to connect the four 72-inch sections of furring strip that will be its legs to the 36-inch crossbar. Furring strips are usually sold in 8-foot lengths, so you'll need to cut the pieces to size before beginning assembly. Beware of splinters. The piece of hardware used in connecting the leg to the crossbar is the T hinge. The long extension off the hinge is called the strap; the short rectangular section is called the pad. Using your right angle as a guide, lay the pads of the hinges (with the hinge spines facing up) on the crossbar opposite one another and 1 inch in from the end. Make certain that the spines are kept parallel with the edge of the wood. Position the screws in the holes and drive them until they are secure (figure 8-1). Beware, do not overtighten wood screws—this can actually loosen them and defeat their purpose.

Mount the hinges

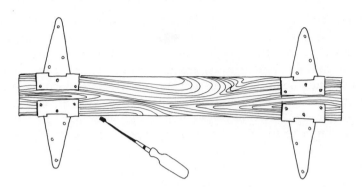

fig. 8-1

Attach the legs

When all of the hinges are connected to the crossbar, lay it in an open area to facilitate attaching the legs. If you're working in a large area, lay them straight out at the hinged corners, perpendicular to the crossbar (figure 8-2). Just position the hinge straps over the ends of the legs and drive the screws. If you're cramped for space, however, work on one side at a time. After attaching two legs on one side, you can swing them up against a wall and lay out the other set of legs for mounting.

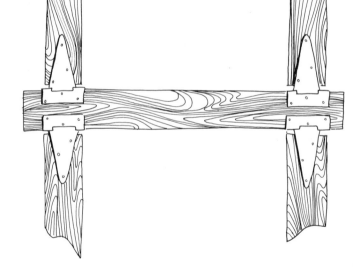

fig. 8-2

Attach the crossbars

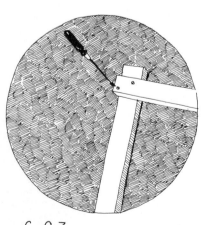

fig. 8-3

Having joined the legs at the crossbar alone, you will notice that each leg can be moved independently of the others. This will make standing the unit awkward and apply a good deal of stress to the hinges. Therefore, to give it greater stability you must now attach the two 34-inch bottom crossbars. With the legs in the same position as for connecting the hinge straps, lay one of the bottom crossbars over a pair of legs so that there is no overhang on either end, about 1 inch up from the bottoms of the legs. Mark two points at each juncture. Using a bit smaller in diameter than the wood screws, drill at these points, through the crossbar and into the leg below. At each hole drive a 1¼-inch No.8 wood screw until the crossbar is snugly mounted (figure 8-3). Do the same for the other pair of legs.

While the legs are lying flat, you have an excellent opportunity to carefully drill all of the adjustment holes for the various design adaptors.

You will need eight holes in each leg if you want your easel to be able to accommodate basic attachments for all three designs. All of the holes should be drilled along the midline of the legs. When drilling, you must be careful not to split the wood—apply even pressure but don't bear down. A ⅜-inch bit is the one to use here. Measuring from the top of the leg, the end hinged to the crossbar, drill holes at 4, 8, 20, 32, 44, 56, 64 and 68 inches (see figure 8-4).

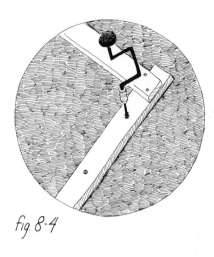

fig. 8-4

Now your easel will stand, but it will probably wobble like a fawn. So, before trying to stand it, you should prepare it for attaching the chain. To do this you'll need the four cup hooks. The hooks will work best if they're mounted about halfway down the legs toward the midline. The exact location on the leg is not really critical as long as it's the same on all four of them. Mark the points with your pencil and twist the hooks into place. If you're having difficulty tightening the hooks by hand, you may find it helpful to use your screwdriver or the claw side of your hammer. To tighten the hook with a screwdriver insert the blade into the hook and rotate it until it is secure. If you use a hammer, grip the hook with the claw and rotate the hammer handle. With all four hooks in place, stand the easel—or at least balance it in a standing position. When this has been accomplished, string a length of 10-pound chain from each hook to its opposite on the other side, remembering that the length of the chain between the hooks determines the angle of the easel. The unit should now stand by itself.

Attach the chain

You've finished the basic easel. Now, if you haven't already done it, you should decide which design or designs you'll want.

The Design-One Adaptor Unit

The design-one attachment, a particularly valuable one for persons doing soft crafts, will provide you with a 3- by 4-foot work surface that can be mounted on your convertible craft easel in just a few minutes. A number of different approaches are offered to enable you to tailor the tool you build to meet your particular needs.

The least expensive way of making design one—with insulation board— will provide a perfectly adequate work surface that is lightweight and relatively durable. Insulation board is a soft, fibrous material that usually can be found in 4- by 8-foot sheets in lumber yards. Some yards will cut the material to size for you for a small fee. Occasionally you can find precut scraps that, with a little trimming, can be made to fit. If you don't want a surplus of insulation board, this is the answer. However, if scraps are hard to come by, all is not lost. Even in whole sheets, insulation board doesn't cost much, and the surplus material is very usable. If you happen to want two design-one boards, a 4- by 8-foot sheet will be almost entirely consumed. And if one is enough, insulation board does have many other practical uses. You can always use a piece of the leftovers as a simple board loom, which can go wherever you go. Just bind the edges of the piece with cloth tape to protect them from denting and chipping. It's also a good material for making bulletin boards. With what you'd have left you could produce one or more. Just paint them or cover them with fabric (maybe a wild print from the local emporium or something you did yourself), screw eye hooks into the back, and attach picture-hanging wire or string to them. It's also good for backing pictures being readied for framing. And it's delightfully easy to cut with a standard handsaw. Just remember when you're working with it that it can break, dent, or chip.

The following list of materials includes all of the things you'll need to assemble a basic design-one adaptor, using insulation board as the work-surface material. Additional materials needed for building special variations of design one are included in the descriptions of those variations.

ASSEMBLY

Wood

Quantity	Material	Cut to	Description
2 lengths	furring strip	48 inches [a]	frame
2 lengths	furring strip	34 inches [a]	frame
1 section	insulation board	34 by 48 inches	face

Hardware and Other Stuff

Quantity	Material
4	corner braces (with accompanying wood screws)
12	No.8 flatheaded wood screws, 1 inch long
4	¼-inch T nuts [b]
4	¼-inch stove bolts, 3 inches long
8	washers for ¼-inch bolts
4	nuts for ¼-inch bolts [c]
1 roll	plastic tape [d]
	paint [e]

[a] Minus the width of the strip.

[b] Optional.

[c] Wing nuts are preferable.

[d] As wide as you can get.

[e] Choose a color that is easy on the eyes. Trying to do knots on a screaming magenta surface can be unnerving.

Build the frame

To avoid damage to the insulation board, we have suggested that you mount it on a frame. Make an L with one longer and one shorter length of furring strip by putting the end of one against the side at the end of the other, forming a 90-degree angle. Fit a corner brace into the lap of the L. Check the outside angle with a square (figure 8-5) to be sure that it's 90 degrees. Try to center the brace relative to the width of the wood and drive in the screws. Prepare the next two boards in the same way. When the second L is completed, position both sets to form a rectangle (figure 8-6). Install the two remaining corner braces. Check to be sure that all your corners are approximately right angles. (The frame will probably be somewhat unsteady so expect it).

Cut the insulation board

If you didn't have your insulation board cut for you, or if you did but it doesn't seem to fit the frame you have just completed, the procedure is simple. Lay the frame on the surface of the board, edge to edge and corner to corner, and trace around it with your pencil (figure 8-7). If you're working with the

right angle

corner brace

fig. 8-5

fig. 8-6

fig. 8-7

whole 4- by 8-foot sheet, you can make maneuvering easier by cutting the sheet in half before attempting anything else. Trim along the pencil lines with a saw. Cutting insulation board will frequently leave a ragged edge. If you have this problem, keep a sheet of medium-grit sandpaper nearby so that you can quickly even things out. Wrap the sandpaper around a block of wood for easy handling. It's wise not to breathe in any of the dust and to wash up after cutting your insulation board. If you happen to be using a board that contains asbestos, these precautions are particularly important. And of course it's always a good habit to wear safety glasses when cutting anything with a saw.

The board and frame are joined with the 1-inch flatheaded wood screws. We have suggested twelve, but you needn't follow this recommendation exactly. The important thing is to space them evenly around the edges of the board. Before putting in the screws, though, it's a good idea to apply tape around the edges of the board to help prevent them from crumbling or fraying. A coat of paint will also help. If you plan on doing both, paint it first and then tape it (figure 8-8).

Join the board to the frame

fig 8-8

Place the prepared board on top of the frame, aligning the corners and sides, being certain there is no overlap. Drive a screw into each of the four corners. If you bear down slightly on the screwdriver, the screw will start itself in the insulation board. However, to decrease the possibility of splitting the wood below, we suggest that you use your drill with the small bit to drill through the insulation board and into the frame at least a short way (figure 8-9). Also, to avoid splitting, make certain that your screws are about ¾ inch in from the corners and edges. Take care not to overtighten them or they will slowly disappear into and ultimately pass through the insulation board. Evenly space the remaining screws around the sides; this should keep the board from buckling on the frame. If it doesn't feel snug, you can always add more. Perhaps the thought of looking at all of those shiny silver screws while you're working doesn't appeal to you. Paint flowers around them, paint them the color of your board, or run another strip of tape over them so you don't have to deal with them at all.

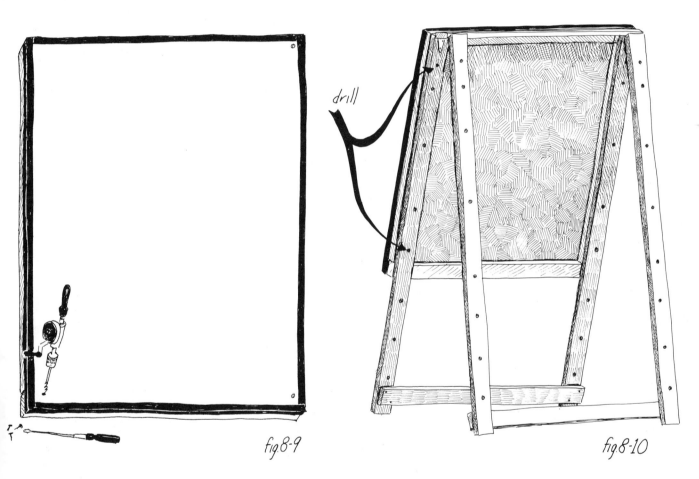

fig. 8-9

drill

fig. 8-10

Now you should drill holes near the corners of the design-one work surface for the bolts that will tie it to the easel. Hold the insulation board up to the easel to determine their exact position (figure 8-10). Use your ⅜-inch drill bit. If you would like the mounting bolts to be completely removable and the easel free for attaching other design units, then you are ready to attach the insulation board. But if you're the kind of person who easily loses his keys or can never find the scissors or scotch tape, then we're sure you'll prefer to have the mounting bolts attached more permanently to the design-one unit. If so, you will need four ¼-inch T nuts. Turn the insulation-board frame over, insert the T nuts into the mounting holes, and tap them into place with a hammer (figure 8-11).

Drill the mounting holes

Optional T-nut mounting

You are now ready to mount the unit on your easel. To do this you'll need the stove bolts, washers, and nuts as well as your screwdriver and pliers. Put a washer on each bolt and screw the bolts through the mounting holes until the washers are firmly against the insulation board. (If you don't use T nuts, push the bolts through the holes and hold them in position.) Lift the board assembly to the easel and push the bolts through the holes in the easel legs. Secure the unit with washers and nuts (figure 8-12). If you plan on changing easel attachments frequently, wing nuts on the mounting bolts are a good idea.

Mount the board
on the easel

insert T nuts

fig. 8-11

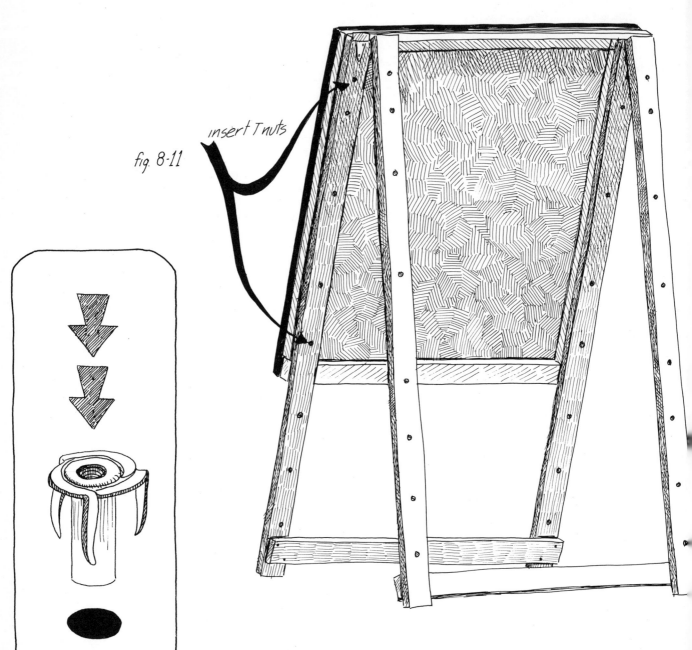

And now it's completed, a huge surface that you can work at comfortably, at almost any angle you could want. Well, don't just stand there—go to work.

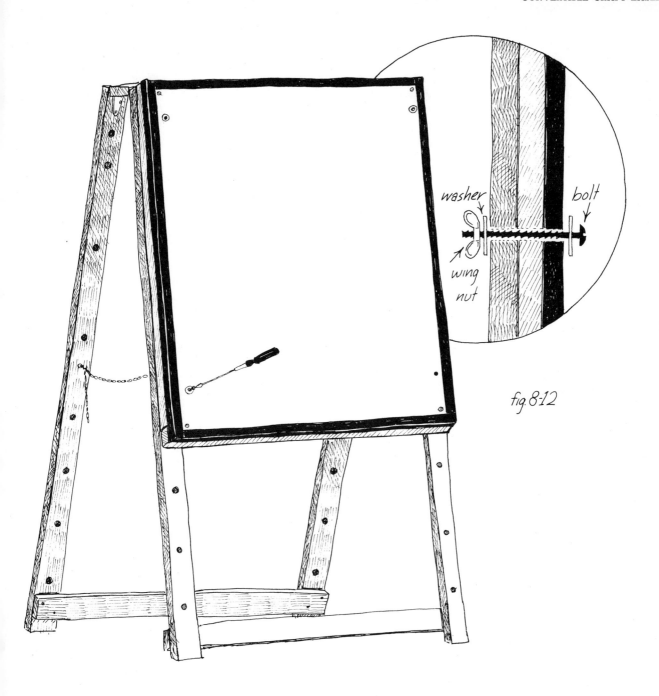

washer

bolt

wing nut

fig. 8-12

Alternative Work Surfaces for Design One

THE CLOTH SURFACE

If you take a "clean slate" approach to your craft, a cloth-covered surface may be most appropriate for you. That way you don't have to look at the pin holes made by your last project, and you can visualize your new project on a seemingly fresh surface. For this you'll need all of the same things that were used in making the painted insulation-board unit. The principal difference is in substituting 2 yards of 48- or 52-inch-wide fabric for the paint and tape. Cotton duck, twill, linen, canvas, or closely woven smooth upholstery fabric are all very suitable, as pin holes will quickly close up and disappear after the pins are removed. In choosing a fabric, try to avoid distracting patterns. Such fabrics may well be quite beautiful, but you certainly don't want to have to strain your eyes in trying to distinguish what you're doing from what you're doing it on. A soft, middle-range color (a pale green or a muted gold) makes it much easier to see what you've done and enables you to do it longer. You'll also need an iron, wide masking or cloth tape, and a staple gun with ¼- to ⁵⁄₁₆-inch staples. (A staple gun is a fabulous tool that's definitely worth having, but if you don't own one, and can't borrow one, you can substitute upholstery tacks for staples.) A sewing machine or needle and thread are optional.

Build the basic unit

Mark the fabric

Assemble the frame as described previously. Trim the insulation board, eliminating the painting and taping procedures. Attach the board to the frame and turn the whole unit face down onto the fabric. Center it, allowing a wide border all around the edges. Trace the edges of the board on the fabric with a pencil (figure 8-13). Also mark the positions of the mounting holes. To mark the holes on the border fabric, fold the fabric over the frame and poke around with your pencil until you find the holes (figure 8-14). Then you should unfold the border fabric. Push your pencil through each mounting

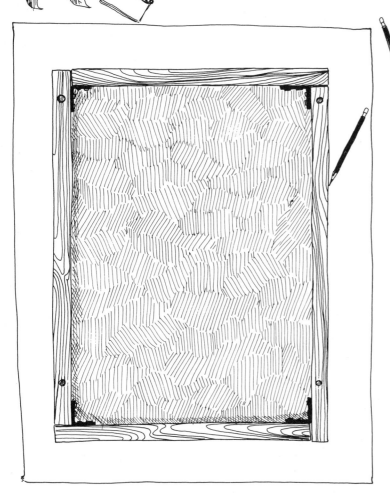

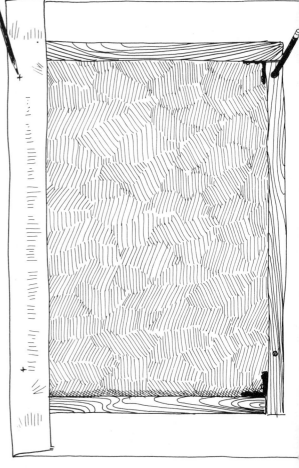

fig. 8-13   fig. 8-14

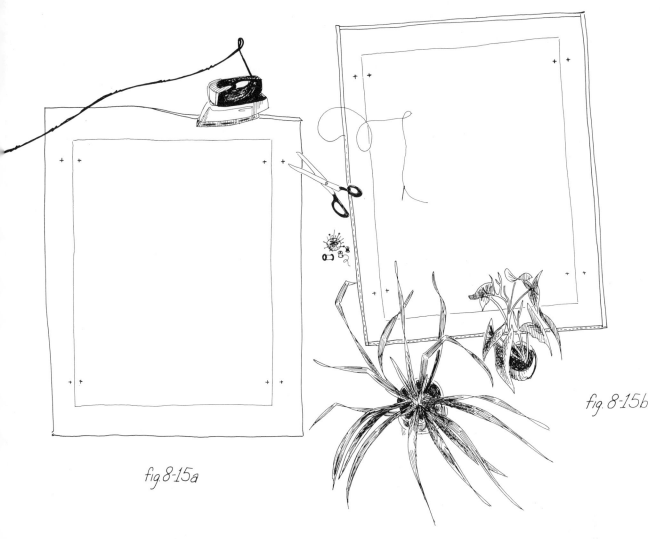

fig. 8-15a

fig. 8-15b

hole in order to mark the fabric underneath. When this is done, you should have eight marks, four on the surface fabric and four on the border fabric (figure 8-15a). With a sharp pair of scissors snip a small cross at each of these points. Fold over the edges of the fabric, about ½-inch, and press them flat with an iron. If you want, you can stitch these edges down (figure 8-15b.) While you have needle and thread in hand, you might also consider running a line of button-hole stitches around the mounting-hole crosses as an added security.

Lay the frame board down on the fabric again, matching the edges to the penciled outline. Fold the fabric over the edges and staple them down close to the frame. Start from the center and work toward the corners (figure 8-16), but do not staple the corners yet. First fold them down into triangular shapes and then staple them flat. Run a border of tape along the edges of the fabric, covering the staples if you can (figure 8-17). Try to make it tight and smooth. When you've finished this, your board is ready to be used. Just bolt it onto the easel.

Reinforce the edges and holes

Staple the fabric to the frame

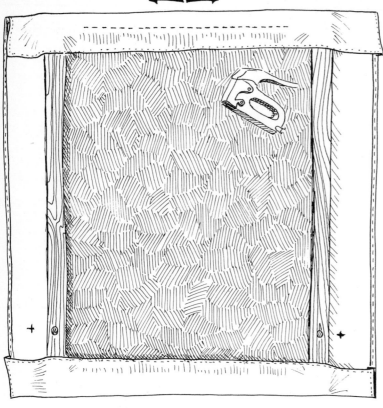

fig. 8-16

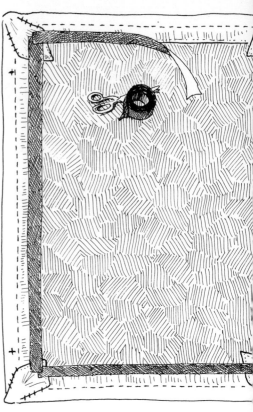

fig. 8-17

THE PADDED SURFACE

Sometimes a heavy padded work surface is a good thing to have. It can be very helpful for macrame and knotting and is especially nice for hooking small rugs. Basically this is a modification of the standard foam pillow used typically by macrame artists—a modification that, in this instance, allows the work to hang vertically. If you want one, all you'll have to do is add a foam pad to the cloth-covered version of design one (figure 8-18).

You'll need all of the tools and materials used in making the cloth-covered workboard. But this time the fabric covering should be at least 52 inches wide or even wider. (A salesman may throw the idea of burlap your way, so be prepared to duck. Burlap is marvelous except it sheds wiry hairs that can easily get all over the piece that you're working on. It itches, too, and can be very rough on your hands.) You'll also have to get a piece of foam rubber—it should be 34 by 48 inches, or a few inches larger on all sides if you want to allow for wrapping around the edges. Following the same basic procedures for making the design-one workboard, assemble the frame and attach the board. However, don't mark and cut the holes for the mounting bolts in the fabric. Position the framed board on the fabric, mark its position (see figure 8-13), remove the board, and lay the foam rubber over these markings. Lay the board over the foam. With a pencil or, better yet, a felt-tipped pen, mark the location of the mounting holes onto the foam rubber.

Disassemble and penetrate the foam at these marks by pushing a long nail or pencil or blade of a scissor or knife through the foam and twisting. This procedure will open holes for the mounting bolts to pass through. Lay the foam and board over the fabric again. Pull the borders of the fabric over the edges of the board and foam (pull relatively tightly). Mark and snip the

Build the basic unit

Mark the foam

Poke the mounting holes in the foam

cloth   foam rubber   frame   fig 8-18

positions of the mounting holes on the fabric borders. Having a friend available to help you may be of particular value at this point.

Sew the edges over into a hem, and they will not fray when you are stapling them down. While you're at it, throw some stiching around the mounting holes. The fabric on this workboard will have to take quite a bit more strain than the fabric on the unpadded board, and all this stitching will help it endure.

Lay the fabric down, along with the foam and board, and line up the mounting holes. Pull one side of the border fabric over an edge of the framed board and staple it down (stapling from the center to the corner, but not at the corner). Move over to the opposite side and pull the fabric tightly. The help of a friend and/or wide-nosed pliers for pulling fabric will make the job of stapling easier. Staple the fabric down close to the interior edge of the wood. Be sure that the mounting holes in the fabric stay aligned with those on the board. Fold the corners into triangles and staple them down. Check the front surface to be sure that it's smooth and tight. If it isn't you'll have to pull up the staples and adjust it. Repeat this procedure with the top and bottom. Run a strip of tape over the edges of the fabric, making an effort to cover the staples. Push bolts with washers through the mounting holes and attach the board to the easel.

Cut the mounting holes
in the fabric

Reinforce the edges and holes

Staple the fabric to the frame

THE CORK SURFACE

Cork—with its rich organic beauty, its deep texture, and color—is particularly worthwhile mentioning as another craft-easel workboard possibility. Not only is it aesthetically appealing but it's entirely practical for use as a surface that will be expected to accommodate push pins, T pins, tacks, and the like without incurring extensive damage. It's somewhat more expensive than other work surfaces we've described; however, with its current popularity

as a decorating material you may be fortunate enough to have access to some scraps that, taken together, could cover a 3- by 4-foot area. If not, you will need either a sheet of natural cork, usually ⅟₁₆ to ⅛ inch thick, or a number of cork tiles. Thin sheets—the kind used for making bulletin boards, coasters, and picture mats—are adequate and not quite so expensive. Cork tiles are usually available in building-supply stores.

As a backing you can use insulation board or ⅜- to ½-inch plywood. An important difference between the two materials is that plywood won't require a support frame, whereas insulation board has to be mounted. This is a point to consider when you're comparing the costs of materials as well as when you plan the time needed to do the job. If you're using thin cork sheeting, you must also consider the difficulties in pressing your pins into a surface backed with plywood. If your cork is relatively thick and you want to use plywood, we suggest using the unfinished construction grade. It's less expensive than finished grades though the lumber yard may not sell cut pieces. However, if as you wander around, you come upon a scrap that appears large enough, ask the price; you might be pleasantly surprised.

You'll also need some glue. There are several products that will work well for this purpose, including white glue. See what your local hardware dealer recommends (maybe he's got a homemade brew that's guaranteed to glue a Studebaker to the side of a passing woolly mammouth). If you're using plywood, you might also keep a piece of medium- to coarse-grit sandpaper handy to knock off splinters with. A sharp utility knife is useful for trimming the cork.

Glue the cork to the board

Lay the board out flat and arrange the cork so that it covers the whole surface. Trim off any excess with the knife. Remove the cork and apply the adhesive as the package directs. Replace the cork. If you're using a piece of sheet cork, start at one end, carefully matching the corners, and slowly roll the sheet down over the surface. Smooth it as you go.

Reinforce the edges

Mount the board

If the edges of the board are rough, run a line or two of tape around to cover them. Hold the board up to the easel and mark the spots where you will drill the four mounting holes. Mount the board onto the easel with stove bolts, washers, and nuts (T nuts if you wish).

A useful compliment to your design-one attachment, regardless of which surface you've chosen, is the material tray accessory described at the end of this chapter. It's perfect for holding all of those odds and ends that you inevitably need while working at your craft—extra T pins, beads, yarn and string, needles, scissors, and so on (figure 8-19).

The Design-Two Adaptor Unit

The design-two attachment for drawing, painting, and collage is similar to design one; the basic work area is a board mounted on a frame. In design two, however, the board has a hard, rather than a soft surface. The best material to use here is Masonite Its surface is smooth and relatively durable; it's lightweight and not expensive. You'll need a piece measuring 34 by 36 inches. Masonite that is ⅛ inch thick will provide sufficient support, although you can get ¼-inch masonite. Unless you have something really unusual in mind, however, what you'd get out of using ¼-inch Masonite probably won't justify its additional cost.

You'll also need something to mount the Masonite on for extra support. The choice is either a support frame made with furring strips and corner

corked surface

fig8-19

braces or a ½-inch sheet of plywood cut to form a square 34 by 34 inches. Although the Masonite panel used is rectangular, the support that it is mounted to is square so that the top of the masonite can overextend it by 2 inches to facilitate the use of easel clips. If you use plywood, all you have to do is spread adhesive over one surface and press the masonite onto it. Contact cement is ideal for this purpose. While this is much easier than building a frame to mount the Masonite on, it is heavier and it will cost more (unless you already have some ½-inch plywood).

First cut your furring strips to size. Following the procedure for making a furring-strip frame as outlined under design one, join the four lengths of wood to form a square measuring 34 by 34 inches. When you have completed the frame, lay the Masonite panel over it (figure 8-20). Align the bottom and the sides. Attach the Masonite securely to the frame by using the ¾-inch flatheaded wood screws (figure 8-21). It's best to space them evenly around the board and position them in from the edges about 1 inch.

Build the frame

Attach the Masonite

ASSEMBLY

Wood

Quantity	Material	Cut to	Description
4 lengths	furring strip	34 inches [a]	frame
1 section	⅛-inch Masonite	34 by 36 inches	face

Hardware

Quantity	Material
4	2-inch corner braces (with accompanying wood screws)
10	No.8 flatheaded wood screws, ¾ inch long
4	¼-inch T nuts [b]
4	¼-inch stove bolts, 2½ inches long
8	washers for ¼-inch bolts
4	nuts for ¼-inch bolts [c]
2	wooden clothespins [d] or easel clips

[a] Minus the width of the strip.
[b] Optional.
[c] Wing nuts are preferable.
[d] With spring action.

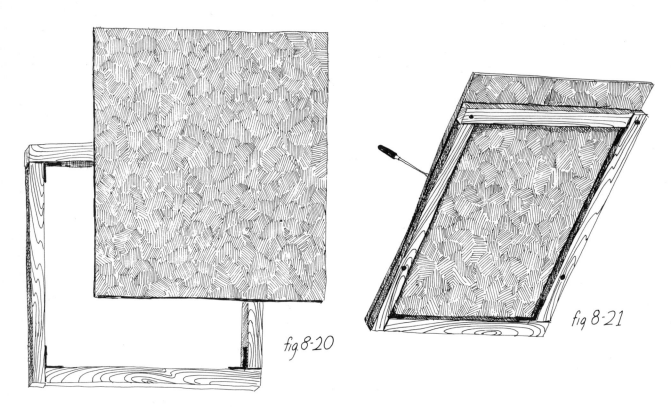

fig 8-20

fig 8-21

Drill the mounting holes

Optional T-nut mounting

Now you need to drill the mounting holes. To correctly position them, hold the frame up to the easel and mark onto the Masonite the holes that fall nearest the corners (see figure 8-10). Use your ⅜-inch drill bit.

As with design one, you can use either removable or permanent mounting bolts. For permanent bolts, turn the frame over and tap ¼-inch T nuts into the holes.

With this part of the assembly completed, take a moment, go to the clothesline, and find some clothespins. Those without springs are practically useless, but the others—the clothespins that children sometimes use as alligator puppets—make very satisfactory easel clips (figure 8-22). There are inexpensive metal easel clips commercially available that will do the same job, but they're sometimes hard to find.

Hanging the design-two workboard on the easel is the same as hanging design one. Just remember that the overlapping Masonite edge goes on top.

fig 8-22

The Design-Three Adaptor Unit

Design three is the option for craftspersons working pieces on frames, like weavings and paintings, or on other solid mounts, like mosaics. It enables you to clamp your work firmly onto the easel and will hold pieces up to about five feet in width or length. Unlike designs one and two, design three can be made entirely out of furring strips.

ASSEMBLY

Wood

Quantity	Material	Cut to	Description
2 lengths	furring strip	62 inches	track
5 lengths	furring strip	34 inches	crosspieces and bottom clamp
4 lengths	furring strip	6 inches	top clamp

Hardware

Quantity	Material
4	No.12 flatheaded wood screws, 1¼ inches long
10 to 12	No.8 flatheaded wood screws, 1½ inches long
7	¼-inch T nuts
6	¼-inch stove bolts, 1½ inches long
1	¼-inch stove bolts, 3 inches long
14	washers for ¼-inch bolts
7	nuts for ¼-inch bolts [a]

[a] Wing nuts are preferable.

After cutting the wood to length, write the letter *T* on one of the 34-inch pieces; this will be the top crosspiece of your design-three attachment. Also indicate the left and right ends of the same piece. On the left leg of the easel find the exact distance from the outside edge to the top hole (figure 8-23a) and measure off the same distance on the left end of the crosspiece. Mark the crosspiece at this point. Repeat this procedure for the right side. In order to be certain that these points on the crosspiece are midline on the wood, bisect the crosspiece by finding the central points (figure 8-23b) and drawing a line through them lengthwise down the wood. With a ⅜-inch drill bit bore holes at the two centered marks (figure 8-23c), turn the piece over, and insert a T nut into each hole.

Mark and drill the mounting holes

Mark the alignment indicators

For further steps in construction, you'll need to rule off alignment indicators on the crosspiece. Locate the halfway point along the midline and mark a set of points ¼ inch off to each side. Then run lines through them perpendicular to the midline. Continue the lines right over the edges (figure 8-24). These lines, as they appear on the edges of the piece, are the alignment indicators.

Mark and drill a bottom crosspiece in the same way, this time using the mounting holes 8 inches up from the bottom of the easel for reference. Insert T nuts into the back side.

Align the track

Clear some floor space and lay the top and bottom crosspieces, T nuts down, parallel and about 5 feet apart. Place the two 62-inch lengths of furring strip, which will be the track, side by side over the top and bottom crosspieces, thereby forming a large capital letter I. Separate the long pieces so that the inside edge of each is positioned on the alignment indicators (figure 8-25). Square off the corners with your right angle. Draw your pencil along the outside edges of the long pieces, marking the top and bottom crosspieces.

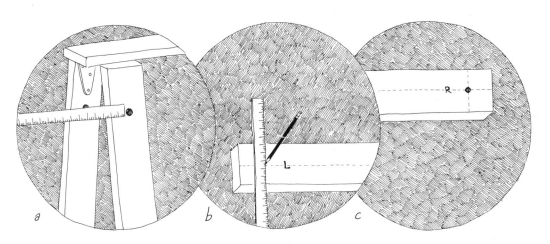

fig. 8-23

When the long pieces are removed, each crosspiece should have two squares drawn upon it. Find the center of these by drawing lines diagonally across them (figure 8-25a). Where the lines intersect indent and drill with a bit smaller in diameter than the wood screws being used. Turn the crosspieces over with T nuts up and right and left positions reversed. Using the alignment indicators, align the crosspieces over the long pieces, making sure that everything is square. Push a nail through the small holes in the crosspieces to indent the surfaces beneath (figure 8-26). Remove the crosspieces once more, and with the small bit again drill about ¼ inch into the long pieces at the points marked. Again replace the crosspieces. Position four 1¼-inch flatheaded wood screws at the drilled holes and drive them into place. (Drive them so that the screw heads are flush with the surface of the wood.)

Predrill the screw holes

Drive the screws

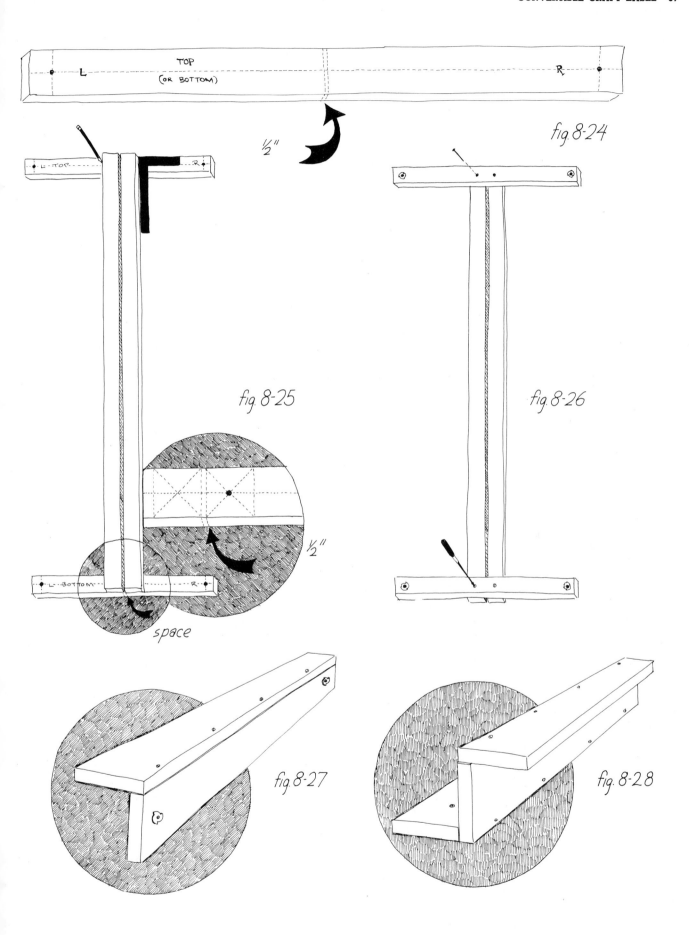

TOP
(OR BOTTOM)

L   R

½"

fig. 8-24

L · TOP ·   R

fig. 8-25

½"

L · BOTTOM ·   R

space

fig. 8-26

fig. 8-27

fig. 8-28

The Work Clamps

To complete design three, you have to make the work clamps. The bottom clamp is 34 inches wide and provides the basic support for your work. It is mounted directly to the easel and its movements are limited by the number of holes up and down the easel legs. The top clamp is only 6 inches wide and works as a stabilizer. Unlike the bottom clamp, it mounts directly to the design-three unit. The long verticals function as a track enabling the top clamp to slide freely in order to accommodate any size piece.

To make the bottom clamp, you'll need the remaining three 36-inch furring strips. With one of them proceed as you did with the crosspieces—that is, follow the same procedure for locating the two mounting holes. Drill these, again using your ⅜-inch bit. Tap the T nuts in place.

It may be useful to think of the bottom clamp as being made in a Z shape. Put the drilled piece up on one of its edges. Lay the second piece, flat side over it extending away from the T nuts, with one edge in line with the side of the first piece and the other edge being supported (figure 8-27). Mark three or four points along the board, ⅜ inch in from the aligned edge, spacing them between 9 and 12 inches apart. Join the two pieces together with 1½-inch wood screws.

The third piece is attached to the unit in the same way as the second was to the first. Turn the joined furring-strip assembly so that the T nuts in the first piece are down (figure 8-28).

Although working with screws may seem to add unnecessary difficulty, the strength of a joint made with nails is no match for one made with wood screws. This is especially critical for the first joint (connecting the first and second pieces), which must support the full weight of your projects. Nonetheless, because of the somewhat delicate character of the procedure described above, you may prefer to use nails. If so, you can strengthen the joints with glue.

When the bottom clamp is completed, drive the remaining two 1½-inch-long stove bolts, with a washer under each head, in place. The units can be connected to the easel at the height of your choice—depending on the size of your piece and whether you sit or stand while working.

To build the top clamp, you'll need the four 6-inch pieces of furring strip. The procedure is essentially the same as for making the bottom clamp; the major difference is in the number of screws used along each joint (two instead of three or four). Also, only one mounting hole is necessary. This hole should be drilled in one of the pieces before you begin assembly. The best place for it is in the center of the piece. Draw diagonals from the corners and drill with the ⅜-inch bit at the point where they cross. Tap a T nut into this mounting hole. Once the hole has been completed, follow the assembly procedures described for the bottom clamp (figure 8-29), extending the assembly away from the T nuts.

Now with the ⅜-inch bit drill a hole in the center of the fourth and remaining piece, using the other top-clamp mounting hole as a template. This last board will secure the clamp (figure 8-30). Drive the long ¼-inch stove bolt, with a washer under its head, through the nut until both the bolt and T nut are secure (figure 8-30).

You may need some help to mount design three, although it's probably not essential. Just hold up the unit behind and against the easel legs. Push bolts through the easel's mounting holes, at 8 and 68 inches up from the bottom, and through the corresponding holes in the adaptor unit. Secure the

Drill the mounting holes in the bottom clamp

Join the pieces of the bottom clamp

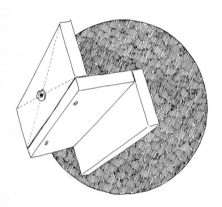

fig. 8-29

Build the top clamp

Mount the unit on the easel

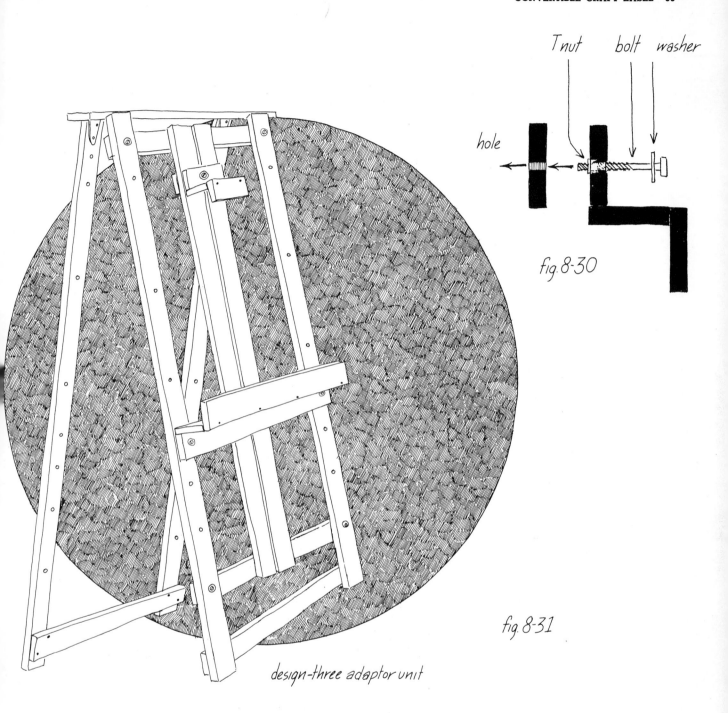

T nut   bolt   washer

hole

fig. 8-30

design-three adaptor unit

fig. 8-31

unit with washers and nuts (figure 8-31). To secure the top clamp to the design-three unit, push its mounting bolt through the track. Insert the end of the bolt into the clamp-board mounting hole and secure the unit with a washer and wing nut. By loosening this nut, you can slide the top clamp up and down.

The Materials Tray Accessory

A useful attachment to the convertible craft easel is the materials tray that can be used for keeping a variety of things convenient to the work area. If you wish, you can also build the removable container-holding insert. If you're worried about things spilling while they're in the tray, the insert is worth the additional time and effort needed in putting it together.

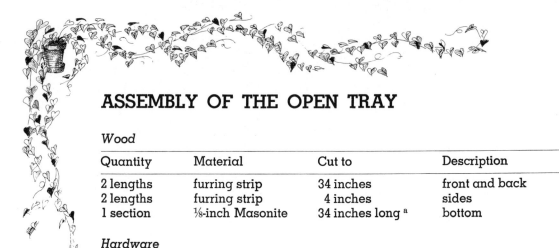

ASSEMBLY OF THE OPEN TRAY

Wood

Quantity	Material	Cut to	Description
2 lengths	furring strip	34 inches	front and back
2 lengths	furring strip	4 inches	sides
1 section	⅛-inch Masonite	34 inches long [a]	bottom

Hardware

Quantity	Material
2	¼-inch T nuts
2	¼-inch stove bolts, 2½ to 3 inches long
4	washers for ¼-inch bolts
2	nuts for ¼-inch bolts [b]
8	No.8 roundheaded wood screws, 1½ inches long
8	No.8 roundheaded wood screws, ¾ inch long

[a] Width is 4 inches plus the combined thickness of two furring strips.
[b] Wing nuts are preferable.

Drill the mounting holes

After cutting all the pieces to size, lay one of the 34-inch furring strips flat and mark two points for mounting holes as described under design two (figure 8-32). Indent and drill through with a ⅜-inch drill bit. Insert the T nuts (figure 8-33) and drive in the mounting bolts with a washer under each head.

fig. 8-32

fig. 8-33

Stand the two 34-inch and two of the 4-inch pieces in the form of a long rectangle with the bolt heads inside. The short pieces should be fitted between the long ones so that the inside distance between the 34-inch sides equals the length of a short piece, or 4 inches (figure 8-34). Now that you've got it together, connect the pieces with the eight 1½-inch wood screws (figure 8-35).

Join the side pieces

fig. 8-34

Mark the Masonite at four equidistant points along each 34-inch edge. Keep your marks about ½ inch inside the edges. At these marks you will screw the Masonite panel to the furring strips with the short screws (figure 8-36). This completes the basic assembly of your tray (figure 8-37).

Attach the bottom panel

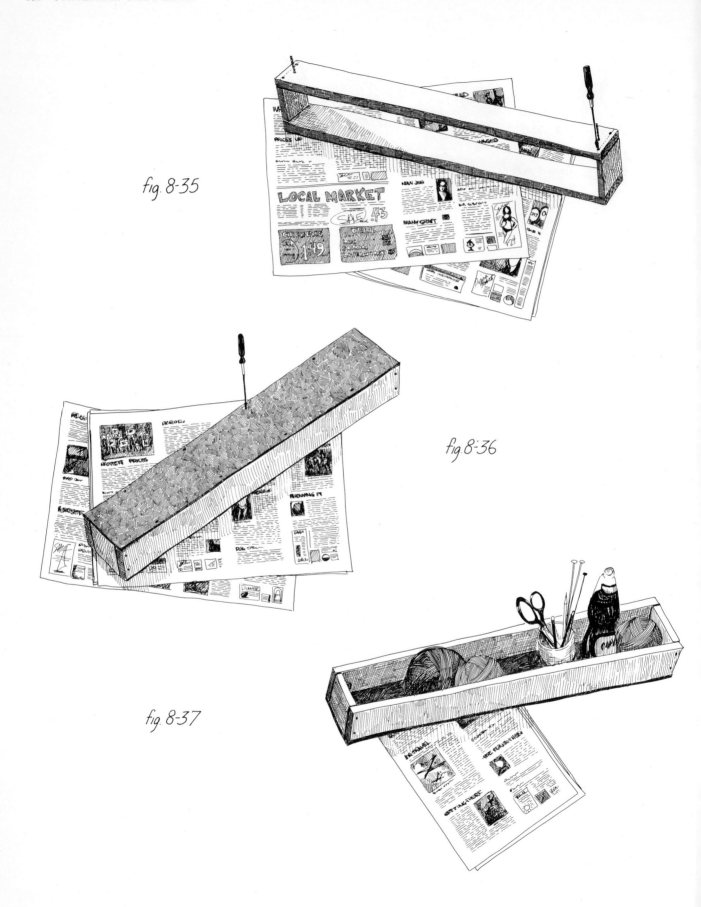

fig. 8-35

fig. 8-36

fig. 8-37

ASSEMBLY OF THE CONTAINER-HOLDING INSERT

Wood

Quantity	Material	Cut to	Description
2 lengths	furring strip	4 inches	stabilizers
1 section	⅛-inch Masonite	4 by 34 inches	face

Hardware

Quantity	Material
4	No.8 roundheaded wood screws, ¾ inch long

Hold the two blocks of furring strip together sandwich style. Stand them on edge on the face of one end of the Masonite panel, aligning them with the Masonite's edge. Trace the inside edge of the pair of blocks onto the Masonite (figure 8-38). Move the blocks to the other end of the Masonite and repeat this procedure. Separate the blocks and place one of them at each of the lines you've just drawn so that the inside edge of each is flush with the line (figure 8-39). Then run your pencil along the outside edge of the blocks. You should now have a set of two pencil lines on each end of the Masonite panel. Align the blocks between each set of lines. Drive the screws 2 inches apart and not too close to the lines (figure 8-40).

Mark the position of the blocks

Drive the screws

Now turn the whole thing over. Measure about ½ inch in from one of the blocks and mark the edge of the Masonite. Measure 3 inches from this point and mark the edge again. Measure another 1 inch and make your mark. Continue measuring off alternating 3-inch and 1-inch distances along the edge of the Masonite until you run out of space (figure 8-41). The distance from the last mark you can fit to the other furring strip should be about ½ inch. At each mark draw a line across and perpendicular to the edges of the Masonite. Using a square here can save you time (figure 8-42). Measure ½ inch in from both edges, marking two points. Connect the points by laying a straight edge across them and running your pencil along the straight edge (figure 8-43). When you've done this, you should have two parallel lines, each positioned in from the edge of the Masonite by ½ inch. You should also have, among other things, a series of eight 3- by 3-inch squares. That's it folks—eight squares spaced 1 inch apart.

Mark the squares on the panel

You now have to cut out the squares. To do this you'll need your drill with a ⅜-inch bit and a coping saw. First, drill holes inside the four corners of each square (figure 8-44). Indent these spots before drilling to prevent the bit from sliding around on the Masonite. Then remove the blade of your coping saw and put it through one of the holes in the first square. Reinsert the blade into the saw frame. Saw along the edges of the square, turning the blade to the appropriate direction at each corner (figure 8-45). Repeat this for each of the remaining squares. When they've all been cut out, you can clean up any rough spots with a piece of fine-grit sandpaper. When

Cut out the squares

you're done, you can insert the unit into the materials tray (figure 8-46) to provide your easel with sections for holding containers—whether jars of tempera, cans of beads, or bottles of cream soda.

Attach your completed materials tray to the easel by simply pushing the mounting bolts through the mounting holes on the legs and securing them with washers and nuts. Your convertible craft easel is now complete.

Mount the tray on the easel

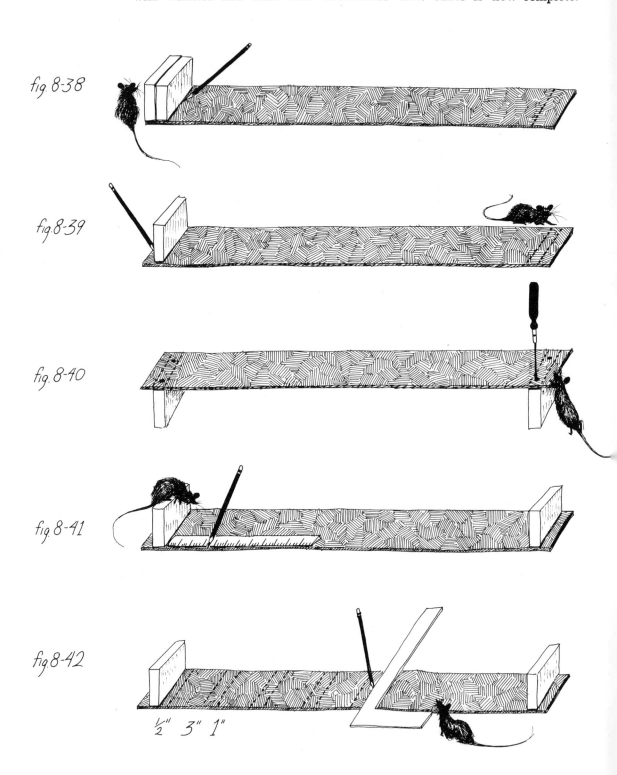

fig. 8-38

fig. 8-39

fig. 8-40

fig. 8-41

fig. 8-42

½" 3" 1"

fig. 8-43

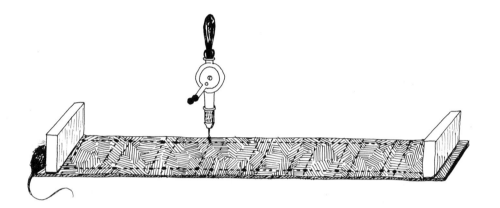

fig. 8-44

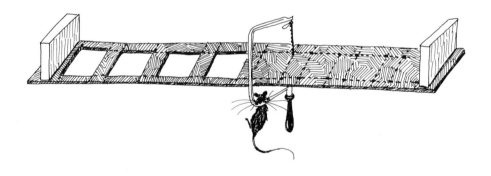

fig. 8-45

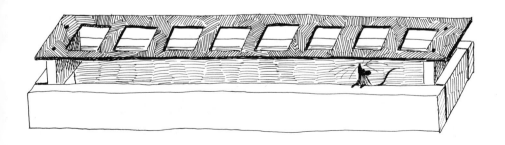

fig. 8-46

9·FRAMES

Why build a frame? What is it good for? Is it really a tool? Is there more than one way to make one? In this chapter we will be discussing frames. That's right, frames. For despite their structural simplicity, frames are a basic kind of crafts tool with many applications. With only slight adjustments in design, they may be used by needlepointers, quilters, weavers, hookers, and/or beaders. There are a number of ways to build them, depending on what you plan to use them for; however, regardless of which type you select, be assured that it should pose no great problems in construction.

To avoid needless repetition, we have chosen to combine instructions for the building of a number of kinds of frames into a single chapter. As with the convertible craft easel (Chapter 8), these are dealt with separately for each variation.

The Needlepoint Frame

This frame is lightweight, easily adjustable, and covers a good range of sizes. It can be made in one afternoon with a minimal investment in materials. The only wood that's involved is 1½-inch lath stripping. One 10-foot length of it should be more than enough for the size we're suggesting.

ASSEMBLY

Wood

Quantity	Material	Cut to	Description
2 lengths	1½-inch lath	30 inches	sides
2 lengths	1½-inch lath	24½ inches	top and bottom

Hardware

Quantity	Material
4	³⁄₁₆-inch stove bolts, ¾ inch long
8	washers for ³⁄₁₆-inch bolts
4	wing nuts for ³⁄₁₆-inch bolts

To cut the lath strips accurately measure, mark, and saw them one at a time. To double-check, hold each pair together on end. If they're a little off, you can trim them to match. When cutting lath, use a relatively fine-toothed saw and, to avoid chipping and splitting, don't press too hard. When you're satisfied with what you've got, lay the shorter pair of pieces aside.

Cut the lath strips

One of the ways that your frame will be adjustable is along the long side. This is achieved by drilling a series of twenty holes in each long side piece, equidistantly from end to end. A ³⁄₁₆-inch bit will be necessary for this purpose. To place the holes correctly, draw a midline along the length of each of the pieces. On one of the pieces measure in ¾ inch from an end. Mark this distance on the midline. Space the remaining nineteen marks 1½ inches apart. If your measurements are correct, the distance between the last mark that you make and the end of the board will be ¾ inch. Repeat this procedure to mark the holes in the other long piece (figure 9-1). When drilling, remember to block up the piece you're working on to avoid bruising either the bit or the surface below (figure 9-2).

Drill holes in the long pieces

fig. 9-1

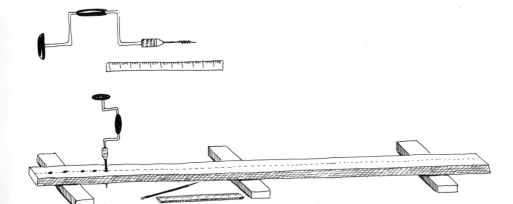

fig. 9-2

Cut slits in the short pieces

So that your frame will also be adjustable along its narrow side, we suggest that you cut slits into the shorter set of pieces for greatest flexibility. To do this, you'll need a small coping saw—the kind of saw that has a removable blade—and your drill with the same bit. As with the long strips, divide each shorter piece with a midline along the length from end to end. Measure 1¾ inches in from one end of one piece. Mark the point on the midline. From that point measure 7 inches along the midline and make another mark. Drill a hole at each of these spots (figure 9-3). Hold a straight edge parallel to the midline and tangent to the edges of the two holes. Draw a line along it, connecting the holes. Do the same on the opposite side of the midline. You should now have an area about ³⁄₁₆ inch wide and 7 inches long running between the holes. Position the blade of your coping saw in one of the holes and mount it in the saw frame. Cut along the lines you've drawn until the strip can be removed. Now, measuring in from the opposite end, repeat this entire procedure. When you've completed the piece, it should have two long grooves cut out of it (figure 9-3). Cut the other short piece to match.

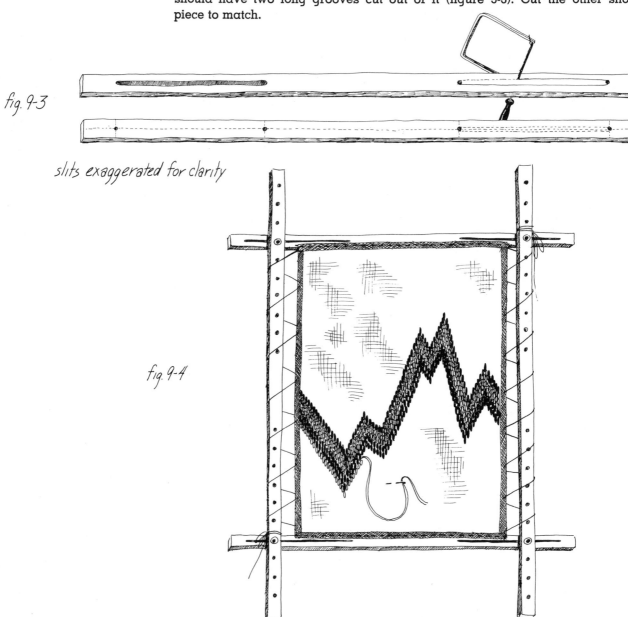

fig. 9-3

slits exaggerated for clarity

fig. 9-4

All that's left to do is to put the frame together. Lay out the frame in a rectangle of whatever proportions are suitable for your work, aligning the holes over the slits, and push the four bolts, with a washer under each head, through. Place washers over the ends protruding from the slits and twist the nuts in place. Your needlepoint frame is now complete (figure 9-4). When not in use, this frame can be easily disassembled and stored. If you want a stand for the frame, see Chapter 10 for instructions. Just make the brace piece 30 inches instead of 40.

Bolt the frame together

The Quilting Frame

We first learned about quilting frames from the people of a small mountain hamlet located in the rich, green heartland of the Catskills. There a fine old crafts tradition, the quilting bee, has been quietly preserved. Meeting together in a manner reminiscent of our remarkable handmade colonial period, they gather together periodically about a large frame to exchange ideas and experiences while sharing in a truly collective crafts process.

If your interest is quilting, this frame is the one that you'll most probably want. It's large, big enough to support a full-sized quilt and a number of sharing friends, fully adjustable, lightweight, and completely disassembleable for easy storage. In fact, in some ways it's quite similar to the needlepoint frame.

ASSEMBLY

Wood

Quantity	Material	Cut to	Description
2 lengths	1 × 4	8 feet	front and back
2 lengths	1 × 4	4 feet	sides

Hardware and Other Stuff

Quantity	Material
2 strips	canvas, 5 inches by 8 feet [a]
4	½-inch stove bolts, 2¼ inches long
8	washers for ½-inch bolts
4	wing nuts for ½-inch bolts

[a] Or drapery tape, 2½ to 3 inches wide.

As with the needlepoint frame, before you can start drilling, you'll have to find the midlines on every board. To locate the first hole in one of the long pieces, measure 6 inches in along the midline and mark the spot with your pencil. From this point measure 3 inches and mark another. Space the next eight points at the same distance. When these are marked, indent 6 inches from the other end and mark off the same number of points. You should

Mark holes in the long pieces

now have a total of twenty marks, ten on each end separated by a space of 2½ feet (figure 9-5). Repeat this procedure on the other long piece.

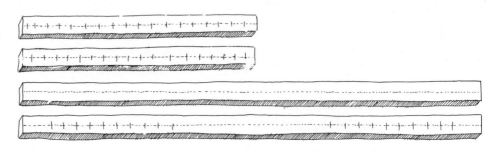

fig. 9-5

Mark holes in the short pieces

Unlike the needlepoint frame, the short pieces on the quilting frame are to be drilled out. However, to mark the first point measure in only 3 inches from the end of one of the short pieces. As before, space the remaining points every 3 inches. There should be fifteen marks in all running from one end to the other (figure 9-5). Repeat with the remaining short piece.

Drill the holes

To drill all of the holes you'll need a ½-inch bit. Remember to block up the piece you're working on to avoid bruising either the bit or the surface below.

Attach canvas tapes to the long pieces

For the next step you have a couple of options open to you. The objective is to run some kind of strong tape along the inside edge of each of the two long pieces, to which you will be able to attach your quilting project. The stuff that you choose should be fairly rugged. The method we have suggested is to cut two strips of canvas, 8 feet long and 5 inches wide. Fold them over in half lengthwise and press them flat. With canvas tacks or a staple gun, tack the loose edges of each one down to a long piece, skirting the holes and allowing some overhang (figure 9-6). This is more than adequate. Or another possibility, which can save some cutting, folding, and pressing, is to use drapery tape. You need only purchase a 2½- or 3-inch width, cut it to length, and tack it down.

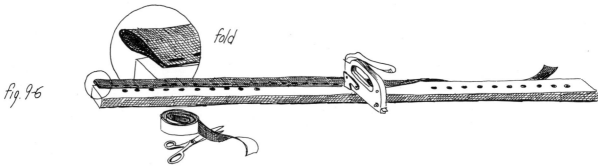

fold

fig. 9-6

Secure the quilt to the frame

Bolt the frame together

At this point, although still unassembled, the frame is ready to go to work. To mount your project, baste it to the tape on one of the long pieces and roll it up, leaving enough of it unrolled to attach to the other tape (figure 9-7). Lash the unattached sides of the project to the holes in the short pieces and put up the tea water. Then, bolt the frame together, inserting washers under the bolt heads and before the nuts. Make sure that it's all at right angles so you don't wind up with a crooked quilt.

fig. 9-7

Obviously this frame is too large to be held in a lap. To support it, four chairs at the corners can be used (figure 9-8), or you can rest it on a couple of saw horses. For extra stability C-clamps at each corner, where the frame rests on the supports, may be used. Naturally this will depend on what you have available. The important thing is to give it good support without sacrificing comfort. When the water comes to a boil, the quilting bee can begin.

Support the frame and quilt

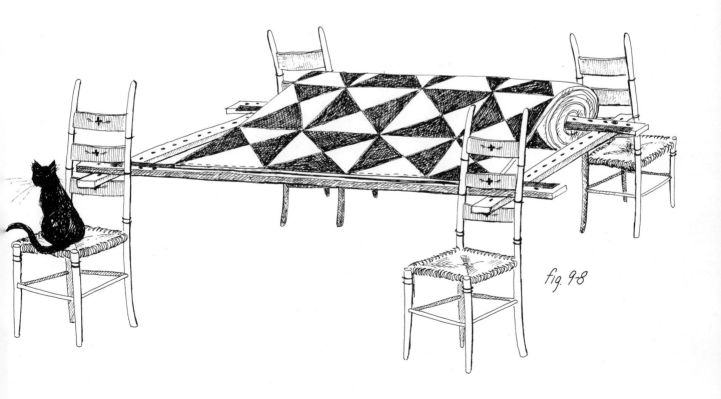

fig. 9-8

The Macrame Frame

If macrame is something that you do a lot of, this frame will be of particular interest to you; it was designed with the macrame artist in mind. Unlike the other frames that we've described in this chapter, this one is freestanding. It provides a firmly supported structure from which to hang your cord, and it serves no other household function. Or—to put it another way—not only is it a place to work, but it's also one where work can be left unbothered.

The size of the frame we describe is 6 feet tall and 3 feet wide. However, if your work or work space will necessitate a larger or smaller version of the frame, this is easily accommodated by modifying the dimensions of all the pieces accordingly. The whole unit is made up of only eight wooden parts: the frame members, the legs, and the head bar.

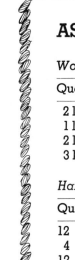

ASSEMBLY

Wood

Quantity	Material	Cut to	Description
2 lengths	2 × 2	72 inches	side frame pieces
1 length	2 × 2	36 inches	top frame piece
2 lengths	2 × 4	36 inches	bottom frame pieces
3 lengths	1 × 6	36 inches	head bar and legs

Hardware and Other Stuff

Quantity	Material
12	10d common nails
4	6d finishing nails
12	6d common nails
2	cork tiles, 12 inches square [a]
2	cloth tape measures
	white glue
	paint, shellac, or varnish

[a] Will be cut further during assembly.

Cut all the pieces to size

If the lumber yard hasn't done it for you, begin this project by cutting all the wooden parts to size. Some careful measuring and a standard handsaw are all that it takes. Then, after all of the pieces have been cut, check those that are to be the same length against one another to be sure that they match before you start putting them together.

Join the side pieces to the top piece

Begin assembly by laying out one of the two 72-inch side frame pieces perpendicular to the 36-inch top frame piece. Butt one end of the top piece over an end of the side piece and join them with two of the 10d nails. Lay the other side frame piece parallel to the first and join it in the corresponding position at the opposite end of the top piece (figure 9-9).

Without changing the position of the section that you just assembled, position one of the two 36-inch 2 × 4 bottom frame pieces on top of the unconnected ends of the side frame pieces. Square it up, and the whole thing should form a large rectangle (figure 9-10). Use four 10d's to tack the bottom frame piece down. Carefully turn the unit over (in doing this, avoid putting too much stress on the joints) and attach the other bottom frame member.

Join the bottom pieces to the side pieces

fig. 9-9

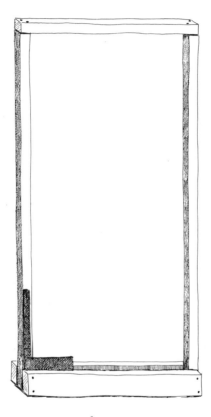

fig. 9-10

Place one of the 1 × 6's, which will be the head bar, in position over the top frame piece so that its top and side edges are flush with the top and side edges of the frame. It is in this position that the head bar should be mounted. Here use 6d finishing nails driven in the pattern illustrated in figure 9-11.

Mount the head bar

The legs are to be joined to the side with twelve 6d common nails. To do this, it's best to stand the frame, balancing it on the bottom frame members. To make hammering easier, try to position the unit so that one of the side frame pieces is adjacent to a wall; there is nothing more frustrating than trying to hammer into a moving object. Once the thing's erect, stand one of the leg pieces on its long edge against the side frame. Mark its center at 18 inches in from both ends and—at least visually—center that mark on the surface tangent to the frame. Use a level to be sure that the structure is standing perpendicular and drive in the first two 6d common nails. These should penetrate the side frame itself. Follow this set with another pair of 6d's, this time entering the end of one of the bottom frame members. Two more nails should be driven through the leg, this time into the edge of the other bottom frame piece. Turn the unit around, placing the completed leg toward the wall, and repeat the same sequence to mount the other leg (figure 9-11).

Mount the legs

Glue the cork to the head bar

Glue the measuring tapes
to the side pieces

When this is done, you can mount the cork. Its purpose is to enable easy tacking of the cords, and for greatest flexibility we recommend that you cover the entire surface of the head bar with it. Cut the cork with a utility knife. You should easily get two usable strips out of one of the tiles. Cut the tiles until you have three strips, or 36 inches in all, the width of the head bar (figure 9-12). To mount them, coat the head bar with adhesive and lay them in place.

To simplify and localize your measuring, you will definitely want to permanently attach a measuring tape to each of the side frame pieces. Start both of them at the bottom of the head bar and glue them in place along the inside edges of the side frames. Except for a coat or two of paint, shellac, or varnish, this frame is finished (figure 9-13).

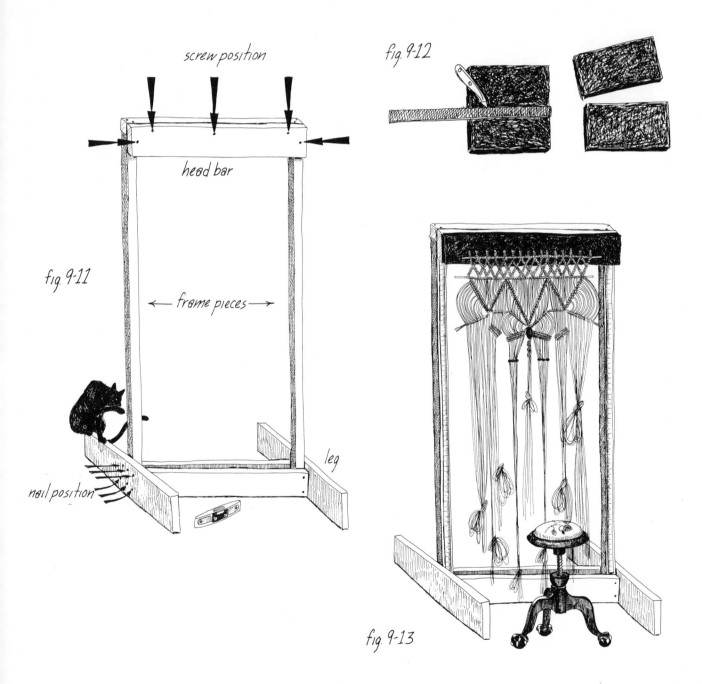

screw position

fig. 9-12

head bar

fig. 9-11

← frame pieces →

leg

nail position

fig. 9-13

10·FRAME STAND

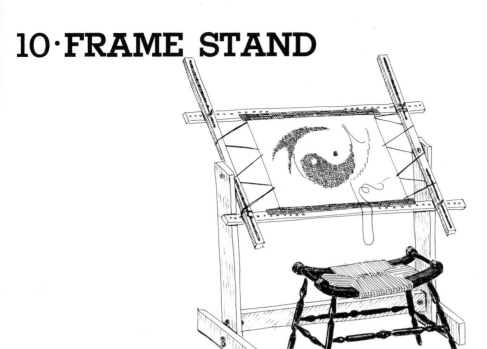

For any of the larger kinds of needlework frames, finding a place to work at it and some way of supporting it can certainly be a problem. Well, here's a solution that involves putting together only five pieces of wood. It's a frame stand, and if you're a person with a big frame and no place to put it, it's intended for you. While we have made a point of giving specific dimensions, these are certainly not intended as the only dimensions possible for this project. It's really a matter of how big the frame is that you're trying to accommodate, and, in this context, the most variable measurement is likely to be that of the brace running between the legs.

ASSEMBLY

Wood

Quantity	Material	Cut to	Description
2 lengths	⁵⁄₄ × 4	36 inches	legs
2 lengths	⁵⁄₄ × 4	18 inches	feet
1 length	⁵⁄₄ × 4	40 inches [a]	brace

Hardware

Quantity	Material
4	¼-inch stove bolts, 2½ inches long
2	¼-inch machine bolts, 2½ inches long
2	¼-inch carriage bolts, 2½ inches long
8	washers for ¼-inch bolts
6	nuts for ¼-inch bolts
2	wing nuts for ¼-inch bolts

[a] Alter this dimension to fit your frame.

Draw midlines on all the pieces

Join the legs to the feet

Drill holes in the legs for mounting brace and frame

fig. 10-1

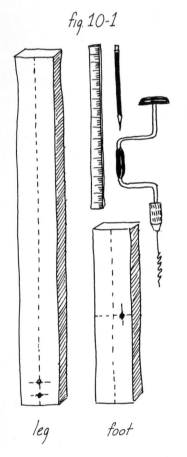

leg   foot

Drill bolt and nut holes in the brace

Mount the brace to the legs

Mount the frame to the stand

Begin by drawing a midline lengthwise down each of the five pieces. Additionally, draw lines across the width of each foot at the center, to divide it in half in the opposite direction as well.

On one leg measure in 1 inch from the end and mark it on the midline. With a ¼-inch bit, drill at this point. Measure off another inch and drill again (figure 10-1). Repeat with the other leg. Lay the drilled end of one leg over a foot piece so that leg and foot are absolutely perpendicular. Mark the locations of the holes onto the foot and bore through it at those spots. Push the stove bolts into the holes and secure with washers and nuts (figure 10-2). Repeat with the other leg-and-foot pair.

On each leg measure 1¾ inches from the top edge of the foot piece and mark another point on the midline. Also, mark off a distance of 1 inch down from the top end of the leg. Drill ¼-inch holes at these marks (figure 10-3).

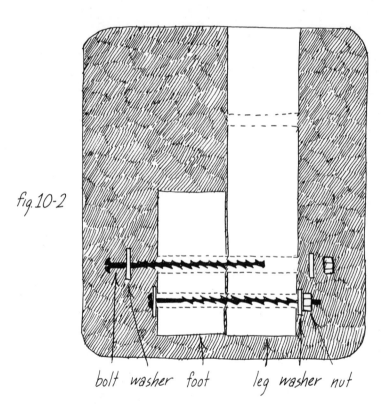

fig. 10-2

bolt   washer   foot   leg   washer   nut

To ready the brace for mounting, measure in 1½ inches from each end of it and mark the points along the midline. This time using a 1-inch bit, bore holes at both points (figure 10-4). Change back to your ¼-inch bit and stand the brace on end. Find the center by drawing diagonals (figure 10-5). Drill at the center, down to the 1-inch hole. Turn the brace over and repeat the procedure.

Using a machine bolt, nut, and washer, connect the brace to one of the legs as illustrated in figure 10-6 (the nut being seated in the 1-inch hole). Do the same on the other end. You may need someone to help you support the thing while you're doing this, but once you've done it, you're finished.

That is, except for mounting the frame. The way this is done will vary with the style of frame being mounted. Here again refer to figure 10-7 to see the different ways of doing it. If your frame is the type illustrated in figure 10-7a, the mounting should be obvious. If it is the type illustrated in figure

10-7*b*, the mounting is essentially the same as for mounting the brace to the legs. Please note, however, that in either case the carriage bolts with washers and wing nuts are used.

One of the particularly neat things about this unit (something we didn't mention before) is that since it's bolted together, it can easily be taken apart again. A nice feature when you're short on space.

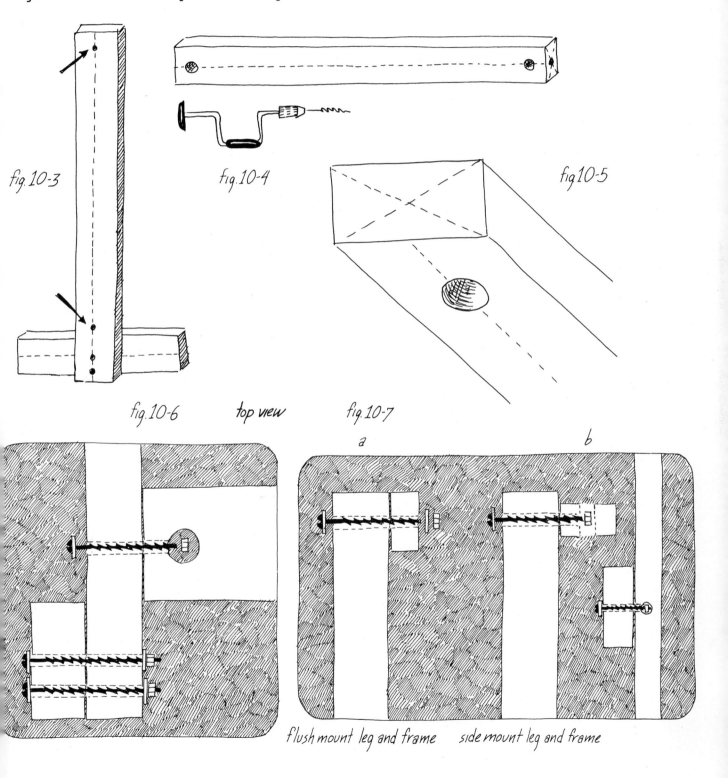

fig. 10-3   fig. 10-4   fig 10-5

fig. 10-6   top view   fig. 10-7
                                 a   b

flush mount leg and frame   side mount leg and frame

11·HOOP STANDS

This chapter is about things that you can do with hoops. A hoop, as any user knows, is a kind of frame—specifically a round one. Its uses include embroidery, appliqué, quilting, and trapunto. If you can think of others that we've omitted, you're probably right. As with so many tools, the number of its uses largely depends upon the ingenuity of its user. To accommodate for this kind of variety, hoops can be found in a wide range of sizes. Unfortunately though, it's not always convenient to have to hold one in your lap, particularly inasmuch as you can't have both hands free. And that's why some of them come mounted on stands. And it's also the reason for what we'll be describing: three practical kinds of stands and the hows for making them.

The first of these is a freestanding table stand, the second a chair stand, and the third a freestanding floor stand. While each is intended for a different kind of application, all make use of one most basic component part—the head. The head is the thing that enables you to attach a hoop to a stand. It's not very large, but it's completely necessary. Its construction is the same, regardless of which stand you choose. The other parts of the stands are essentially variations on a theme, each involving some length of post and some kind of base. Following is a list of the wood and hardware needed to assemble each type of stand. Although the dimensions given for the base of the table stand are specified for a hoop 9⅝ inches in diameter, it is possible to make the base longer or shorter to accommodate whatever diameter of hoop you have. But, whatever the diameter is on your hoop, its band should have a width of at least ⅞ inch. This is true for all three stands. The reason for this is that to bind it to the head securely, two screws are used at each mounting point. They just won't fit if the hoop is too thin, and a joint made with only one screw will surely fail.

ASSEMBLY

Wood

Quantity	Material	Cut to	Description
1 [a] length	1 × 1	2⅞ inches	head
1 [a] length	2 × 2	variable [b]	post
1 section	½-inch plywood	4¾ by 12½ inches [c]	base for table or chair stand
4 lengths	5/4 × 3	14 inches	feet for floor stand

Hardware

Quantity	Material
1 [a]	3/16-inch stove bolt, 1½ inches long
2 [a]	washers for 3/16-inch bolt
1 [a]	wing nut for 3/16-inch bolt
2 [a]	No.1 flatheaded wood screws, 7/16 inch long
2	No.5 roundheaded wood screws, 1½ inches long [d]
4	screw-on rubber legs, approximately ¾ inch in diameter [d]
2	No.5 flatheaded wood screws, 2 inches long [e]
8	No.5 roundheaded wood screws, 2¼ inches long [f]

[a] Twice this amount for the table stand.
[b] Depends on the stand—7 inches for the table stand, 14 inches for the chair stand, and 34 inches for the floor stand.
[c] In the table stand these critical dimensions are specified for a hoop 9⅝ inches in diameter. The length can be varied to accommodate the size of your hoop, however. If your hoop is larger, add the amount larger to the 12½-inch length of the base. If smaller, subtract.
[d] For table stand only.
[e] For chair stand only.
[f] For floor stand only.

The Head

Start with the head. Although it's the smallest wooden part, it'll take more time to prepare than any of the others. To make it, you should have a vise; however, a large one isn't really necessary. If you don't already own one and don't have access to someone else's, you can purchase a small one quite inexpensively. They're always useful to have around. In order to do the cutting necessary to shape the head, it's quite important to be able to hold the block stationary, and without a vise this job can really be a problem.

Measure and label the cuts

There are four cuts in all. Mark the first by drawing a line on the block's end, ¼ inch in from one edge and perpendicular to it. We'll label this line *A* (figure 11-1*a*). On the opposite end measure in 3/16 inch from side opposite line *A* and draw another line. We'll label this one *B*. Lay the block so that the side you just measured from is facing up. On that side measure ⅞ inch from the end that you just marked. Draw a line across the side at this spot. This will be line C. And from the opposite end, measure 1 7/16 inches and draw another line parallel to the last. We'll call it *D*.

Mount the head block in the vise so that the end with line *B* on it is facing up. Using a saw with a fine-toothed blade, carefully cut at this line

Make the cuts

down ⅞ inch. Then change the block's position so that the side with lines C and D on it is facing up. Cut at line C, down to the cut from B. A corner of the block will fall off, exposing the mounting surface. Now gently cut down ½ inch at line D. Finally, turn the block so that the end with line A drawn on it is facing up. Cut at line A down to the cut from D. A huge chunk will fall off, exposing the tongue (figure 11-1b).

Drill the mounting hole in the head

Put your saw aside and place a ¼-inch bit in your drill. Make a mark on the tongue centered relative to the sides, and ⁷⁄₁₆ inch from the end. Drill it out gently (figure 11-1c). Once you've gotten this far, your biggest problems are over. Just smooth the thing off with sandpaper, and you've completed the head. Or rather, one of the heads—if you're making the table model, you've got to make two heads. Oh well, at least now you've got experience.

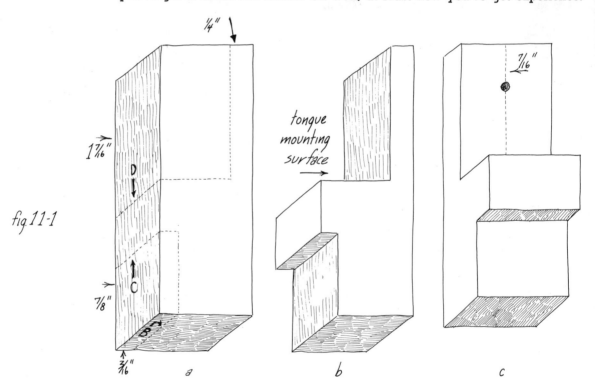

fig. 11-1

a   b   c

The Post

With the head cut, we move on to the post. This must be fashioned to accept the head. The length of the post varies, depending upon which stand you are building (see the note in the materials list). Also, if you are building the table stand, you will need two posts.

Drill the mounting hole in the post

Draw midlines, running lengthwise down each side of the 2 × 2. These will make it easy to drill the necessary holes in the correct locations. You can begin by marking the position of the first hole along one of the midlines, about ⅝ inch down from one end. Use a ¼-inch bit to drill it out. This hole will be for the mounting bolt (figure 11-2a).

Now turn the post onto one of the adjacent sides and, using a ½-inch bit, drill a hole on the midline 1½ inches down from the same end that you measured from to drill the mounting-bolt hole. Let's call this the clamp hole (figure 11-2a).

Drill the clamp hole

Now you can put your drill aside and take out your pencil, straight edge, and saw. On the end that you have been measuring from, mark off ⅛ inch on either side of the midline. Draw lines from these points to the clamp hole, keeping them parallel with the wood's edges. If you've done it right, you should now have a ¼-inch-wide strip drawn on the post piece, which runs between the end and the clamp hole (figure 11-2a). Cut this strip out with your saw (figure 11-2b).

Cut the clamp slit

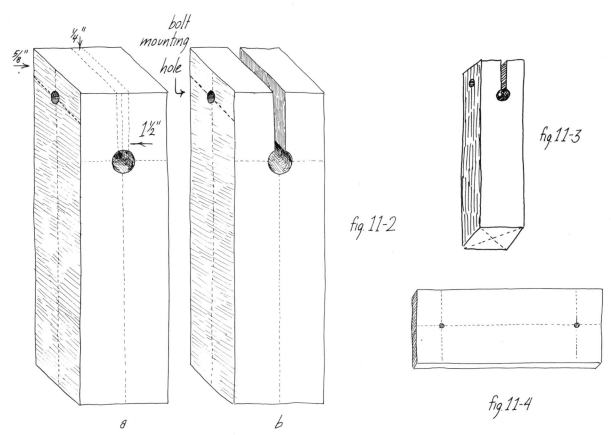

bolt mounting hole

5/8" ¼" 1½"

fig. 11-2

a   b

fig. 11-3

fig. 11-4

The Table-Stand Variation

For the table stand you need two heads and two posts. To begin the final assembly, connect the posts to the base. This is done with the two 1½-inch roundheaded wood screws. The position is critical. Take one of the two posts and find the center of the bottom end—the end opposite the slit you just cut—by drawing diagonals (figure 11-3). Depress this point with an awl. Repeat with the other post. Then draw a midline lengthwise across the base piece. Measure in 1¹¹⁄₁₆ inches from each side along the midline and mark the spots for drilling (figure 11-4). Choose a drill bit that's smaller in diameter than the shanks of the screws and bore the two holes through the base. Clamp the base in a vise and mount the posts to it, one at a time. Hold each of them up so that its marked center is aligned with the hole (figure 11-5) and drive the screw until the post has been secured. If you're having problems doing this, it may be best for you to remove the screws and predrill the holes in the posts.

Once the posts are in place, mount the rubber legs, one on each corner of the base. This should raise the unit sufficiently to prevent the screw heads from touching any surface beneath.

Mount the heads into the posts by fitting the tongues on the heads into the clamps on the post. You may need to sand the tongues a little to get them

Mount the posts to the base

Mount the rubber legs to the base

Mount the heads to the posts

to fit. Align the ¼-inch screw holes and push the stove bolts, with a washer under each head, through (figure 11-6).

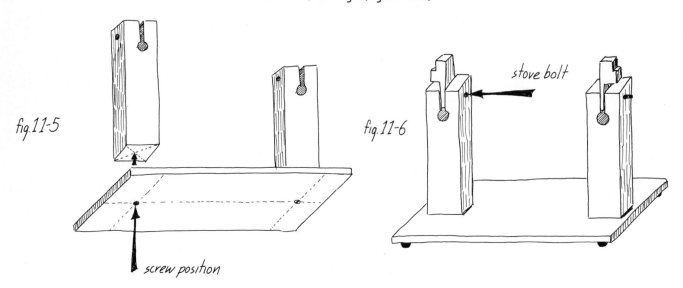

fig. 11-5

screw position

fig. 11-6

stove bolt

Mount the hoop to the heads

Now it's time to mount the hoop to the heads. This is done by predrilling holes in the hoop and driving the 7/16 flatheaded wood screws through them and into the mounting surface on each head. In order to correctly place these holes, it's a good idea to slip the hoop into position over the heads and trace the outlines of both onto the inside surface of the hoop (figure 11-7). This way you'll be sure to hit the mark if your holes fall within the lines. Within each outline drill two holes, one above the other. Put the hoop back over the heads. Try to drive the screws so that their heads sink into the wood far enough to prevent them from sticking out (figure 11-8). Tilt the hoop in whatever position is comfortable for you to work in. Slip on a washer and wing nut over the protruding shank of each bolt and screw them tight.

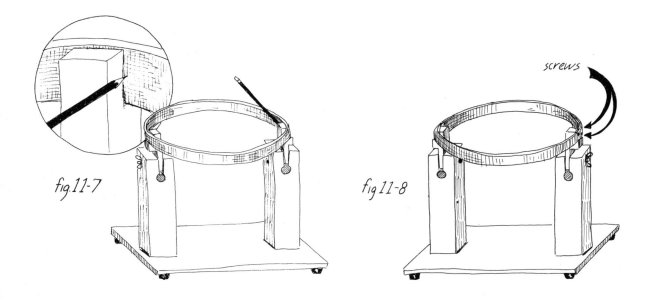

fig. 11-7

fig. 11-8

screws

The Chair-Stand Variation

The chair stand, unlike the freestanding table stand, requires only one post and head. This makes the assembly of this design a somewhat faster matter. Additionally, it can be used almost anywhere, requiring nothing more than a chair and, of course, you.

The joining of the post to the base is quite similar to the procedure with the table stand. The differences are really nothing more than small variations. For one thing, mounting is achieved with two diagonally placed 2-inch flat-headed screws (figure 11-9) rather than one centrally located 1½-inch flathead. To accommodate this difference, the screws used in the chair stand are somewhat smaller in diameter and the pilot holes that are drilled for them should be countersunk—a basin should be made into which the screw head can be seated (figure 11-10). Because there is only one post and it will be expected to bear the full stress that you put on it while working at the hoop, it may also be advisable to reinforce the joint with glue. Naturally, do this before putting in the screws.

Mounting the hoop is a far easier matter on the chair stand—the reason being that, with only one head to affix it to, there will be no need to go through the somewhat time-consuming process of trying to determine the precise points on the inside of the hoop where the heads should be attached. It really doesn't matter with this stand. And of course, there's time saved too in the fact that you only have the one set of hoop screws to drive (figure 11-11). When the hoop has been mounted to the head and the head has, in turn, been bolted to the post, this unit is ready for use. Simply place the base across the seat of your chair, sit on it, and you'll be set to work. If over a period of time you find that sitting is becoming increasingly difficult, consider tacking a small foam rubber pad onto the base. And if you like, cover it with a piece of original stitchery.

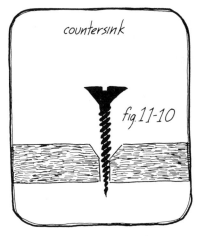

countersink

fig. 11-10

Mount the post to the base

Mount the hoop to the head

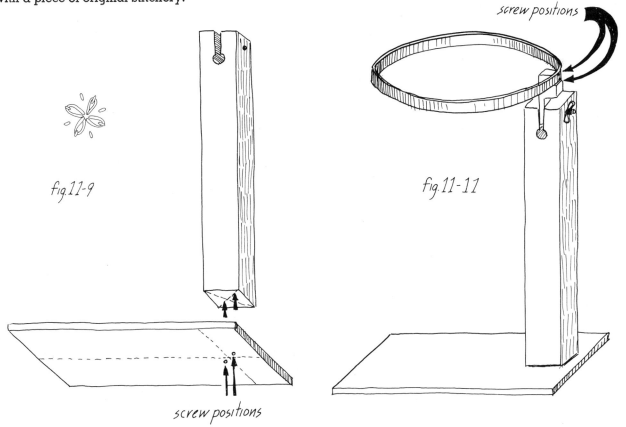

fig. 11-9

fig. 11-11

screw positions

screw positions

The Floor-Stand Variation

To construct a freestanding floor stand, you'll again be able to follow many of the same steps as for the table and chair stands. The basic difference in this design, besides the length of the post, is the structure of the base. This time, we're not suggesting plywood. Rather, we're recommending four foot structures made of ⅝ × 3's. This should provide ample support to enable the unit to stand independently without making the thing too heavy or otherwise awkward to move about.

Each foot is attached to the post quite simply with two 2¼-inch round-headed wood screws. No special cutting is required. In fact, all you have to do is align each piece at the bottom, so that the bottom end of the post is flush and square with the bottom end of the foot, and drive in two screws, preferably on a diagonal (figure 11-12). To position them correctly, measure in the width of the post from one end of the foot and draw a line. Then, within the area described by that line, mark two points for the screws, keeping them far enough from all edges to prevent splitting. When all four of the feet have been mounted, you can attach the hoop to the head and connect them with the post as described for the table stand. This will complete the unit. The only other thing that you might want to do is coat it with varnish or shellac to finish it off a bit. This is, of course, applicable for any of the stands. You may even want to chisel or cut decorative designs in the pieces to make them look like those pictured at the beginning of the chapter. To work with it, simply stand it between your legs, adjust the angle of the hoop to suit you, and begin.

Mount the feet to the post

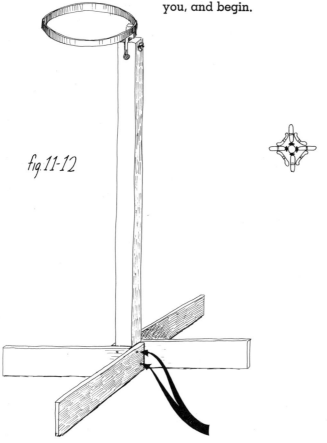

fig. 11-12

12·FLOOR LOOM

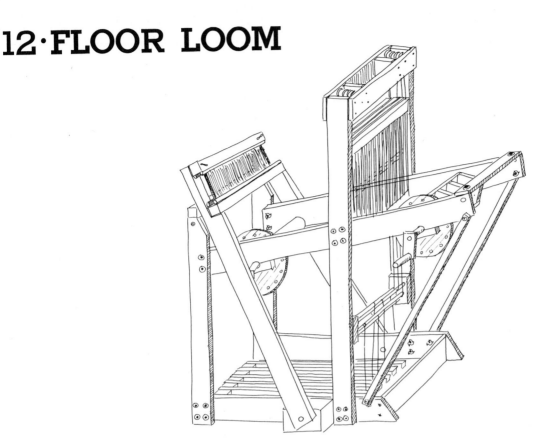

We came upon our first large loom quite by accident. It was among the properties of an old Woodstock weaving school that had closed its doors several years prior to our making our discovery. Most of the other tools and supplies had been sold at auction, and now only a very few, unwanted, artifacts remained. They were housed in a large old barn that friends of ours had recently purchased to make into a home and sculpting studio. Unfortunately, to complete this conversion, those "fossils" would have to be disposed of.

Knowing of our interest in the crafts, our friends contacted us about identifying one of the larger and more mysterious relics before dumping it. We jumped at the opportunity of getting a glimpse at what was later to become the very basis for our interest in craft-tool making.

It was a loom—a fine old colonial loom, assembled in its entirety with wooden pegs—complete with two harnesses, bent heddles, a badly weathered reed, two foot-worn treadles, and an aging warp. And the first time we saw it, it was barely discernible in a far corner of the dimly lit building, disrespectfully littered with bits and fragments of the carcasses of household furnishings and battered garden tools.

Removing it required excavation. We cleared a path first. Then, we carefully dismantled it, labeling each part as it was removed. We carried it out piece by piece, loaded it onto our friends' pickup, and joyfully brought it home. After scrubbing it all down, we began to reassemble it. It was so satisfying to see the way it came together. Every part had its place. And it was all so delightfully simple. It's amazing to be able to look at something that at first appears so complex and realize how logically uncomplex it actually is.

The loom design that we'll be describing here, however, is not that of our old classic. It is, rather, quite a bit less cumbersome, both in overall size and weight. Yet the basic structural concept is the same. And that's one remarkable thing about looms, and about weaving in general: regardless of the kind and number of variations, the basic theme doesn't change. Actually our loom design, despite its smaller stature, is a more flexible tool than its giant ancestor, having two more harnesses and four more treadles. Also, it won't require a room of its own.

Building it may take some time, but if you've always wanted one, the wait will be well worth it. We're recommending that you assemble it in stages. This will help to simplify the process. The stages we have outlined are the basic frame structure, the warp beam, the cloth beam, the treadles and harnesses, and the beater bar.

If you're not sure about where you can go to find heddles, harnesses, or a reed—as well as any other weaving accessories you may need (see also Chapter 14)—consider writing to either of these suppliers who do business by mail: School Products Company, 312 E. 23rd St., New York, N.Y. 10010; or Dick Blick, P.O. Box 1267, Galesburg, Ill. 61401.

ASSEMBLY OF THE BASIC FRAME STRUCTURE

Wood

Quantity	Material	Cut to	Description
2 lengths	1×4	39½ inches	top-center frame pieces
2 lengths	1×4	3⅝ inches	tray end blocks
1 length	$½ \times 5$	30 inches	tray bottom
2 lengths	$⁵⁄₄ \times 4$	47 inches	side-center frame pieces
2 lengths	$⁵⁄₄ \times 4$	30⅛ inches	side-base pieces
1 length	$⁵⁄₄ \times 4$	35 inches	back-base piece
1 length	$⁵⁄₄ \times 3$	35 inches	front-base pieces
2 lengths	$⁵⁄₄ \times 3$	30 inches	side-front frame pieces
2 lengths	$⁵⁄₄ \times 4$	41⅝ inches	side frame pieces
2 lengths	$⁵⁄₄ \times ⁵⁄₄$	31½ inches	back supports
1 length	2×2	39½ inches	breast beam
1 length	2×3	37¼ inches	back beam

Hardware

Quantity	Material
8	6d finishing nails, 2 inches long
26	4d finishing nails, 1½ inches long
8	No. 10 roundheaded wood screws, 1¼ inches long
4	No. 12 roundheaded wood screws, 2¾ inches long
4	No. 12 flatheaded wood screws, 2¾ inches long
2	³⁄₁₆-inch carriage bolts, 5½ inches long
30	³⁄₁₆-inch stove bolts, 2½ inches long
4	³⁄₁₆-inch machine bolts, 3¾ inches long
36	washers for ³⁄₁₆-inch bolts
30	T nuts for ³⁄₁₆-inch bolts
6	hex nuts for ³⁄₁₆-inch bolts

To put the loom together, we're suggesting that you begin with the front and back top-center frame pieces, the two end blocks, and the tray bottom. These are all components of the accessories holder, a convenient feature of this particular loom design and a basic structural part of the frame itself. To get started, take one of the top-center frame pieces and measure in 4 inches from each end. Mark these locations with lines drawn across the width of the board and parallel to the ends (figure 12-1). Along the inside edge of each of these lines, align and nail one of the end blocks (figure 12-2). Use four of the 6d finishing nails, tacking two, one above the other, into the end of each. Position this assembly so that the two blocks are standing vertically on the top-center frame piece. Measure the remaining top-center frame piece like the first one and position it atop the blocks, being sure that the lines and blocks match up. Nail it down with the remaining 6d's (figure 12-3).

Turn the completed section so that the edges of the frame pieces and blocks are facing up. Lay the tray bottom over it so that its edges are aligned with those of the top-center frame pieces and the end blocks (figure 12-4). Secure it with the 4d nails, using about nine on each side and four on each end (figure 12-5). When you've hammered the last one, you've completed the tray.

Attach the end blocks to top-center frame piece

Attach the tray bottom

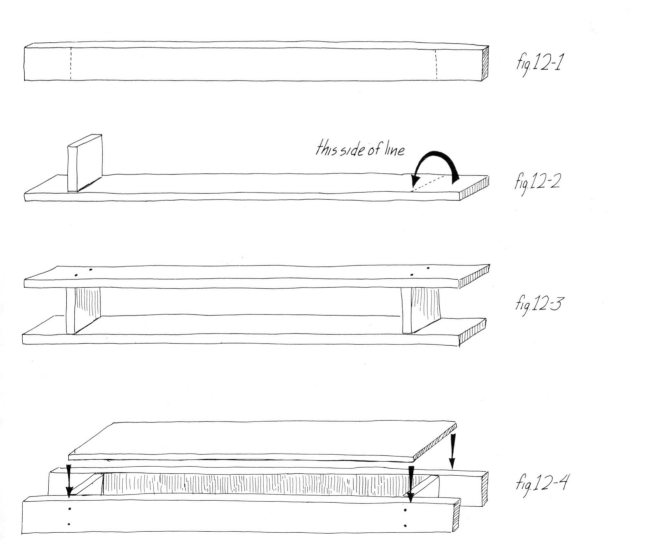

this side of line

fig. 12-1

fig. 12-2

fig. 12-3

fig. 12-4

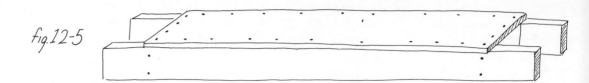

fig.12-5

The next logical step is to attach the side-center frame pieces to it. Position the tray assembly on its side again, so that the face of a top-center frame piece is up, and slide an end of one of the side-center pieces into the placement illustrated in figure 12-6, sandwiched between the ends of the top-center frame members. Hold it so that the outside face of the side-center piece is flush with the ends of the top pieces while drilling two pilot holes for the No.10 roundheaded mounting screws. Then drive the screws. Position the remaining side-center piece in the same manner at the opposite end of the tray structure and secure it with wood screws, too. Now turn the whole thing over and put in the remaining four screws.

Attach the side-center pieces

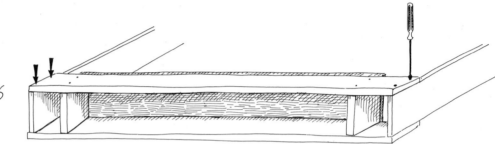

fig.12-6

At this point the overall assembly should be relatively secure. However, for added corner stability we've added two 5½-inch-long carriage bolts. These are to be mounted one on each side so that the shaft of each bolt runs adjacent to the interior face of each of the side-center frame pieces (figure 12-7). Position both bolts near the top edge of the top-center frame pieces and be sure to align the holes in both front and back pieces so that the bolts will go in straight. Use a bit to drill them out that's equivalent in diameter to the bolts themselves. Secure the bolts with hex nuts.

Mount the long carriage bolts into the top-center assembly

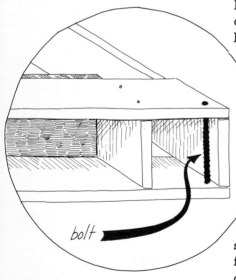

fig.12-7

bolt

Cut off a back corner from each side-base piece

Assembling the base is the next order of business, but before you do, you should trim off a back corner of each of the two side-base pieces. Measuring from one of the corners, with a protractor in hand, draw a line marking about a 75-degree angle relative to the length. Cut along the line (figure 12-8). (A rather quick alternative would be a miter box.) This will eliminate one corner. Do the same on the other side piece.

Stand the two side-base pieces parallel to one another and separated by about a yard, and position the back-base piece between them as illustrated in figure 12-8. Connect the three pieces with the four No.12 roundheaded wood screws, two at each joint, being sure to line up the upper edge of the back-base piece with the end of the upper edges on the side-base pieces and the

Attach the back-base piece

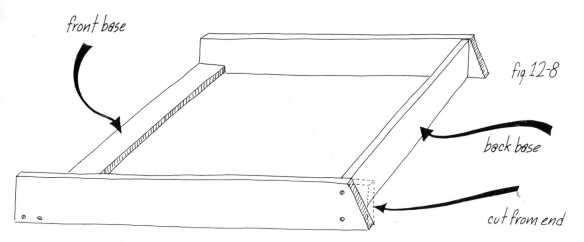

front base

fig. 12-8

back base

cut from end

lower edge of the back piece perpendicular with the lower edges of the side pieces. Here, as before, start the screws with pilot holes in order to prevent splitting.

Once these three parts are tightly joined, you can attach the front-base piece. Unlike the back, however, this piece is laid flat for mounting. Position it at the opposite end of the side-base pieces (figure 12-8). Drill two pilot holes at each end, countersinking all four of them. Drive in four No.12 flatheads.

Attach the front-base piece

To unite the completed base unit to the center frame structure, you'll be using bolts and T nuts. Four on each side will do the job well. You can find the location of the joint by measuring in 20½ inches from the front end of each of the side-base pieces. That's where the front edges of the side-center frame pieces belong (figure 12-9a). It's easiest if you can hold the center frame unit up vertically at this position when drilling the mounting holes, but to do it you probably need some help. If no one's willing or no one's around, the alternative is to lay the center frame on either the right or left side and hold the base vertically during the drilling and mounting. With a ⅜-inch bit, drill four holes on each of the sides, placing them about ¾ inch in from all edges as illustrated in figure 12-9b. Tap a T nut into each of them from the base side. Drive the stove bolts from the center frame in.

Mount the center frame assembly to the base

When the base–center-frame structure is standing, you can attach the side-front frame pieces. Here again T nuts and stove bolts are used. But before we get to the mounting, you've got some trimming to do. On one end of each piece, measuring crossways, mark a point 1⅝ inches from one edge. From that point draw a diagonal line to a point marked 2 inches down on the edge opposite the one measured from for the first point (figure 12-10). Saw along the diagonal. This trimmed end is the top of both side-front frame pieces. Set your saw aside.

Cut off a top corner from each side-front frame piece

Measuring up from the bottom end of each of the side-front frame pieces draw a line across the board at 1⅛ inches. Measure up 2½ inches more and draw another line. Between these two lines mark three points for drilling

Mount the side-front frame pieces to the base

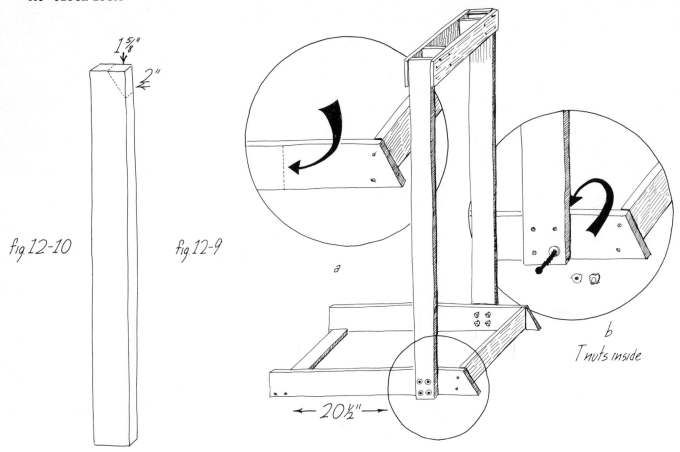

fig. 12-10

fig. 12-9

a

b

T nuts inside

← 20½" →

1 5/8"

2"

Attach the side frame pieces to
the center frame assembly

Attach the side frame pieces to
the side-front frame pieces

Mount the back support pieces

mounting holes as illustrated in figure 12-11a. Drill them out with your ⅜-inch bit. Then hold one of the front frame pieces in position against the side-base piece and mark the positions of the holes onto the base. Drill at these points. Tap T nuts into the holes from the inside of the base (figure 12-11a) and secure the side-front frame piece with the stove bolts. Mount the other side-front frame piece in the same way.

Once both side-front frame pieces are mounted, the side frame pieces can be attached. These should be put in on an angle. To accomplish this, measure up 28¾ inches along the front edges of the side-center frame pieces and 29¼ inches along the back edges. The top edge of each of the side frame pieces should be aligned with both points for correct mounting. As a kind of guide, draw a line on the inside face of each between these points. Measure down about 3⅝ inches from this line and draw another, parallel to it (figure 12-12). Between these, mark four places for mounting holes on each side-center piece and drill them out. Hold each of the side frame pieces up in the mounting position—being certain that they just overlap the side-front frame pieces—and mark the locations of the holes on them. Drill the four holes in each of the side frame pieces and tap in T nuts from what will be the inside. To attach them, position each on the inside face of the center frame, line up the holes, and put in stove bolts from the outside (figure 12-13).

Next bolt the side frame pieces to the side-front frame pieces. Mark the points for drilling on the side pieces so that you'll be drilling from the inside out. Bore two holes in each piece. Again install T nuts from the inside and screw in the bolts from the outside (figure 12-13).

For more back support on the side frame pieces to hold up the weight of the warp beam, the back support pieces are added. Inasmuch as the side frame should already be pretty secure, these pieces need not be very heavy and can be mounted with only one bolt at each end. Begin on the side frame pieces themselves, marking a point ½ inch up and ½ inch in from the bottom rear corner of each. Now on the two supports measure ¾ inch from each end of each and mark (figure 12-14a). Drill at these four points. Tap T nuts on the inside faces of both side frame pieces and bolt on the supports. But, before you

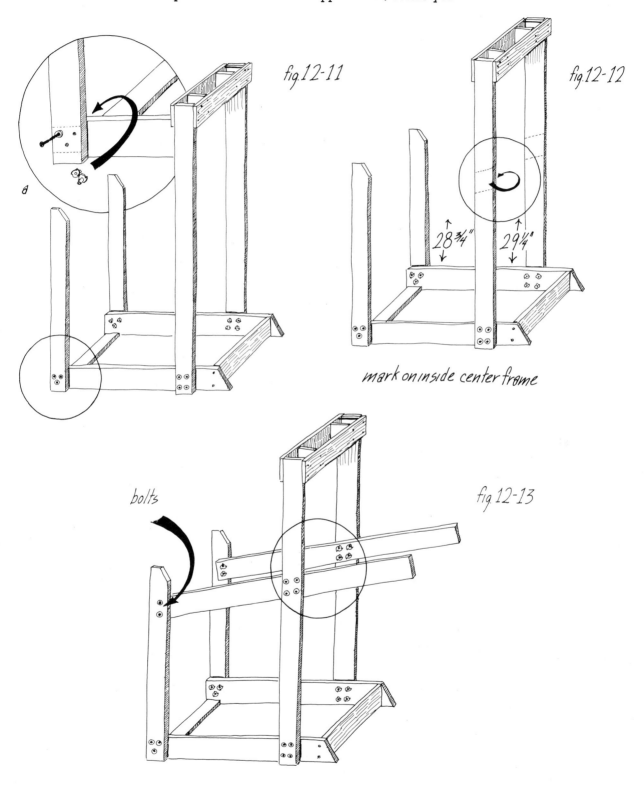

fig. 12-11

fig. 12-12

28 ¾"   29 ¼"

mark on inside center frame

bolts

fig. 12-13

tighten them up, swing each of the supports into position, as illustrated in figure 12-14. This way, when the bolts are tightened, they will be holding the supports correctly for attachment to the base. The necessary drilling can easily be done with the pieces being supported in this way. When locating the bottom holes in the base, be certain that you don't drill them too near the edge of the wood.

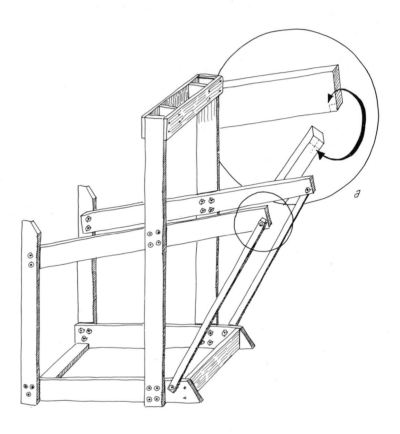

fig 12-14

Mount the breast beam on the side-front frame pieces

At this point, all that it'll take to complete the loom frame is the addition of breast and back beams. These are attached with machine bolts. The breast beam should be mounted at the front of the loom, across the top ends of the side-front frame pieces. Inasmuch as 2 × 2 lumber is really only about 1½ by 1½ inches, the tapering that you did on the frame ends should comfortably accommodate the beam. Locate the centers of these ends by drawing diagonals across them, running corner to corner (figure 12-15a), and, using a ⅜-inch bit, drill at these points down about 1½ inches into the frame. Now measure down that distance plus ¼ inch beyond it and mark a point on the outside face on each of the side-front frame pieces, centered beneath the holes you just drilled (figure 12-15a.) At this spot bore a ⅝-inch hole through the wood (figure 12-15b). On the beam itself measure in 9/16 inch from each end (figure 12-15a) and drill 3/16-inch holes at these points (figure 12-15b). Rest the beam in its mounting position, align the holes, put washers on two of your machine bolts, and push them down through the holes (figure 12-15c). If all of your measurements are accurate, you should be able to see the bolt ends in the ⅝-inch holes. Using a set of wrenches or pliers, twist and tighten hex nuts onto the bolts (figure 12-15d).

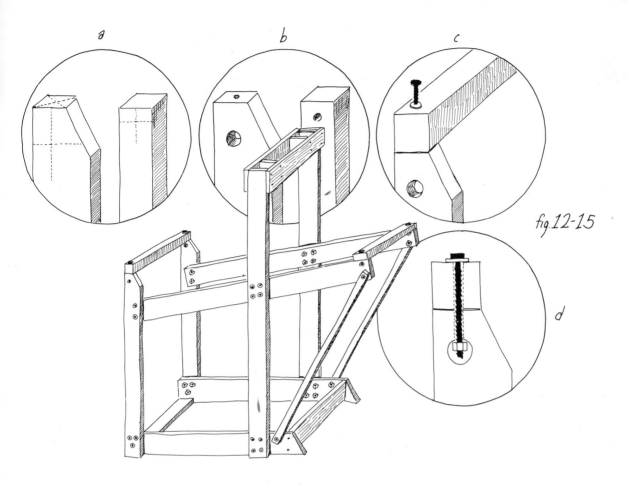

fig. 12-15

Follow the same basic procedure for mounting the back beam. Here, however, a 2 × 3 is to be used. Begin by drilling a hole in each end of the beam first. Try to keep them about centered on the wood, and set ½ inch from the ends. When the holes are made, position the beam on the side frame pieces so that it's flush with the ends of those pieces and mark the location of the holes onto the edges of the frame. Drill at these points. As before, drill a ⅝-inch hole through each face, 1¾ inches down from the top edge, to enable you to place and secure the nuts. Once the back beam's bolted down, the frame is finished (figure 12-15).

Mount the back beam on the side frame pieces

ASSEMBLY OF THE WARP BEAM

A warp beam can be made in several different ways. On the old loom that we told you about earlier a log was used. It was about the same diameter as a phone pole and was bored at one end to accommodate pegs that functioned as handles for lifting and turning it. Of course, it was heavy, requiring the two of us to move it, and, fortunately, there are other options. The type that we suggest will be far less difficult to manage. It's made up of sixteen wooden parts, as described in the following list.

Wood

Quantity	Material	Cut to	Description
5 sections	¾-inch plywood	5½ inches square	beam plates
1 section	¼-inch plywood	10 inches square ᵃ	locking disk
4 lengths	1-inch half-round molding	34¾ inches	warp bars
2 lengths	⅝ × ⅝	6 inches	beam mounts
1 length	1-inch dowel	39½ inches	shaft
1 length	⁷⁄₁₆-inch dowel	2¼ inches	locking peg
1 length	1 × 3	5½ inches	crank arm
1 length	1-inch dowel	4½ inches	handle

Hardware and Other Stuff

Quantity	Material
9	No.7 flatheaded wood screws, ⅞ inch long
20	No.7 flatheaded wood screws, 1⅜ inches long
4	No.7 roundheaded wood screws, 2 inches long
1	No.7 flatheaded wood screw, ¾ inch long
2	No.1 roundheaded wood screws, ¼ inch long
1	1⅛-inch screw eye
1	piece of string or rawhide, 12 inches long

ᵃ This will be cut further during assembly.

Drill the shaft holes into the beam plates

It's easiest to prepare all five beam plates at one time. This way all of them should wind up trimmed and drilled in the same way. Start by drawing intersecting diagonals across each of them. This will provide you with the locations of the centers, and, if all of the squares are exactly the same size, all should correspond well. Using a 1-inch bit, drill a shaft hole at the center of the first one and lay it over the second one, taking care to match the sides. If things are as they should be, the point where the diagonals on the second piece intersect should be centrally located relative to the edges of the hole bored into the first. Drill the remaining shaft holes, checking each in the same manner.

Drill the secondary holes into the beam plates

Adjacent to each shaft hole, drill another hole, leaving just enough space between the holes to avoid splitting (figure 12-16a). This time a ¾-inch bit should be large enough. The purpose of these secondary holes is to allow for screws to bind each of the beam plates to the shaft.

Cut off the corners of the beam plates

Next, remove the four corners of each of the pieces. To do this properly, so that the same amount will be removed from each, measure in from the

fig. 12-16

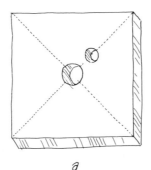
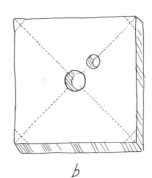
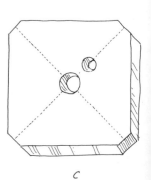

a   b   c

corners ½ inch along the diagonals and mark them at this distance. Using a right angle, draw a line through each of these marks, perpendicular to the diagonal that it intersects (figure 12-16b). Cut along these with your saw thereby eliminating the corners (figure 12-16c). Again, it will be wise to check your work as you do it—that is, check to be certain that the positions of the marks on each piece match the cuts taken from the first piece. When you've cut your last corner, the beam plates are complete.

Another item that requires some preparation is the locking disk. Take the 10-inch-square piece of plywood and draw diagonals across it from corner to corner. Place the point of a compass where the lines intersect and draw a circle with a radius of 4¾ inches (figure 12-17). Cut out the disk.

The diagonals you drew should divide the disk into quarters. Bisect each quarter into eighths (figure 12-18). Then bisect each eighth into sixteenths. Bisecting is easy using a compass. Place the compass in the center of the disk and draw a small circle (about a 1½-inch radius). Then place the point of the compass at the intersection of this circle and one of the large diameters you have already drawn. Draw a small arc on each side of the diameter line. Then, *without changing the radius of the compass,* move to the next diameter line and draw two more arcs (figure 12-19). Continue all around the disk. Wherever two arcs intersect draw a line to the center of the disk. When all such lines have been drawn, the sections have been bisected (figure 12-20).

Now set your compass to a radius of 4¼ inches and place the point at the center of the disk. Draw a circle (figure 12-21a). At the sixteen points where the circle and diameters intersect you'll have to drill ⅞₆-inch holes.

Cut out the locking disk

Divide the locking disk into sixteenths

Drill the locking holes and the shaft hole into the locking disk

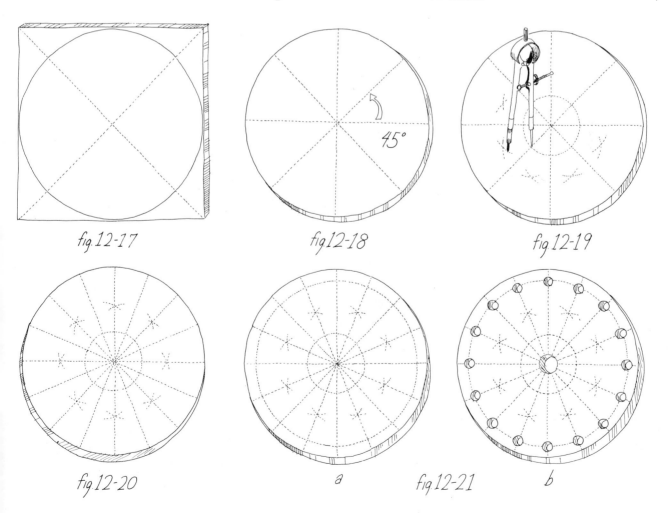

fig. 12-17   fig. 12-18   fig. 12-19

fig. 12-20   a   fig. 12-21   b

Take care in positioning them, to avoid misalignment problems later. When they're done, drill out the center using a 1-inch bit (figure 12-21b).

A final bit of preassembly is the attachment of the locking disk to one of the beam plates. For this purpose use four of the No.7 ⅞-inch flatheaded screws. Countersink and drive the screws through the disk and into the plate (figure 12-22) so that the heads are flush with the surface of the disk.

Insert the shaft through the shaft hole so that 3⅜ inches of it is left extending through the disk. Install it by drilling a pilot hole through the side of the secondary hole of the beam plate (figure 12-23a). Hold the shaft firmly as you bore a short way into it. When the No.7 ⅞-inch flathead is tightened, the shaft won't move independently (figure 12-23b). Space the next beam plate about 7 inches from the first. And space the remaining three at 8½, 8½, and 7 inches respectively (figure 12-24). Lock all of them in position, one at a time, as you did with the first.

Attach the locking disk

Mount the beam plates on the shaft

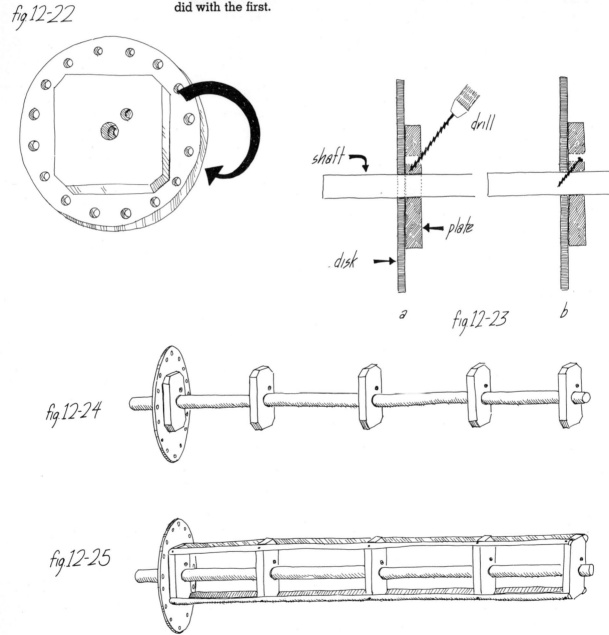

fig. 12-22

drill

shaft

plate

disk

a   fig. 12-23   b

fig. 12-24

fig. 12-25

To attach the four warp bars at the trimmed corners of the beam plates, your twenty 1⅝-inch flatheads will be used, one at each corner (figure 12-25). To prevent a mixup, mount them one at a time. Check to be sure that all of the heads of the screws are nested well into the wood, but take care when tightening them not to split the molding.

The beam can now be installed on the frame. Doing this will require that you connect the beam mounts to the side-frame pieces. Place each of them 6 inches in from the back along the bottom edge. Use the 2-inch flatheads to mount them, positioning them two on each piece with 4 inches between. Once they're on tight, find the midpoint of one mount lengthwise and mark it on the cleavage line where mount and side are joined. Position the point of your 1-inch drill bit at this spot and, of course, bore holes right through (figure 12-26a). Repeat with the other mount. When both are made, remove one of the mounts. Raise the beam into position, fitting an end of the shaft into the mount that's left and lift the other end to where the remaining mount will be rejoined. Screw on the remaining mount (figure 12-26b).

Mount the warp bars on the beam plates

Mount the warp beam on the frame

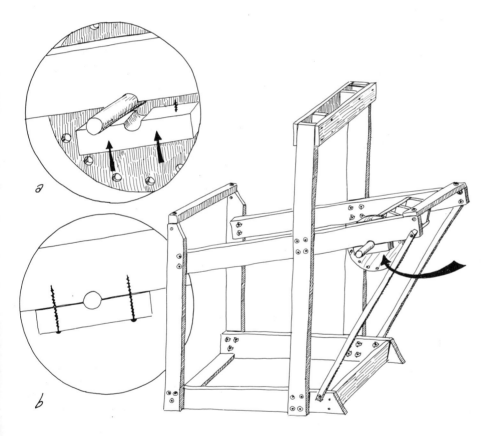

fig.12-26

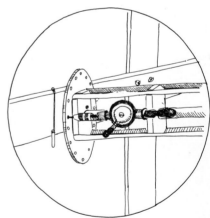

fig.12-27

Drill the locking hole into one side frame piece

Attach the locking peg to the frame

Only a few things remain. For one, you've got to drill a hole into the side frame that will be aligned with the holes in the locking disk. This is best accomplished by boring right through the disk (figure 12-27). Alignment is thus assured. Try not to go all the way through the side frame—an inch in is enough. As for the peg that will be pushed into the hole in order to hold the beam, we're recommending that you attach it permanently to the loom with a short length of string or rawhide. Drill a small hole through one end of the peg and attach the string. Then tie the other end to an eye screw mounted nearby along the top edge of the side frame.

Install the crank

To make turning the beam an easy matter a crank should be installed. In the 5½-inch-long 1 × 3 intended for this purpose, bore a 1-inch hole at each end. Stick the 4½-inch length of dowel in one of them; this will be the handle (figure 12-28a). To prevent it from slipping out, screw two ¼-inch roundheaded wood screws into it, one on each side of the crank arm (figure 12-28b). Fit the other hole over the protruding beam shaft. Drill a pilot hole for the ¾-inch flathead through one of the edges of the crank arm and into the shaft. Countersink and drive the screw until beam and crank move as one (figure 12-28c).

fig 12-28

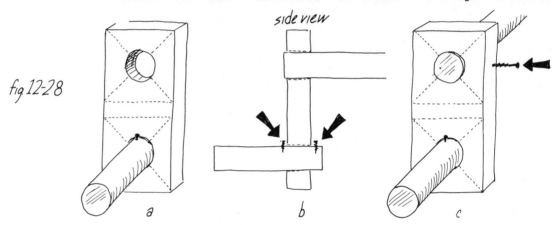

side view

a   b   c

ASSEMBLY OF THE CLOTH BEAM

The cloth beam is really quite similar to the warp beam insofar as both utilize a locking disk and peg as well as a crank. In fact the preparation of these components is about the same as just described. There are some differences in the overall structures of these two units that make them entirely distinguishable. The following list of materials should amplify this point:

Wood

Quantity	Material	Cut to	Description
1 length	closet bar	34¾ inches	shaft
1 length	¹¹⁄₁₆-inch dowel	5 inches	long extension
1 length	¹¹⁄₁₆-inch dowel	2⅜ inches	short extension
1 section	¼-inch plywood	10 inches square [a]	locking disk
1 length	1 × 3	8½ inches	crank arm
1 length	1-inch dowel	4½ inches	handle
2 lengths	⅝ × ⅝	6 inches	beam mounts
1 length	⁷⁄₁₆-inch dowel	2¼ inches	locking peg

Hardware and Other Stuff

2	No.2 flatheaded wood screws, ¾ inch long
4	No.1 roundheaded wood screws, ¼ inch long
1	No.7 roundheaded wood screws, ¾ inch long
4	No.7 flatheaded wood screws, 2 inches long
1	1⅛-inch screw eye
1	piece of string or rawhide, 12 inches long
	white glue

[a] This will be cut further during assembly.

You can begin this project by drilling a 1½-inch hole into each end of the beam shaft (figure 12-29). Use a bit that's ¹¹⁄₁₆ inch in diameter and be certain that the holes are as centered as you can make them. When that's done, fill them with glue and tap in the long and short shaft extensions. Set the piece aside to dry.

Prepare the locking disk as for the warp beam, the only modification here being that the hole drilled at the center should be ¹¹⁄₁₆ inch. Mount it by sliding it over the long extension—this may require a little pressure—and gluing and screwing it to the beam shaft (figures 12-29 and 12-30). Small No.2 flatheaded screws have been recommended here due to the limited area that you'll have to work with.

Attach the extensions to the shaft

Attach the locking disk to the shaft

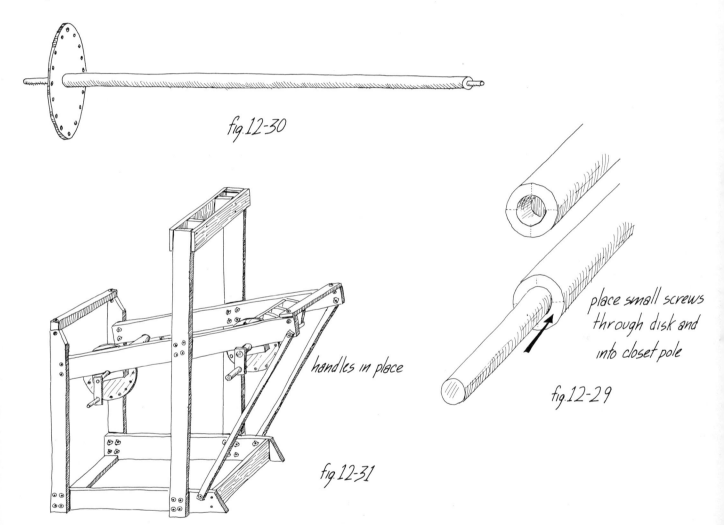

fig.12-30

handles in place

fig.12-31

place small screws
through disk and
into closet pole

fig.12-29

Adding on the crank is no different here than for the warp beam. Just keep in mind that on the cloth beam the shaft will require a slightly smaller hole (¹¹⁄₁₆ inch). Mounting the unit to the frame is the same as well (figure 12-31). Here too the shaft hole should be ¹¹⁄₁₆ inch. When drilling out the frame for the locking peg, remember to align it well with the holes in the locking disk. Once this all has been done, twist in the screw eye, bore a small hole through one end of the locking peg, and tie it on.

Install the crank

Attach the locking peg

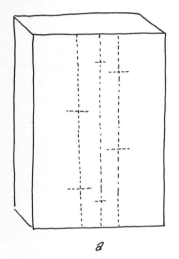

fig. 12-32

a

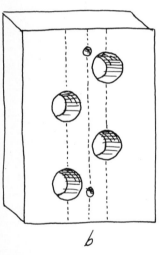

b

Drill the holes into the pull blocks

Mount the pull blocks and harness pulls to the frame

ASSEMBLY OF THE TREADLES AND HARNESSES

Now you have to add the treadles and harnesses. While the latter can be bought commerically, treadles are something you'll have to make. Actually, there is a bit more to it than that. After all, a treadle by itself is nothing more than a pedal. And a pedal that isn't connected to anything isn't much at all. So when we speak of treadles, what we mean is treadles and the system by which they are attached, which in conjunction with the treadles enables us to lift the harnesses. The parts to put all this together are as follows:

Wood

Quantity	Material	Cut to	Description
2 lengths	$\frac{5}{4} \times 4$	5 inches	pull blocks
4 lengths	1-inch dowel	37 inches	harness pulls
5 lengths	$\frac{5}{4} \times 3$	1¾ inches	treadle mounts
2 lengths	$\frac{5}{4} \times 3$	1 inch	end mounts
6 lengths	$\frac{5}{4} \times \frac{5}{4}$	26 inches	treadles

Hardware

Quantity	Material
4	$\frac{3}{16}$-inch stove bolts, 2 inches long
4	washers for $\frac{3}{16}$-inch bolts
4	nuts for $\frac{3}{16}$-inch bolts
7	No.7 flatheaded wood screws, 1⅝ inches long
1	$\frac{3}{16}$-inch steel rod, 16¾ inches long
2	steel rods,[a] 5 inches long
8	1½-inch pulleys

[a] Having a diameter that can accommodate the pulleys you use.

Drill the pull blocks first. They'll need six holes apiece of two different sizes (figure 12-32). Begin with a $\frac{3}{16}$-inch bit. Measure widthwise across the pieces and divide each in half with a line running lengthwise. Indent about ¾ inch in from each end of the line and at those points make your holes. Now change to a bit slightly larger than 1 inch. Draw lines on one block parallel to your first line and set in 1½ inches from the sides (figure 12-32a). On the left line make marks at 1 and 3 inches up from the bottoms; on the right line make marks at 2 and 4 inches. When all four are marked, drill them out (figure 12-32b). Lay this block over the other one, carefully aligning the edges. Mark the position of each of the holes onto the second block. Drill at these marks.

Thread the pull blocks over the harness pulls before mounting on the frame. Now mark the frame at the position on the side-center frame pieces where all of this will be located—that is, 10 inches off the floor. Using the marks as your guide, hold the pulls up to the frame, aligning the bottom of each pull block with the mark that you've made, and bolt them in place (figure 12-33). If your work's been accurate, the harness pulls should turn freely in place and be in no danger of falling out.

In order for you to attach the treadles, you must now set up the mounts. First they must all be bored to accept the $\frac{3}{16}$-inch steel rod. And in doing this,

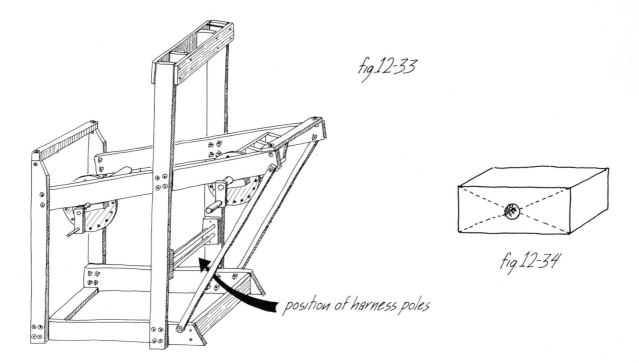

fig. 12-33

position of harness poles

fig. 12-34

it is very important that all of the holes line up with one another. To assure this, mark the center of the long sides of each of the blocks. This can easily be done by drawing diagonals. Then make certain to drill exactly on the marks (figure 12-34). Check them as you go along just to be on the safe side. After the five treadle mounts are done, do the same for the end pieces; however, with these don't drill all the way through—leave about ⅛ inch.

At this point you can attach the treadle mounts and one of the end mounts to the front-base piece with the 1⅝-inch flatheaded wood screws. Be sure to countersink and put one screw in each mount. To place them properly, position the left end mount 7½ inches from the left side-base piece. Space the rest 1¼ inches apart (figure 12-35).

Drill the center holes in the treadle mounts

Attach the treadle mounts to the front-base piece

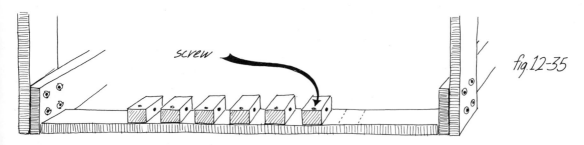

screw

fig. 12-35

With six of the seven mounts in place, you're ready for the treadles. But, again, before you can mount them, you'll have to drill them. Measure in about ¾ inch from one of the ends of each of them. With each piece mark the point centrally on one of the faces and drill right through using the same ³⁄₁₆-inch bit. Before you install them, you also ought to drill a series of holes partway down the adjacent face of each of them, starting from the opposite end (figure 12-36). Use an ⅛-inch bit, drill about four holes per treadle, and space the holes about an inch apart.

To attach the treadles, place one in each space between the mounts,

Drill the holes into the treadles

Install the treadles

align the holes with those drilled into the mounts, thread the metal rod through, and slip the right end mount into position over the end of the rod. Screw down the right end mount to secure the rod (figure 12-37).

fig. 12-36

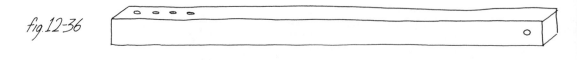

fig. 12-37

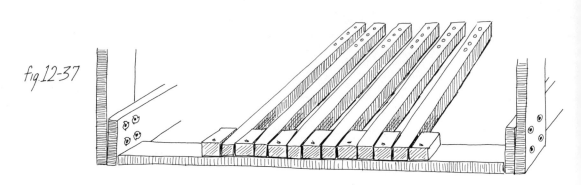

Install the pulleys into the top-center assembly

Now it's time to install the pulleys. Here again you'll need your drill. Choose a bit that will produce a hole large enough to snugly accommodate one of the 5-inch-long steel rods. And drill two holes, one at each end of the back top-center frame. More specifically, position each 2½ inches in from the end and about 1 inch down from the top edge (figure 12-38a). When the bit has passed through the back piece, continue drilling until you have depressed the inside surface of the front piece about ½ inch. Withdraw the bit and insert a steel rod in each hole. Thread four pulleys over each and seat them in the front-piece depressions (figure 12-38b). Lock the pulleys on the rods with an allen wrench (that's the kind of tool made to fit into the screws with hexagonal holes instead of heads).

fig. 12-38

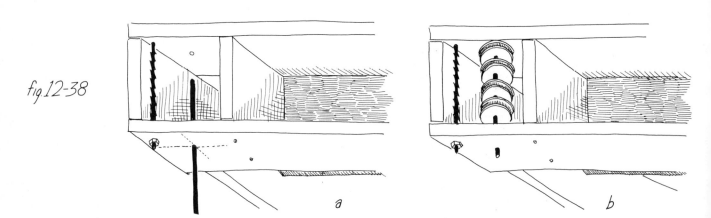

a   b

As we mentioned earlier (see page 126), harnesses can be purchased complete with heddles from commercial suppliers, and for the price we think this is worthwhile. To string them up, refer to the figure 12-39 directly. In fact, if you decide to make your own harnesses–perhaps you have a strong preference for homemade string heddles–the basic pattern remains unchanged.

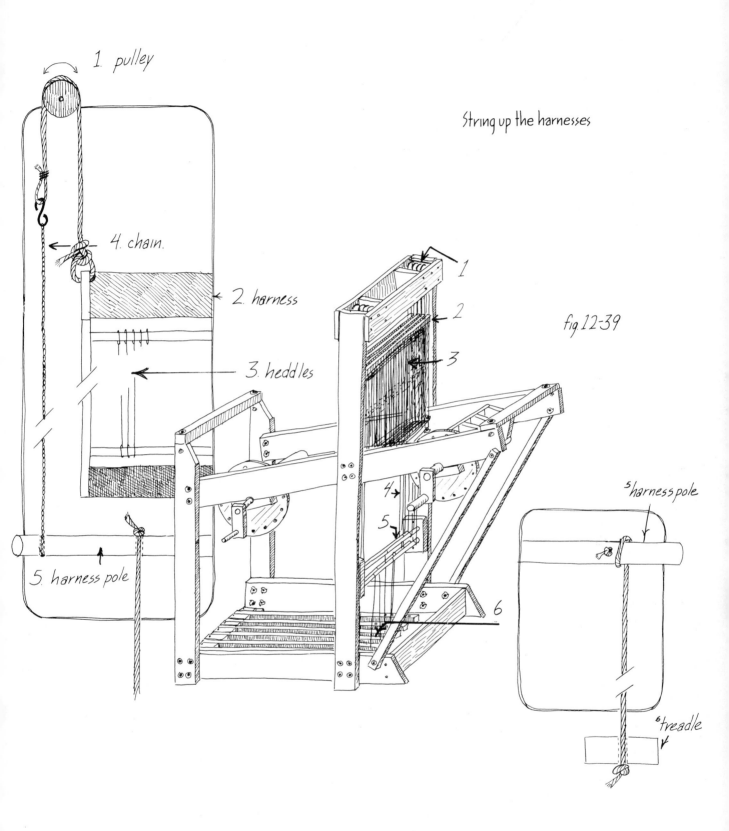

1. pulley

String up the harnesses

4. chain.

2. harness

3. heddles

fig. 12-39

1

2

3

4

5

6

5. harness pole

⁵harness pole

⁶treadle

ASSEMBLY OF THE BEATER BAR

A loom isn't a loom without a beater bar. While we're not suggesting that you make your own reed (a long process requiring much patience and far more difficult than simply ordering from one of the suppliers listed on page 126), you will, nevertheless, need a place to mount one. Here's what's involved:

Wood

Quantity	Material	Cut to	Description
2 lengths	$\frac{5}{4} \times 4$	37 inches	sides of beater bar
2 lengths	2×2	44½ inches	top and bottom reed holders
4 lengths	½-inch quarter-round molding	44½ inches	holder rims
1 length	4×4	12 inches	spacer block
1 length	1-inch dowel	5½ inches	right side pivot
1 length	1-inch dowel	3 inches	left side pivot

Hardware and Other Stuff

Quantity	Material
2	³⁄₁₆-inch carriage bolts, 4½ inches long
2	wing nuts for ³⁄₁₆-inch bolts
2	No.12 flatheaded wood screws, 3 inches long
4	No.12 roundheaded wood screws, 3 inches long white glue

Drill the pivot holes into the beater-bar

The most involved thing that you have to do is to prepare the beater-bar sides. To begin with, you'll need to drill two holes large enough to accommodate 1-inch dowels. While these should not be oversized, they should be large enough so that the dowels may be slipped into them without force. Position one at an end of each of the side pieces. They should be drilled at midline and set in from the edge about 1½ inches (figure 12-40).

Remove a corner from the top end of side

Now a corner at the opposite end of each piece should be removed. The size of the segment being eliminated is 1¾ by 8½ inches (figure 12-41). Near this end of each beater-bar side a slit just over ³⁄₁₆ inch in width must be made.

Cut a slit in the top of each beater-bar

Using a bit of equivalent diameter, drill two holes along the midline *of the edge*—the first about ⅞ inch in from the end and the second 1½ inches from the first (figure 12-42). Cut out the area between them to form the completed slit.

The top and bottom reed holders also require some drilling. In the top piece a ³⁄₁₆-inch hole near each end is all that's needed. This should be located along the midline a little more than ½ inch in from the end (figure 12-43).

Drill mounting holes in the top reed holder

Inasmuch as these holes are to be aligned with the slits in the sides of the beater bar, these two pieces may be used to assure correct placement of the holes.

As to the bottom reed holder, the holes needed are a somewhat different matter. Here the need is for pilot holes only. Use a bit slightly smaller in

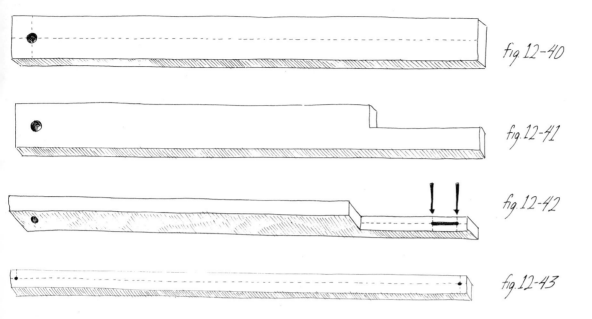

fig. 12-40

fig. 12-41

fig. 12-42

fig. 12-43

diameter than that of the shank of the wood screws and bore at the midline, a little more than ½ inch in from each edge. When both holes have been completed, position the piece relative to the beater-bar sides as illustrated in figure 12-44. Mark the locations of the holes onto the beater-bar sides and continue to drill at these spots.

To get the parts together, begin by gluing the surface of the bottom reed holder and beater-bar side pieces that will be joined. Then, before things dry up, lay the three parts in the form shown in figure 12-44 and drive in the two flatheads, making certain to countersink. Let the unit sit for a while before going further to allow the glue to develop a good bond. The top reed holder should not be glued; rather, it is attached to the sides with carriage bolts and wing nuts to permit easy adjustment up and down in the slits.

Drill pilot holes in the bottom reed holder

Attach the reed holders to the beater-bar sides

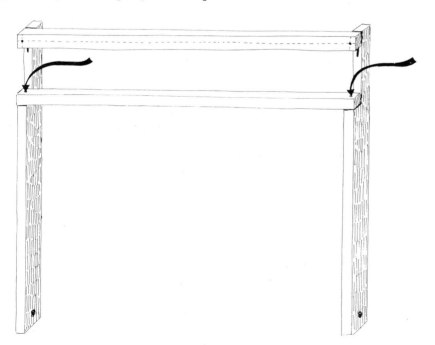

fig. 12-44

Glue the holder rims onto the reed holder

Both top and bottom holders should now be fitted with the holder rims. Glue alone is all that's needed. One pair of rims belongs to each holder, and of course they're mounted along the edges as shown in figure 12-45.

fig. 12-45

Mount the spacer block

Drill the pivot holes into the base

Insert the pivots

As of now the unit can hold a reed. But so far it's still not attached to the loom. Here's where that spacer block and those little pivots come into play. Mount the spacer block on the right side-base piece so that one end is butted up against the side-center frame piece (figure 12-46). Secure with glue and the four roundheads driven from the inside.

Now drill a 1-inch hole a little above the midline of the spacer block and 5½ inches from the side-center frame piece. Make this hole 2 inches deep. Also in the corresponding location on the left side-base piece drill a 1-inch hole all the way through. Coat the insides of these holes with glue. Align the beater-bar frame with these holes (figure 12-47) and insert the appropriate pivots.

fig. 12-46

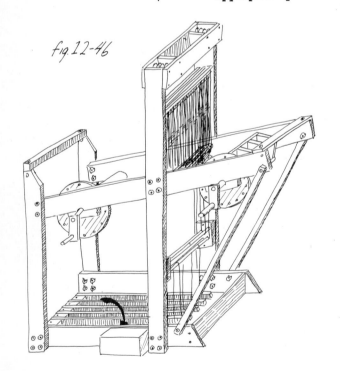

fig 12-47

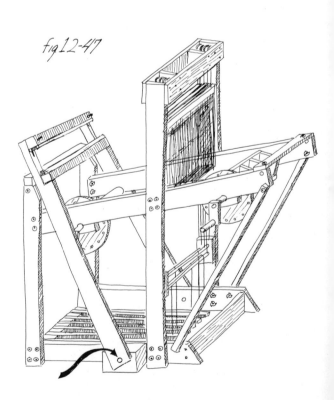

13·INKLE LOOM

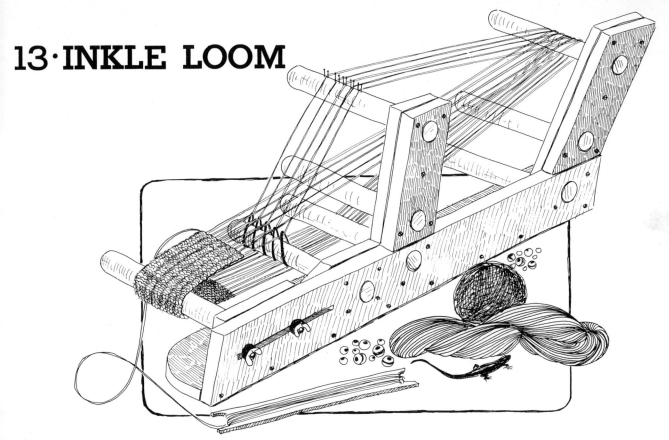

The inkle loom is most frequently thought of as a tool for weaving belts, straps, and the like. But it's in no way limited to these kinds of projects. Actually, it can be used in very much the same way as any other small loom with limited warp space. Sewn together, several pieces woven separately on an inkle loom can produce a truly fascinating tapestry. And, like the basic frame loom, it invites experimentation. For anyone interested in a rather unique alternative to either frames or floor looms, we definitely recommend the inkle.

In design the inkle loom is really quite simple, involving no moving parts. And it's because of this simplicity that it's quite easy to personalize. There seem to be almost as many variations in the construction of these looms as there are builders. The one we've chosen to describe comes from a good friend and fine craftsman.

ASSEMBLY

Wood

Quantity	Material	Cut to	Description
1 length	1 × 4	42 inches	side board
1 length	1 × 4	41⅛ inches	base
1 length	1 × 4	10⅝ inches	center plate
1 length	1 × 4	7⅞ inches	center plate
1 length	1 × 4	13¹⁄₁₆ inches	back plate
1 length	1 × 4	10⅝ inches	back plate
1 length	1 × 3	7 inches	heddle plate

1 length	1 × 3	9¼ inches	slider plate
8 lengths	1¼-inch dowel [a]	9 inches	posts

Hardware and Other Stuff

Quantity	Material
27	No.8 flatheaded wood screws, 1¼ inches long
2	¼-inch roundheaded stove bolts, 1¾ inches long
2	wing nuts for ¼-inch bolts
2	washers for ¼-inch bolts
	No.18 finishing nails, ¾ inch long [b]
	white glue

[a] Or closet pole.

[b] Quantity will vary with the number of warp threads you anticipate using.

Label the ends and sides of the side board and base

To simplify the process of putting this loom together, we're suggesting that you take a moment out to label two of the key parts—the side board and the base. Label the ends of both of them *F* (front) and *B* (back). It doesn't matter which is which as long as each is marked. In the same manner label the sides *R* (right) and *L* (left). When we refer to these pieces, you should have little difficulty following what we say.

Draw a line running lengthwise down the side board from *F* to *B*, dividing the board in half. We'll call this line the midline. Measure in along the midline 1½ inches from *F* and mark it by drawing a ¼-inch-long line perpendicular to the midline and pointing toward *R* (figure 13-1). Measure down the midline another 12½ inches and draw another ¼-inch-long perpendicular pointing in the same direction. Connect the ends of the little perpendiculars with a line, thereby forming a long, narrow rectangle on the *R* side of the midline. Bore a ⁹⁄₃₂-inch hole at each end of this rectangle. Using either a coping or saber saw, cut along the long sides of the rectangle in order to remove the area between the two holes (figure 13-2). This will produce a slot that will later enable you to adjust the tension on your warp.

Cut the slider slot in the side board

fig. 13-1

fig. 13-2

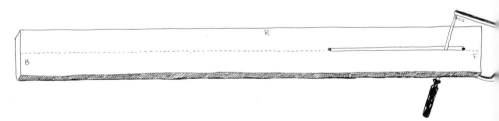

Round off a corner of the base

To insure that your loom will be comfortable to work at after it's been assembled, we're suggesting that you round off the *F* corner on the *L* side of the base. The easiest way to do this is by using the same saw that you used to cut out the slot. You can mark off the area to be trimmed with an old margarine tub. Trace the curve onto the wood (figure 13-3) and saw along the line.

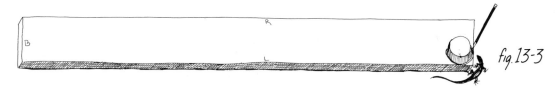

fig. 13-3

When the work on the side board and base has been completed, you can join the two with screws and glue—R on the base being butted against L on the side board. Coat the surfaces with the glue and mount seven flatheaded wood screws along L on the side board, keeping them set in from the edge about ⅜ inch. Space them evenly and set the two end screws about an inch in from F and B to avoid splitting (figure 13-4).

Join the side board and base

fig. 13-4

The next step is to assemble the center plate. This too is done with screws and glue. Join the two pieces so that the edges of both will be flush at one end. Spread glue over the surfaces being attached and lay the pieces in position. Drive in five flatheaded wood screws as illustrated in figure 13-5a.

Assemble the center plate

The back plate is put together in the same way. However, after putting it together, you'll have to do some trimming. As illustrated at the opening of the chapter, this plate is not mounted vertically but rather on an angle of 75 degrees relative to the base. To achieve this, cut 15 degrees off both ends of both pieces (figure 13-5b). Unless you've got a miter box, mark your cuts using a protractor and saw off the ends.

Assemble and trim the back plate

Preparing the heddle plate also involves a little cutting. Here you need to cut 40 degrees off on one end of the piece. Mark the area to be removed (figure 13-5c) and trim it off with your saw.

Trim the heddle plate

There's no cutting on the slider plate. But there is drilling. You'll need two holes large enough in diameter to accommodate the ¼-inch bolts. Position them on the midline and set them back about ⅝ inch from each end. When both have been drilled, change bits. This time you'll need a larger one, something around 1¼ inches in diameter. The goal is to make a hole that's large enough to handle a 1¼-inch dowel but not too large or it won't fit snugly. Ideally you should be able to tap the dowel in with a mallet. Position this hole on the midline, about 2⅛ inches in from one end. Drill it out (figure 13-5d).

Drill the mounting holes and post holes in the slider plate

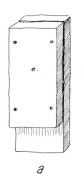

a

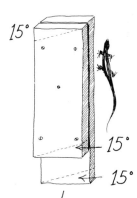

15°
15°
15°

b

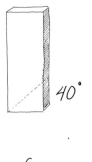

40°

c

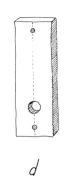

d

fig. 13-5

Mount the back plate

To mount all of the stationary plates to the side base assembly, do the following: Attach the back plate to the *B* end of the side-board–base assembly. Fit it into position over the side board so that the slanted edge of the back piece just meets the top corner of the side board. Connect it with glue and screws, two driven from the side board and one from the plate (figure 13-6). Take care to install all screws near the edges—within about ⅝ inch, but not so close that the wood begins to split. Measure down 22⅛ inches from the *F* end and mount the center plate the same way on the *B* side of the mark. On the *F* side of the center plate and adjacent to it attach the heddle plate. This piece, however, doesn't require a screw from the plate side; instead, drive in four from the side board.

Mount the center and heddle plates

Now lay the whole unit side board down. Draw midlines down the back and center plates. On the back plate mark off three points along the midline; position the first 2⅞ inches from the top, the second at 7⅝ inches, and the third at 10⅛ inches (figure 13-6). On the center plate, again measuring from the top, mark one at 1⅛ inches, the second at 6⅜ inches, and the third at 8⅝ inches. Measuring from the top of the heddle plate, mark one point only at 1⅜ inches. Space it approximately 3¼ inches from the seam between the heddle plate and the center plate. Drill 1¼-inch holes at each mark. This completes the drilling. To install the posts, line the holes with glue and tap them in (figure 13-7).

Drill the post holes and install the posts into the stationary plates

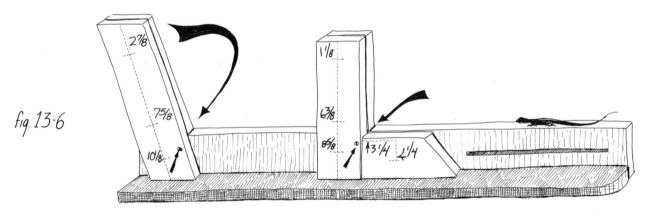

fig. 13-6

Mount the slider plate and post

All that remains now is the slider plate and post. Here too, install the post by spreading glue around the inside surface of the hole and tapping it in. To connect the slider, use the stove bolts. Put them through the holes from the plate side and tighten the washers and wing nuts against the slot on the side board.

Tack on the warp separators

The only other thing that you might want to do is tack some pairs of ¾-inch finishing nails (brads) across the top post on the center plate. This can aid in keeping the warp separated, but it's a matter of personal preference.

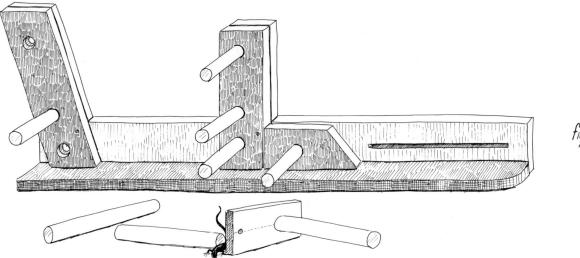

fig. 13-7

14·WEAVING ACCESSORIES

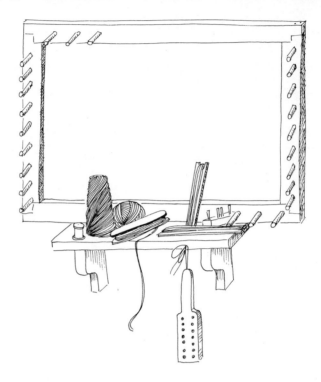

If you're a loom weaver, then you almost certainly know that a loom isn't all that it takes to weave. In order to do all the things that need to be done in preparation for working at the loom, several little, and not so little, related devices are involved. And of them, most can be easily and quickly assembled with only a few basic tools if you have a good pattern to work from. None of them should take more than an afternoon to put together.

Heddle Jig

A heddle jig is a simple tool that enables you to tie your own string heddles, which are somewhat easier on the warp than the metal type. It's made of a single block of wood and four dowels whose dimensions are given in the materials list.

ASSEMBLY

Wood

Quantity	Material	Cut to	Description
1 length	1½ × 3	12 inches	base
4 lengths	⅜-inch dowels	4½ inches	pegs

Other Stuff

	white glue		

Stand the base block on edge. Draw a line lengthwise along the surface that's facing you, dividing the surface in half. Measure 1³⁄₁₆ inches in from one end of the block and mark it on the midline. From that point measure 4⅛ inches and again mark the midline. And from there measure 1⅜ inches, and from there 4⅛ inches. The last mark should be 1³⁄₁₆ inches from the end (figure 14-1). At each of these four points drill a 1½-inch-deep hole using a ⅜-inch bit.

When all four holes have been drilled into the base, fill them part way with the glue and tap in the dowels with a small hammer or mallet.

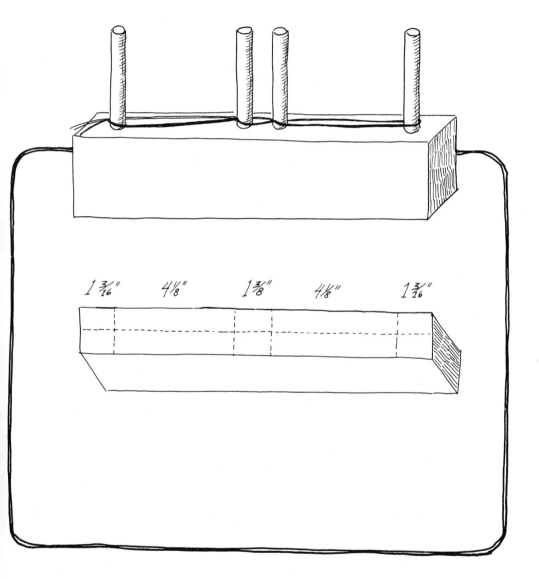

1³⁄₁₆"   4⅛"   1⅜"   4⅛"   1³⁄₁₆"

fig 14-1

Warping Frame

Building a warping frame is not all that different from making a heddle jig; both involve drilling holes and putting dowels in them. Beyond that, the warping frame is nothing more than any other frame—that is, four lengths of wood joined at the ends to form a rectangle. And, as with so many other tools, for the price that's being asked for them ready-made, it pays to build it yourself.

ASSEMBLY

Wood

Quantity	Material	Cut to	Description
2 lengths	⅝ × 3	26½ inches	short frame pieces
2 lengths	⅝ × 3	38½ inches	long frame pieces
22 lengths	½-inch dowel	4 inches	pegs

Hardware and Other Stuff

Quantity	Material
8	No.8 roundheaded wood screws, 2 inches long
2	1-inch screw eyes
	white glue

It's best to begin this project by doing some measuring and marking. First, draw the midlines down each of the frame pieces. Now measure in 1¼ inches from each end of one of them and mark points on the line. From each of these points draw a perpendicular to one of the side edges. With these lines drawn, you will have formed a small, 1¼-inch, square at each end of the frame piece (figure 14-2). Do the same on the other three sections of the frame. Carefully cut out each of the squares, following the lines you've drawn.

Cut out squares at the ends of the frame pieces

fig. 14-2

Now you will be able to fit the frame together as illustrated in figure 14-3; its dimensions when assembled are 29 by 38½ inches. To permanently connect the pieces, we're suggesting two screws and glue at each corner. With the frame laid out flat on your work surface, you can mark the screw positions with an awl. Inasmuch as they will be crossing over one another, the screws at each joint should be screwed in at different levels. This means that if two of the screws are driven in from a point ⅜ inch down from the top surface of a frame piece, the other pair that are mounted perpendicular to them from the adjacent frame member should be driven at a point that is ¾ inch down (figure 14-3a). Once you've located all of the points, predrill the screw holes using a 5/64-inch bit. This will help prevent splitting. Coat the surfaces being connected with glue before installing the screws.

Glue and screw the frame

When the whole thing is together, set it aside for awhile to permit the glue to really set up. Allow at least a half hour for most general purpose household white glues.

Allow the glue to set up

The next step is to drill out the holes for the pegs. For the purpose of orientation, set the frame out so that the side of the frame that's closest to you is one of the shorter ones (figure 14-3). From the left side measure in 3¾ inches and mark the spot on the midline. From this point mark off another seven points, spacing them all 3 inches apart. Now measure along the left

Mark the peg holes onto the frame

frame member 3¼ inches from the corner and mark that point along its midline. From there measure 3 inches and mark the next point. A third and final point should then be marked 3 inches from that one. Repeat this process, locating another three points on the opposite side of the frame, starting from the corner that is diagonally opposite. Also, mark off eight points on the other short piece that correspond to those on the first.

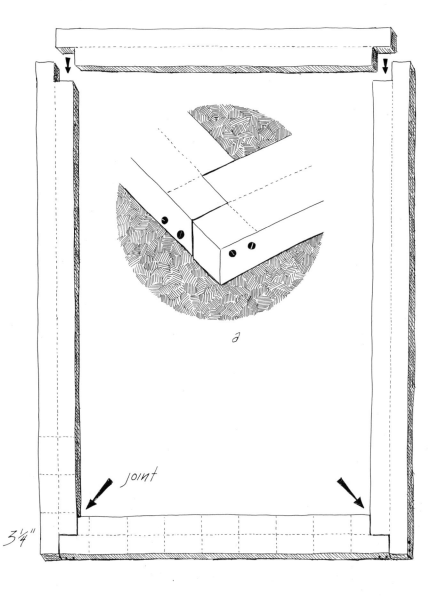

fig. 14-3

joint

3¼"

At each of the points that you've found drill a hole ½ inch in diameter. However, don't bore all the way through; instead make each of them about 1 inch deep. Partially fill them with glue and put in the pegs. To enable you to store it easily or to work at it vertically, mount the two eye hooks along one of the long sides, taking care to space them evenly (figure 14-4).

Drill the peg holes, coat with glue, and insert the pegs
Mount the eye hooks

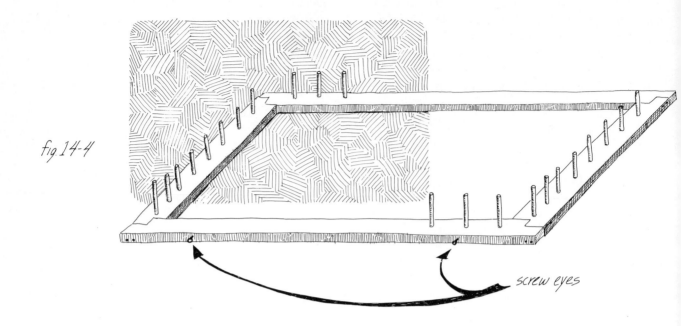

fig. 14-4

screw eyes

Warping Paddle

To make a warping paddle, you need only a small piece of plywood or the equivalent and about an hour to spare. It's the perfect companion for your warping frame. There are two ways to do this project. One is with a coping saw, and the other is with a saber saw. But regardless of which cutting tool you'll choose, the only other tools you'll need are a drill, a pencil, and a ruler.

ASSEMBLY

Wood

Quantity	Material	Cut to	Description
1 section	¼-inch plywood	2½ by 10 inches	the whole thing

Other Stuff

Material
varnish

Drill the holes

Cut out the shape

Start with the pencil and ruler and mark a line ⅜ inch in from each long side. Along each line mark off seven points. Measuring from one end, mark the first one in each row ⅝ inch in; then mark the remaining six with the same distance between them (figure 14-5a). At each of these points drill a ¼-inch hole.

When all of this has been done, all that's left is to cut out the shape of the paddle. To provide a guide for sawing, draw the contours out on the surface of the wood (figure 14-5b). Basically, it's very much like the shape of a popsicle, the kind they sold off the backs of white refrigerator trucks.

Leave the chocolate-covered ice cream part—the area with the holes in it—intact, except for rounding the edges, and trim down the popsicle stick to about 1⅛ inches wide and 4 inches long (figure 14-5c). Sand the whole thing off, coat it with varnish, and put it to work.

Drill the side coves

fig.14-5

a   b   c

Flat Shuttle

A flat shuttle, or shuttle stick, is one of the simplest things you can make. And typically, when you do, you don't just make one. It's another of those single-piece-of-wood projects that require only one of two tools from the workshop.

ASSEMBLY

Wood

Quantity	Material	Cut to	Description
1 length	¼-inch lath	18 (or 22) inches	the whole thing

Other Stuff

	Material
	wax

Once the piece of wood has been cut to the size you want, depending mostly on the width of your warp, find the midline dividing it lengthwise. At each end measure in ¼ inch and mark the spot on the line (figure 14-6a). Fit your drill with a 1-inch bit and drill holes at both of these points. When you do this, you'll immediately notice that the bit is cutting through the edge of the wood. The effect that this creates, with the aid of some sandpaper, is what distinguishes a flat shuttle (figure 14-6b) from the piece of wood that it was when you started. Before you put it to use, be sure that all of the little rough spots have been cleaned away. A coat or two of wax is a good finishing touch.

fig. 14-6

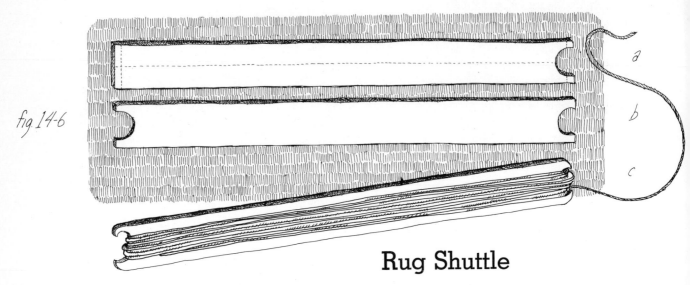

a

b

c

Rug Shuttle

A rug shuttle can be made of two lath strips and three short pieces of dowel, and, if you plan to weave a rug out of strips of rag, it's kind of nice to have around.

ASSEMBLY

Wood

Quantity	Material	Cut to	Description
2 lengths	¼-inch lath	21 inches	sides
3 lengths	5⁄16-inch dowel	2⅞ inches	separators

Other Stuff

Material
white glue
wax

The first step in putting together a rug shuttle is to prepare the parts. Specifically, this means rounding off the ends of the lath strips. One way to do this is to trim down the corners with a saw and sandpaper them round. Another method is to mark the desired curve on the ends with a pencil (figure 14-7a), and cut them out with a coping saw (figure 14-7b). It really doesn't matter how you do it, just as long as it gets done and the ends wind

Round off the ends

up smooth. Also, sandpaper the thickness of the lath down to a point at the corners (figure 14-7c).

Then draw a midline down both pieces and mark off three points along it—one at the center and one 8 inches to either side. At these marks drill holes $\frac{5}{16}$ inch in diameter (figure 14-7d).

Coat the inside edges of the holes with glue. Also coat the ends of the dowels. Let them sit for a moment and then tap the dowels into the holes in one of the sides. Tap the remaining side onto the other end of the dowels, sandwich style (figure 14-7e). After the glue sets up, go over the whole thing with fine sandpaper, and, as with the flat shuttle, consider a coat of wax.

Drill the separator holes

Attach the separators to sides

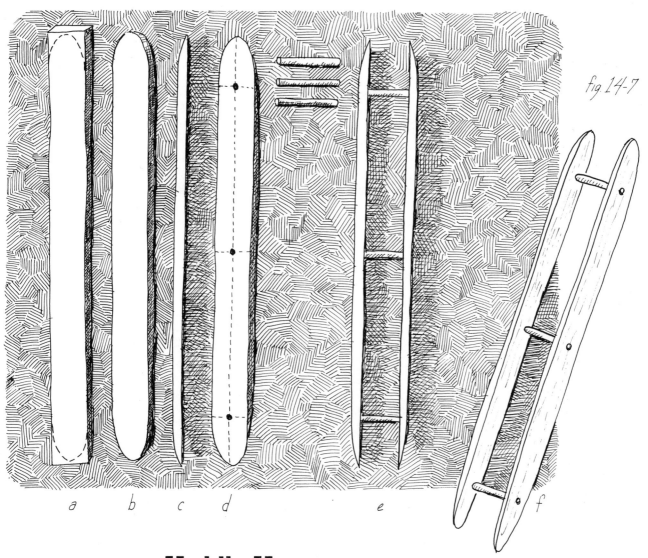

fig. 14-7

a   b   c   d   e   f

Heddle Horse

Heddle horses help make two-harness looms into four-harness looms and pave the way for even further expansion. We learned about them from a friend that spent a year in Sweden studying, of all things, *vavning* (weaving). And we have made use of them ever since. Preparing them is about as difficult as making a flat shuttle. Currently we have four in use.

ASSEMBLY

Wood

Quantity	Material	Cut to	Description
1 length	¼ × 1	12 inches	the whole thing

Before you locate any points for drilling or mark off any section for cutting, draw the midline and find its center. At that spot draw a line perpendicular to the midline, running from side to side (figure 14-8a). For convenience we'll call this line *A*. Draw another line parallel to the midline, halfway between the midline and one of the sides (figure 14-8b). Call this line *B*. Where *B* intersects *A*, drill a hole about ³⁄₁₆ inch in diameter (figure 14-8c).

Draw a line from above the hole from where *A* meets the side down to where the *B* terminates at the end of the wood. Make another from the same point on *A* to the other end of *B* (figure 14-8d). Carefully cut along these lines with your saw (figure 14-8e).

Finally, at a distance of about ¾ inch from each end, along the newly cut edge and set in from that edge about ¹⁄₁₆ inch, mark a point. Bore a ¼-inch hole at each point. As with the flat shuttle, these holes will overextend the edge of the wood, thereby leaving them open on one side to function as hangers (figure 14-8f). Smooth the horse down with sandpaper and you can mount it on your loom (figure 14-8g).

Drill the hanging hole

Trim off the top

Drill the hanger coves

fig 14-8

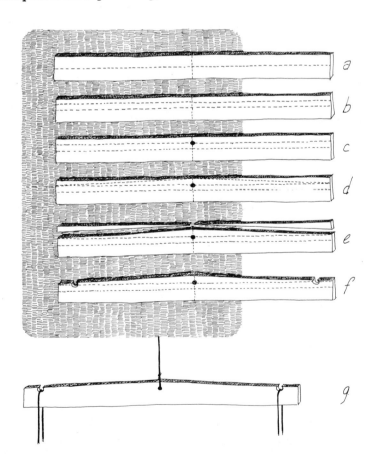

a

b

c

d

e

f

g

15·SPOOL RACK

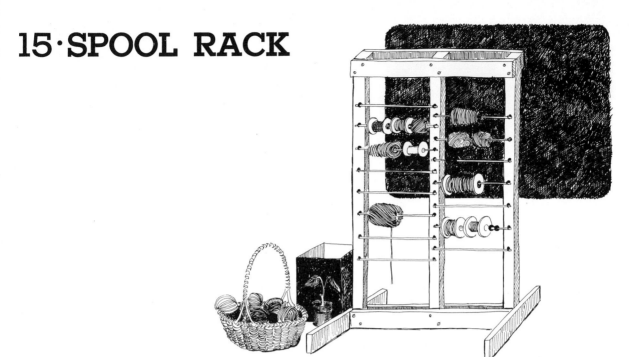

Here's a tool that an awful lot of soft-crafts people we know have said they would like to have. But, ironically, until now almost none of them do. It's a spool rack, and it's the best way we know to keep everything straight in a busy soft-crafts studio or, for that matter, in a home sewing room. Although such racks have been around for quite a long while, the cost of ready-mades seems to be just high enough to make buying one worth putting off time and time again. But somehow, it's just about impossible to keep yarns and such in order in an old shoe box or grandmother's old sewing chest, and, no matter what you intend them for, shelves tend to get cluttered with everything from candy wrappers to incense burners. And that's why we're giving you a spool rack that you can build yourself.

This spool rack is really very easy and not expensive at all. Basically, it's a freestanding frame designed to hold spools that have been threaded onto dowels that can be hung onto and removed from it with ease.

ASSEMBLY

Wood

Quantity	Material	Cut to	Description
3 lengths	2 × 2	48 inches	beams
4 lengths	⁵⁄₄ × 3	30 inches	front and rear head and base pieces
2 lengths	⁵⁄₄ × 3	18 inches	feet
15 lengths	¼-inch dowel	48 inches	spool rods

Hardware

Quantity	Material
32	No.6 roundheaded wood screws, 2 inches long
30	cup hooks

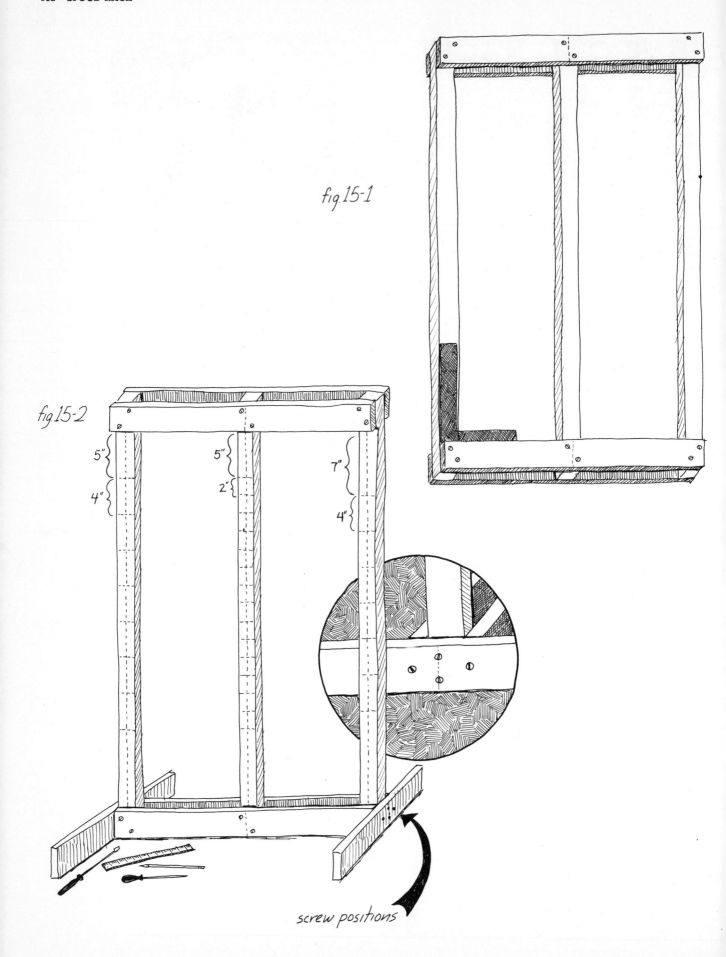

fig. 15-1

fig. 15-2

5"

5"

7"

4"

2"

4"

screw positions

Start by laying the three beams parallel to one another and about 12 inches apart. Place a head piece over them at one end. Adjust the right and left beams relative to the edges of the head piece. With your pencil mark the center of the head piece, 15 inches from an end. Now align the central beam relative to that mark. At each point where the head overlaps a beam you will drive two screws, on a diagonal (figure 15-1). Before driving any screws, check the angles between the head and beams to be certain that they're 90 degrees. If things don't quite check out, make all necessary adjustments and then start putting in the screws. Don't tighten them, though—not yet.

Mount one head piece

With the head piece somewhat attached, position the base piece on the opposite end of the beams. Align it in the same way as you did the head piece—that is, relative to all three of the beams (figure 15-1). Mark the screw points and check to see that everything is square. Drive the screws, this time all the way. Afterward, tighten the ones at the head. When this is done, flip the unit over and repeat the process with the remaining head and base pieces.

Mount the base pieces and the head piece

All of this being done, the basic frame is complete. But it still won't stand—not until you add the critical ingredient, the feet. To do this, balance the unit up on one of its sides. If you can, get someone to hold it. Mark the centers of each foot, 9 inches from an end, and hold one of them up at the bottom end of the side beam so that it overlaps the ends of the base pieces. Try to keep it perpendicular and flush with the bottom while marking screw-hole locations, two over the beam, one over the front base piece, and one over the rear base piece (figure 15-2a). Drive the first screw down through the foot and into the beam, but don't tighten it until you've checked to be sure that everything is still properly aligned. Do the same with the remaining three screws. When this foot is secure, turn the whole unit onto its other side and install the other foot in the same way.

Mount the feet

With all screws completely tightened, you can stand the frame right side up. At this point you should sharpen your pencil and get your ruler. Draw a midline down each of the three beams. On the left beam measure down 5 inches from the underside of the head piece and mark it on the midline. Do the same on the center beam. On the right beam measure down 7 inches (figure 15-2). Again on the right beam measure down 4 inches from the point you just marked and make another mark on the midline. From this spot measure 4 inches again and make yet another mark. Repeat this until you've marked off a total of seven points on the right beam. Go to the left beam and do the same thing, beginning at the mark that you've already made—except this time don't stop until you have a total of eight marks. On the central beam space your marks every 2 inches and make a total of fifteen of them.

Mark the rod positions on the beams

Depress each of the marks that you've made with an awl and drive a cup hook in at every one. These hooks will hold the rods. Lay eight of them into the hooks in the left and central beams and lay the remaining seven into the remaining hooks. To remove them, just lift them out. If you fill up all fifteen rods with spools and have still more to mount, all that you have to do is add some hooks on the back side of the rack.

Install the hooks and lay on the rods

16·SILK-SCREEN PRINTING UNIT

It was on one of those brush-painted autumn days in the Catskills that we were to meet Dmitri, a college dropout in his mid-twenties who had given up the study of medieval European history for a squeegee and a screen. Neither of us knew him personally, nor, for that matter, had we seen any of his work. In fact, until that day in mid-November, we had known pitifully little about the whole process of silk-screening. And that's part of why we were going to his home in Pine Bush—to find out more. We faithfully followed the directions he had given us by phone, got lost twice, consumed one twelve-ounce bag of potato chips and two large chocolate bars with peanuts, and arrived late in the day.

The place he was living in was the recreation hall of an old summer camp, a large white frame building with red shutters and trim. Dmitri greeted us at the door. We entered a large, open room. It was well lit, wood-paneled, and barely furnished except for a pair of sturdy wooden tables near the window. On one of these were several assorted cans, jars, and gallon bottles, and on the other a paint-spotted silk-screen printing unit. A clothesline hung between two hooks that had been screwed securely into opposite pine-board walls. From this several prints were suspended on clip-type clothespins. Dmitri was in the middle of a "run."

We spoke with him as he worked and watched respectfully as he easily commanded his craft. It was fascinating. With each push of the squeegee that he gripped firmly in his hands, a new print was born. After completing several, he decided to stop. He covered his inks and began to wash up. The smell of kerosene was everywhere as he bore down on a small scrub brush to rub away his stencil. Occasionally he glanced over at his work, and, although unspoken, his satisfaction was apparent.

Since that time we've had a great deal of contact with this medium. And it seems that people everywhere are becoming more interested in making prints. Apparently being able to produce an art product in multiples that can be widely distributed at prices people can afford to pay is an attractive idea. Silk screening, of course, is particulary desirable ·because nothing very elaborate is needed to produce good results.

The printing unit is the principal tool for the process of silk-screen printing. This is made up of two main parts—a screen and a base. In building the unit, the fabric for the screen will probably be your largest single investment. However, you'll find that with some care the investment will take you a long way. In going out to buy the fabric, there are a couple of considerations to make. One is whether or not to use silk. Although the name of the process certainly suggests this, there are other options open to you. One of the marvels of our technological society is its skill in making synthetics, and it is that very fact that provided us with a choice. Synthetic silk-screen fabrics aren't bad, and they do cost less. Your decision to go with naturals or synthetics is entirely a matter of personal preference. We've heard pros and cons about both.

The other consideration is that of mesh. This refers to the degree of fineness and coarseness of the material. Mesh ranges from number 00, the finest, to number 18, the coarsest. The nature of your work, the kind of detail that you would be expecting your screen to reproduce, should be considered in making this decision. If you're interested in good overall performance, a number 12 or 14 will probably be a good choice.

If you plan to build a large frame that is sturdy, the 2×2's that we've suggested will do the job well. For a smaller frame, 1×3's are adequate. A piece of ⅝- to ¾-inch plywood or particle board provides a solid printing bed. No matter what you're using, however, be certain that the wood is not warped. A warped silk screen can really be annoying. Also, it's much easier to fit things together when there are no bends to tackle. If the wood you're using is unfinished, plan on sanding it smooth before assembly in order to remove splinters. You certainly don't want to run the risk of pulling or tearing your precious fabric. Begin with a relatively coarse grade of sandpaper and work your way up to fine. Remember the higher the number, the finer the grit.

We have suggested and illustrated certain dimensions. But, again, the size of the unit is really up to you. We do advise, however, that you make it large enough to handle the full range of sizes that you would ordinarily be producing. If the unit is a little too large for a particular job, you can always mask out the unneeded space. If, on the other hand, you haven't made the screen large enough, you're stuck.

ASSEMBLY

Wood

Quantity	Material	Cut to	Description
2 lengths	2×2 [a]	32 inches	front and back frame pieces
2 lengths	2×2 [a]	28 inches	side frame pieces
2 lengths	2×2 [a]	24 inches [b]	posts
1 section	¾-inch plywood [c]	32 by 36 inches [d]	printing bed

Hardware and Other Stuff

Quantity	Material
8	No.8 flatheaded wood screws, 3 inches long [e]
8	3½-inch corner braces [f] (with accompanying wood screws)
1 piece	screen fabric,[g] cut to 30 by 34 inches [h]
2	flat cabinet hinges [i] (with accompanying wood screws)
4	cup hooks
2	screen-door springs
	2- or 3-inch-wide masking tape [j]
	white glue
	shellac

[a] 1 × 3 is adequate for a smaller unit.

[b] Can be smaller if the unit is smaller.

[c] Or ⅝-inch plywood or particle board.

[d] These dimensions are not critical so long as they are greater than the frame.

[e] If 1 × 3's are being used, use 1⅝- or 1¾-inch-long No.8 flatheads.

[f] Or 4 flat corner angles and 4 corner braces.

[g] Silk or synthetic.

[h] Any dimensions slightly larger than those of the frame will work.

[i] With removable pins.

[j] Or packing tape.

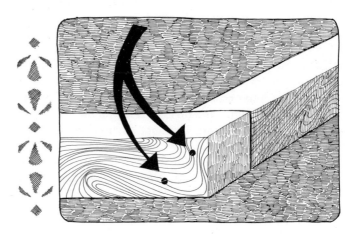

fig. 16-1

Assemble the frame

Naturally you will want the pieces of your frame to be joined securely. After you've cut them, arrange them as illustrated in figure 16-1. If you are using 1 × 3's instead of 2 × 2's, stand the pieces on edge so that the 3-inch dimension will constitute the thickness of the frame. Coat the ends with white glue and attach them with wood screws, two at each joint (figure 16-1). Be sure to countersink. You can check to be certain that the corners are right angles by fitting a metal carpenter's square or even the corner of an old switch plate at the joints and squaring up where necessary. Although we've used butted joints in the assembly shown, if you have the equipment and experience to do so, you may elect to miter instead. Either way, the important thing is to be sure that the pieces fit well together. For further reinforcement at the corners, use corner braces or flat corner angles. If you use corner braces, mount them on the outside rather than within (figure 16-2). If you decide on flat angles, mount them on the face of the frame opposite the one to which you will be tacking the fabric.

corner brace

fig. 16-2

Attaching the screen to the frame is similar to stretching a canvas. If you've done that, you should be rather good at doing this. If you haven't, now is the time to learn. You'll make the task easier if you have canvas pliers and a staple gun at hand. If you don't have either, see if you can find someone you know who does. After all, there is no point laboring over something that can be greatly simplified by the application of a couple of tools. If you can't locate them, however, don't despair, simply find a friend to substitute for the stretching pliers. A staple gun is somewhat more difficult to find a substitute for; a tack hammer and small carpet tacks can be used, but it will mean a greater investment of time and energy. Lay the fabric in position on the frame, aligning the warp with an edge. If the material has been cut well, this shouldn't be difficult. If not, do the best you can; it isn't really critical. Tack the center of each side down, moving from side to opposite side, and pull taut. Bear in mind that, unlike stretching canvas, the silk is attached directly to the edge of the frame that is facing up, rather than around the sides. Beginning on one of the longer sides at the center staple, tack up to one corner, pulling firmly between each staple (figure 16-3). Repeat this on the same half of the opposite long side, pulling not only between staples but across the frame as well. Complete the long sides and then repeat the procedure with the short sides (figure 16-4). If all has gone well, the fabric should be stretched smoothly over the frame. (If perchance there should be a pucker or a ripple, then you have to make some adjustments. Use a small screwdriver to gently pry up the staples that need to be removed, taking special precautions not to damage the silk.) When this is finished, cut off the excess fabric (figure 16-4).

With the silk firmly secured on the frame, you'll want to tape around the edges, both inside and out, to prevent the paints from collecting between the fabric and frame. Use the wide masking or packing tape for this purpose. Run a border around the silk, covering the staples (figure 16-5). Now turn the frame over. Here run the tape so that it fits snugly into the corners, adhering half to the wooden frame and half to the silk itself (figure 16-6). To seal, coat the tape, both inside and out, with shellac (figure 16-7).

Attach the silk screen

Reinforce the silk screen with tape

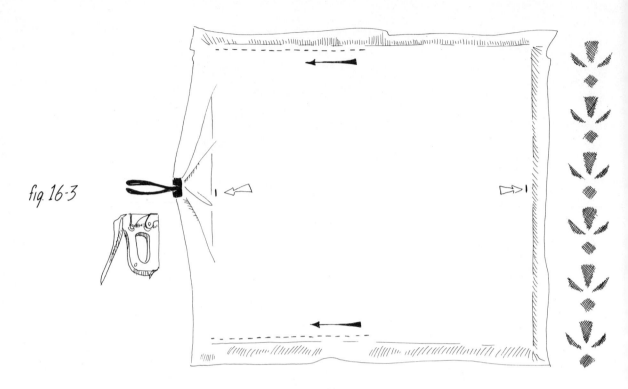

fig. 16-3

Mount the hinges on the frame

For attaching the screen frame to the printing bed, you'll need two hinges with removable pins. To mount the hinges on the frame, turn the frame fabric side up and measure in about 1½ inches from each end of one of the long sides. Mark these two points and position the hinges on the inside of these marks. This should provide adequate separation for the hinges and also leave enough distance from the edges of the frame to prevent splitting (figure 16-8). Drive the mounting screws into place.

fig. 16-4

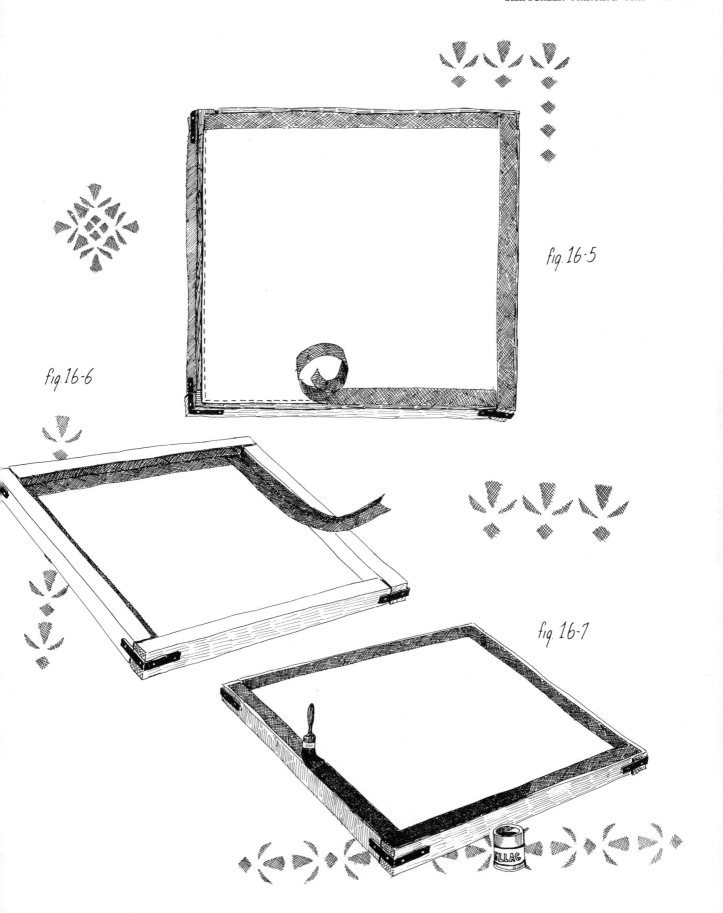

fig. 16-5

fig. 16-6

fig. 16-7

Sand the printing bed

Attach the hinges to the printing bed

The printing bed should be smooth. If it isn't, go over it with sandpaper. Any irregularities on this surface might effect the quality of the finished print. When you're entirely satisfied with the surface, lay the screen in position on it, silk side down. Mark the locations of the hinges' mounting holes onto the surface and drive in the screws (figure 16-9).

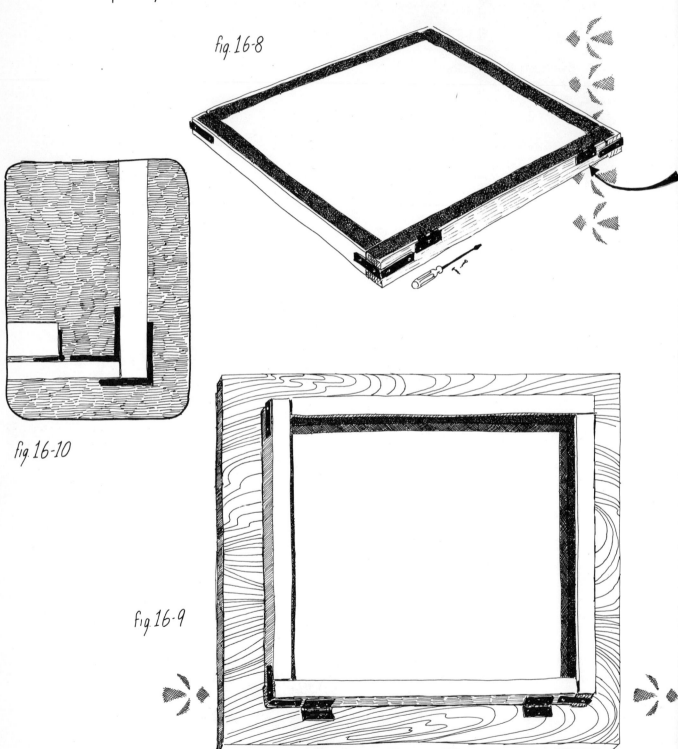

fig. 16-8

fig. 16-10

fig. 16-9

To facilitate removing finished prints and replacing them with fresh paper during the printing procedure, it is desirable to have a way to hold the screen off the printing bed. This is very important for a smooth, efficient printing operation. There are many ways of doing it, but the one most commonly in use seems to be the most practical to recommend. To make it, you'll need the two vertical posts. To attach each, you use two corner braces and some white glue. Hold one of the posts up vertically near one side against the rear edge of the printing bed. Seat the first brace between the post and the printing bed (figure 16-10) and secure it to the printing bed with mounting screws. Hold the post up in position against the brace and mark the mounting holes onto the post. Brush glue over the surface of the post to be butted against the printing bed. Now holding the post snugly in place, drive the screws. The second brace is attached to the outside of the joint, from the rear of the post to the underside of the printing bed (figure 16-10). Carefully propping the unit up into a manageable position, hold the brace in place and mount it. Repeat the entire procedure one more time near the other side of the rear edge.

Install the posts

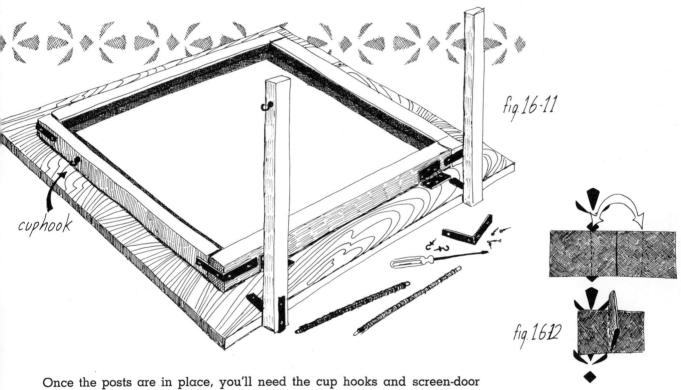

cuphook

fig. 16-11

fig. 16-12

Once the posts are in place, you'll need the cup hooks and screen-door springs to finish the job. Mount one of the hooks on each of the posts, down from the top about 2 inches (figure 16-11). Mount the other toward the front of the side piece of the frame. Repeat on the other side. Attach each spring between the hooks on each side. In its rest position your screen should be suspended above the printing bed.

Mount the hooks and springs

For registration you can make up some masking-tape tabs by cutting 2-inch-long strips of tape, folding them back in half, and folding one of the halves down over itself (figure 16-12). These can be affixed to the surface of the printing bed wherever necessary and removed, relocated, and replaced with ease. Select a spot somewhere on the unit where the wood is particularly appealing and sign your name. The unit is complete.

Make the registration tabs

Sign your name

17·INK PLATEN

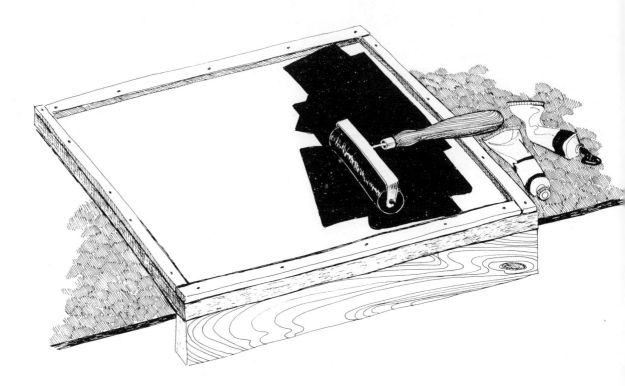

Maybe you don't think that it's worth spending your time to build an ink platen. And perhaps you're right. It's entirely possible that you've currently got something in your studio that you find perfectly adequate for the purpose —something that provides a good, smooth, easy-to-clean surface that's neither too big or too small, that clings to the edge of your workbench and doesn't slide about, and that is durable enough not to require frequent replacement due to chipping, bending, cracking, shattering, and the like. If this is where you're at, read no further.

However, if you're unable to boast of all these features and have been sort of casually looking around for something better, the ink platen that we describe may be of particular interest to you. Basically, it's a sheet of glass mounted on a backing board and edged with strips of lath. Not very complicated. Yet the unit is durable and should satisfy the tastes of most platen consumers.

The size that we're basing our measurements on is that of the glass working area, 12 by 15 inches. In general, this size is small enough not to be cumbersome while being adequately large for rolling out two colors. If, as may well be the case, you've already got an unmounted and unprotected piece of glass that you've been using for inks, simply do your figuring on that basis. If you're buying fresh, we recommend double-strength glass for added durability. The only thing is, have the piece cut to size where you get it. It's not the same as single-strength; you'd find it far more difficult to trim it to size at home. We've tried it. It just didn't work out.

ASSEMBLY

Wood

Quantity	Material	Cut to	Description
1 section	½-inch plywood [a]	13½ by 16½ inches [b]	backing board
1 length	furring strip	16½ inches [c]	lip
1 length	¾-inch lath	8 feet [d]	edging

Hardware and Other Stuff

Quantity	Material
1 panel	double-strength glass, cut to 12 by 15 inches
4	No.16 finishing nails, 1½ inches long
20	No.18 finishing nails, ¾ inch long
1 piece	old newspaper,[e] bigger than the glass
	masking tape
	white glue
	ceramic-tile adhesive compound
	shellac

[a] Or particle board or whatever you have around.
[b] Or 1½ inches larger on all sides than the glass.
[c] Or equal to the long side of the backing board.
[d] Will be cut further during assembly.
[e] Or newsprint

The first step in constructing the unit is to attach the lip to the lower surface of the backing board. This can easily be done by standing the strip on edge along and beneath a long side of the backing board and tacking it into place with the No.16 finishing nails. For added strength coat the surfaces to be joined with white glue before driving the nails. And, of course, hammer them in from the backing board down (figure 17-1).

Now set the unit down just long enough for the glue to begin to set up. Find your lath and a saw. You'll need to cut four pieces, one for each side. Measure the first side off and mark the length on the lath strip. But don't cut yet. Subtract the width of the strip, or ¾ inch, from that length and mark the spot. With your saw carefully cut off the piece. Do the same for the other required pieces, remembering to cut each of them ¾ inch shorter than the actual length of the corresponding side of the backing board.

Once the pieces have been cut as described, lay them out on the surface of the board so as to assure correct placement and good fit. Coat the surfaces to be joined with a little white glue and tack the lath strips into place with the No.18 finishing nails. When in place, the inside dimensions of the lath frame should conform to the dimensions of your piece of glass.

Lay the piece of glass onto a sheet of scrap paper—newsprint is fine. Trace around the edges of the glass with a pencil. Remove the glass and cut out the shape you have drawn. Place the cutout into the lath frame. To hold it down, you can use rings of masking tape (figure 17-2). Coat the unit with shellac, excluding the area that has been covered. Set it aside to dry.

Once the shellac is hard, you can install the glass. Remove the paper and coat the surface that it covered with adhesive. A white adhesive like

Attach the lip to the backing board

Cut the lath strips to size

Attach the lath strips to the backing board

Tape the newspaper cutout into the lath frame

Coat the unit with shellac

Glue the glass to the unit

the kind that is sometimes used to install ceramic tiles is best here so that the inks can be easily seen. Spread the material with a trowel or spatula so that the entire surface is covered. When you've done this to your satisfaction, lay the glass in position. Basically the unit is now complete. If, however, after using it a couple of times, you find that ink is building up in the slight separation that may exist between the glass and the lath frame, clean these areas thoroughly and fill them in with adhesive compound.

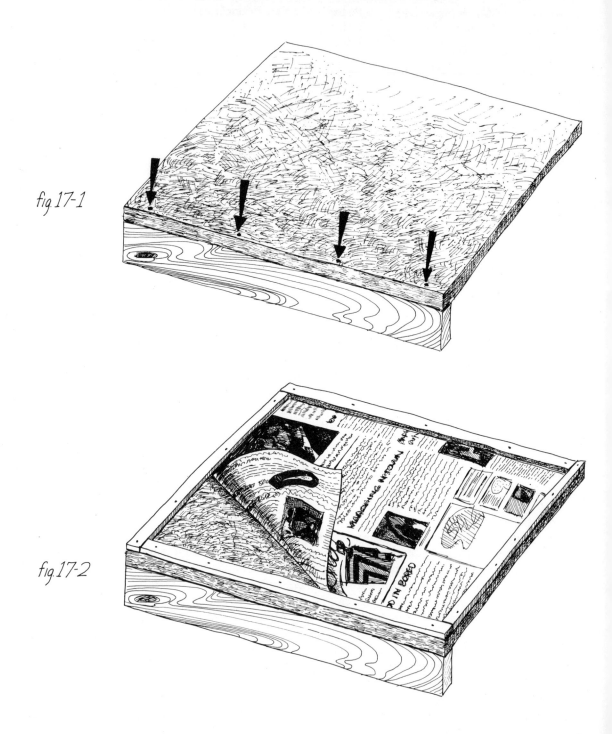

fig. 17-1

fig. 17-2

18·BENCH CLAMP

A bench clamp is a very useful device that can be made out of three pieces of wood. Its purpose is to hold blocks, typically wood or linoleum, for cutting and engraving. If you are an experienced relief printer, then you well know the value of this simple tool. After all, what can be more annoying than attempting to carefully cut a delicate design into a virginal linoleum surface as the block jerks and slowly slips across the table? With a minimal investment in time and materials, this problem can be easily and permanently resolved.

The basic components of the bench clamp are the stop piece, the surface piece, and the clamp piece. The stop piece is that part of the tool against which the block is held. The surface piece is what the block is seated on. And the clamp piece holds the entire unit securely against the edge of your workbench or table. The two basic criteria for a good bench clamp are that it be strong enough and big enough. Regardless of what kind of material you plan on cutting, the clamp has to be able to support your strength when you bear down with the cutting tool. The bench clamp that we built and describe here is 8 inches deep and 10 inches wide. Inasmuch as the largest block we typically use is no more than 8 inches in one dimension, we've found this size to be perfectly comfortable. The size of your clamp is really dependent upon the size of the largest block you'll be using. If you make a bench clamp that's larger than necessary, you can always make up for this by filling in the space between the block you're cutting and the stop piece with an appropriate-size piece of scrap wood. It's always easier to adjust a larger clamp than to try to fudge with one that's too small.

All the lumber that you'll need is one small piece of ½- to ¾-inch plywood

(we used ½-inch construction-grade plywood, rough on both sides) and two
pieces of furring strip as long as the longest dimension of the plywood. A
bench clamp is one of those kinds of projects that's well suited to scrap
wood. If you have some wood around that's approximately the right dimension, by all means don't hesitate to use it—that is, so long as it's not dry-
rotted and/or cracked in strategic places. To put the thing together, all you'll
need is six nails and some glue.

ASSEMBLY

Wood

Quantity	Material	Cut to	Description
1 section	½-inch plywood	8 by 10 inches	surface piece
2 lengths	furring strip	10 inches	clamp and stop pieces

Hardware and Other Stuff

Quantity	Material
6	ringlock nails, 1¾ inches long
	white glue

First, cut all the pieces to size. Keep an extra length of the furring strip with
the unit components to be used as an aid in construction. Place one of the

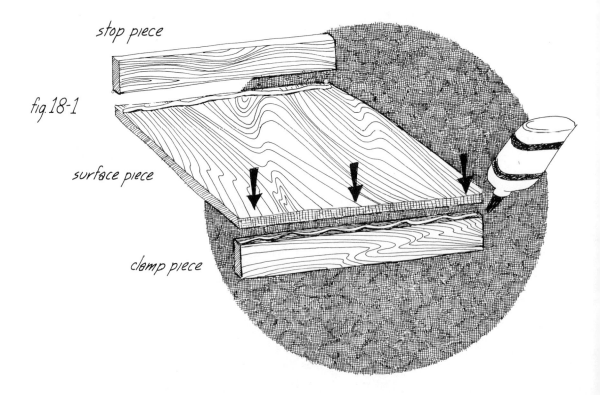

stop piece

fig. 18-1

surface piece

clamp piece

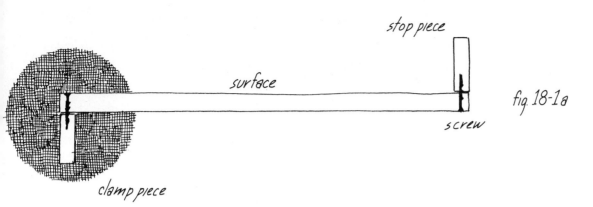

fig. 18-1a

stop piece

surface

screw

clamp piece

furring strips, the clamp piece, beneath the surface piece. Position it along an edge of corresponding length (figure 18-1). Raise the opposite edge of the surface piece, using the extra piece that you've set aside. When the clamp piece is correctly aligned, raise the surface piece slightly and apply the glue along the top edge of the furring strip. Lower the surface piece into position. Gently hammer three ringlock nails through the surface piece into the wood below, one at each end and one in the center. (Ringlock nails have a textured shank that enables them to grip really well.) Now turn the unit over and repeat the procedure to attach the stop piece.

The thing about bench clamps is that they're so easy to put together that if perchance the one that you've built falls apart someday—after having been used as a launching pad by your six-year-old son or crushed beneath the orthopedic shoe of your three-hundred-and-forty-two-pound Uncle Max from Hackensack—you can build a replacement in almost no time at all. This is also important, of course, if you should find that the one you've build is a little too small.

Attach the clamp piece and the stop piece to the surface piece

19·POTTER'S WHEEL

Wendell Mendelson is somebody that we made up. But you may recognize his problem. Wendell just loved to throw pots. And every spare moment he had, he would do just that. He loved clay, he loved what it could do, and just about everyone loved what he did with it. Wendell lived in a small town in a rural place, a town noted for the fine pieces of art that its residents produced. And Wendell knew many of them as friends. And, coincidentally, many of his friends also loved clay, and a few had large, comfortable studios. That's where Wendell would do his work—in those large, comfortable friends' studios. For Wendell, despite the great beauty of his work, couldn't afford his own tools. That is, the big ones—a wheel and a kiln.

For the longest while things were going along quite well. Wendell was able to turn his pots among his friends, and nobody really minded at all. But then it happened. One day Wendell moved to the city, to a large apartment house. And there wasn't a potter's wheel to be found in the whole towering place. What was Wendell to do? He got depressed. He couldn't throw his beautiful pots. He began to wander through the city in search of a wheel, something that he could afford. He looked and looked and months went by.

Then Wendell got an idea. "What if I build my own wheel?" he thought. "But how would I ever do that?"

Well, Wendell, this project may be your answer. Here's a kick wheel that should do the job—a floor model with a built-in bench. The following is a list of materials that you'll need to construct the entire unit. If it's not easy to locate suppliers in your area who handle items needed, consider writing to any one of the following: Sculpture House, Inc., 38 E. 30th St., New York, N.Y. 10016; Stewart Clay Company, 133 Mulberry St., New York, N.Y. 10013; or Dick Blick, P.O. Box 1267, Galesburg, Ill. 61401.

ASSEMBLY

Wood

Quantity	Material	Cut to	Description
4 lengths	4 × 4	42 inches	table legs
2 lengths	4 × 4	42 inches [a]	seat legs
1 length	2 × 4	30 inches	top-left frame piece
1 length	2 × 4	38 inches	top-right frame piece
1 length	2 × 4	35¼ inches	top-back frame piece
1 length	2 × 4	32 inches	top-front frame piece
1 length	1 × 4	30 inches	left foot
1 length	1 × 4	38 inches	right foot
1 length	1 × 6	38 inches	center foot
1 length	2 × 4	32 inches	middle-back brace
1 length	2 × 4	19 inches	seat brace
1 length	2 × 2	32 inches	lower-back brace
1 length	2 × 2	31 inches	seat-to-back brace
1 length	1 × 4	53 inches [a]	left-side brace
1 length	1 × 4	58 inches [a]	right-side brace
1 length	1 × 6	22 inches	seat
1 section	¾-inch plywood [b]	28 by 35¼ inches	table top
1 section	¾-inch plywood [b]	18 inches square	kick-wheel bottom
1 section	¾-inch plywood [b]	32 inches square [a]	kick-wheel top
1 section	¾-inch plywood [b]	14 inches square [a]	throwing wheel
2 lengths	1 × 6	18 inches	kick-wheel sides
2 lengths	1 × 6	17¼ inches	kick-wheel sides
2 lengths	1 × 6	28¾ inches	table sides
1 length	1 × 6	35¼ inches	table back
1 length	1 × 4	35¼ inches	table front
1 length	1 × 3 [c]	18 inches	stabilizer board

Hardware and Other Stuff

1	¾-inch cold-rolled steel rod,[d] 36 inches long
2	⅜-inch cold-rolled steel rods, 16 inches long
2	ball-bearing flange pillow blocks for ¾-inch rod (with accompanying wood screws)
1	threaded flange for ¾-inch rod (with accompanying wood screws)
1 cubic foot	concrete [e]
1 pound	16d common nails
1 pound	6d common nails
1 pound	4d finishing nails
4	10d finishing nails
3	⅜-inch stove bolts, 1½ inches long
3	T nuts for ⅜-inch bolts
1 length	string,[f] 32 inches long
1	large paper clip
1 length	wide flat metal edging, 37¾ inches long
	waterproof wood adhesive
	tincture of green soap

[a] Will be cut further during assembly.
[b] Exterior grade.
[c] Or 1 × 4 or 1 × 6 or just about anything.

[d] Threaded at one end.
[e] Sakrete.
[f] Or thread or fishing line.

The easiest way to begin is by assembling the left side of the unit first. The pieces needed here are two of the table legs, the top-left frame piece, and the left foot. With the table legs laid out on their sides, tack the left foot into place on their ends, using six 6d common nails, forming a big U (figure 19-1). Lay the top-left frame piece over the opposite end of the legs, securing it to the side faces with four 16d's, two in each leg. This completes the left side, minus the brace, a piece that will be added later.

Attach the left foot and the top-left frame piece to a pair of table legs

Now for the right side. Here you use the remaining set of table legs, one of the seat legs, the top-right frame piece, and the right foot. Start by marking the foot 30 inches from one end to establish the exact position of the right front leg. Lay the table legs out with about 2 feet between them. To one of them, tack the end of the foot that you've just measured from with three 6d nails. Carefully align the other leg with the mark that you've drawn on the foot, so that it will fall inside that mark relative to the other foot. Nail it down also.

Attach the right foot to the other pair of table legs

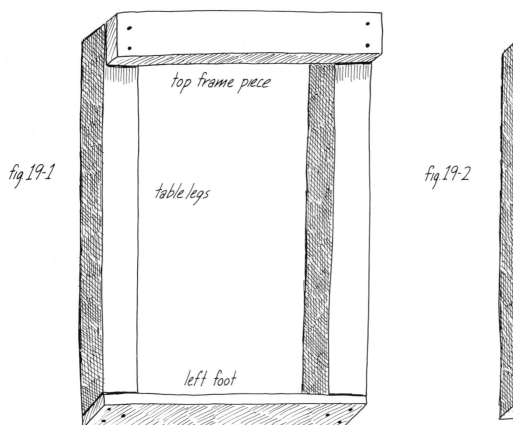

top frame piece

table legs

fig. 19-1

left foot

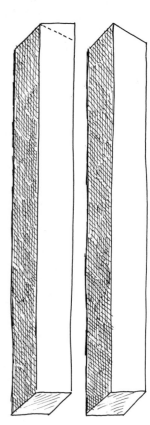

fig. 19-2

To prepare the seat leg, cut an angle of about 25 degrees off one end (figure 19-2). Use a miter box if you have access to one. It's by far the easiest way; it'll hold your saw at the angle you want and guide the blade through. If you don't have one, a protractor, even the inexpensive plastic variety, will suffice. Mark one of the faces of the wood for cutting and carefully begin to saw. Be particularly watchful when making this cut to insure that your saw goes straight all the way. Problems here could result in a shaky seat. When this one's done, you'll do well to prepare the other seat leg.

Miter the ends of the seat legs

Repeat the whole procedure one more time with your miter box nearby. This time, if you don't have a miter box, use the first seat leg as a template to make your mark on the second. When both seat legs are finished, they should match up. Take either one of them and lay it in position against the right foot, the mitered end up, the mitered face toward the table legs (figure 19-3). Using 6d common nails, fasten the foot to the seat leg. To complete the side, position the top-right frame piece over the legs at the ends opposite the foot. Make certain that, when the unit is standing, this frame piece will be on the right side looking from the seat leg. Check to be sure that its edges are flush with the outside faces of the corner legs. When it looks good, tack it down with 16d's (figure 19-4).

Attach the right foot to one seat leg

Attach the top-right frame piece to the legs

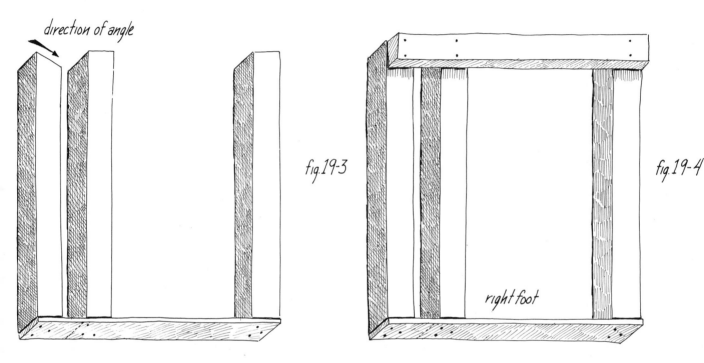

direction of angle

fig. 19-3

right foot

fig. 19-4

With both the left and right sides completed, you can move on to the back. Unlike the sides, this section cannot be built separate from the others. In fact, the first thing you should do is stand both the left and right side units on their feet with about 2 feet between them in preparation for mounting the top-back frame piece. If no one's around to help you hold the sides up, you'll probably have to position them next to something for support. Align the back frame piece with the other top frame members so that its ends are flush, both left and right. Of course, this too may be a bit awkward if you're doing it alone. Here it may be useful to drive a nail in on one side for support only. But don't drive it in all the way, and, by all means, don't use a 16d. A long and relatively fine nail will hold things together adequately and will provide the flexibility needed to enable making adjustments on the end being permanently secured. For final nailing use 16d's as with the other 2 × 4's (figure 19-5). Pull out the support nail when you're done.

Measuring down 22 inches from the bottom of the back frame piece, you can position the top of the middle-back brace. Unlike the frame, however, this piece is mounted to the inside face of each of the back legs (figure 19-5). Again, use 16d's to secure the 2 × 4, and, for lack of a better choice, a construction nail may be used to hold the piece in position while mounting it.

Mount the top-back frame piece

Mount the middle-back brace

Although there is yet another brace to be attached to the back section, it's best to come back to that one later.

In the meanwhile, turn your attention to the top-front frame piece. As with the middle-back brace, it is mounted on the inside. If it's been cut accurately, it should slide comfortably between the two top-side frame pieces. If it's a bit snug, tap it into position with a hammer. If it's loose, try using a small wedge of cardboard to hold it in its place. When correctly positioned (figure 19-5), nail it to the legs using two 16d common nails on each end.

Mount the top-front frame piece

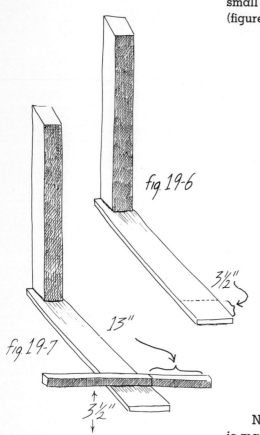

fig. 19-6

fig. 19-7

13"

3½"

Attach the center foot to the other seat leg

Attach the center foot to the lower-back brace

Attach the lower-back brace to the back legs

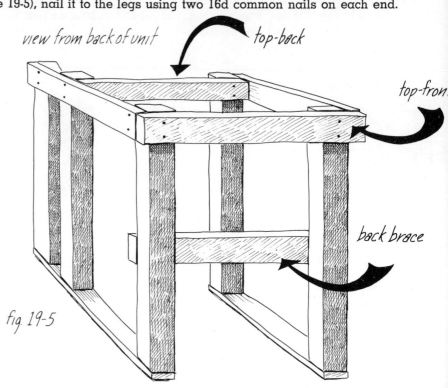

view from back of unit

top-back

top-front

back brace

fig. 19-5

Now for that lower-back brace. Unlike the middle-back brace, this brace is made of a 2 × 2. And before you can mount it, you should attach it to the center foot. Prior to making the connection, however, this foot should be fastened to the bottom end of the remaining mitered seat leg with three 6d common nails. In doing this, be sure that the leg is positioned in the left front corner of the foot (figure 19-6), and that the mitered top faces the back.

When the leg and foot are one, you can position the lower-back brace. On the center foot measure 3½ inches from the end opposite the seat leg. At this point draw a line across the board (figure 19-6). The lower-back brace will be mounted on the inside of this line. Now measure 13 inches from one end of the brace and make a mark. Lay the brace on your workbench or worktable and place the foot over it, using the inverted leg as its support (figure 19-7). Align the foot with the lines you have drawn so that 3½ inches of it extends beyond the brace and 13 inches of the brace extends beyond the same edge of the foot that the seat leg is mounted on. Check with a square to be certain that foot and brace are perpendicular, and tack them together with your 6d's.

Turn the completed section over so that the foot is at the bottom. Fit it into the frame so that the lower-back brace is resting on all three feet and is butting against the back legs (figure 19-8). Use 6d commons and nail it to the legs.

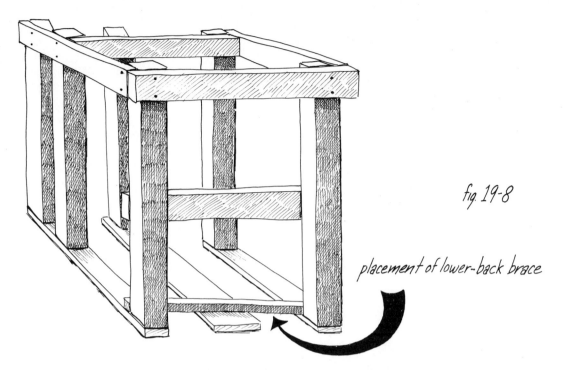

fig. 19-8

placement of lower-back brace

That center seat leg is bound to be a little wobbly. This problem can be handled in two steps. The first is to mount the seat. Place it across the mitered ends of the legs, with its upper edge flush with the front faces of the seat legs and its right end butted against the top-right frame piece (figure 19-9). Attach it with a couple of 6d's in each leg.

Mount the seat

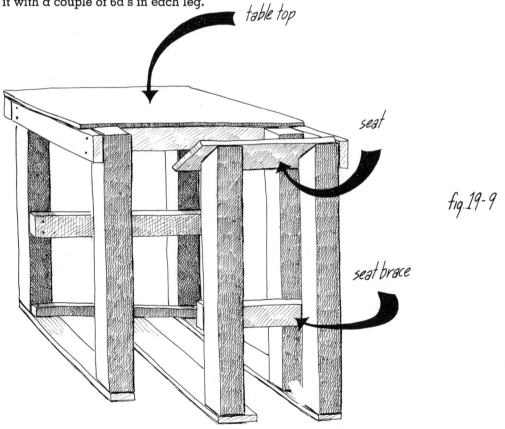

table top

seat

fig. 19-9

seat brace

Mount the seat brace

Along the inside of the right seat leg, measure down from the bottom of the top-right frame piece 22 inches. Mark the spot with a pencil. This is where the top of the seat brace will be located. Position the brace between the two seat legs, across the sides that face the interior of the unit, so that it's correctly aligned with your mark. Sit a level on it. Keeping one end aligned with your mark, move the other end up or down until the brace looks level. Mark the center seat leg. Before nailing, put the level aside and get yourself into a comfortable position. Hold the brace securely at the marks and use four 16d's to secure it (figure 19-9).

Lay the table top in position

The table top will be mounted directly to the top frame members. If all has gone well, the piece of plywood that's been cut for this purpose should fit the frame without overlap. If it doesn't, check your corners to be sure they're square. If that doesn't do it, trim the piece down to size. Lay it in position, but don't tack it down (figure 19-9).

Drill the plumb-line hole in the table top

Now you can make your measurements to locate the hole through which the axle will pass. Measure from the back of the table along the left and right sides, a length of 17⅝ inches. Mark the table at these points and connect the marks with a line. Measure 17⅝ inches along this line and mark the point—the very point where your shaft is to be located (figure 19-10). Now that you've got the point marked, you'll need to drill a small hole through it, from which a plumb line can be dropped to determine the position of the bottom ball-bearing flange pillow block, which will be mounted on the center foot. A ⅛-inch bit will do this job well. You'll also need about 32 inches of string, thread, or fishing line, a pencil, and a small weight, such as a large paper clip or a nail. Tie one end of the line to the pencil and feed the other through the hole. Pull as much of it through as the pencil will permit. If the string is either touching or almost touching the surface of the foot, you may have to cut it a bit shorter before tying on the weight. When the weight is attached, it should be able to swing freely immediately above the surface. Make certain the table top is still properly aligned. Where the weight comes to rest will indicate the point on the center foot at which to mount the pillow block (figure 19-11). Be sure to mark this place accurately. Withdraw your plumb line.

Determine the position of the pillow block on the center leg

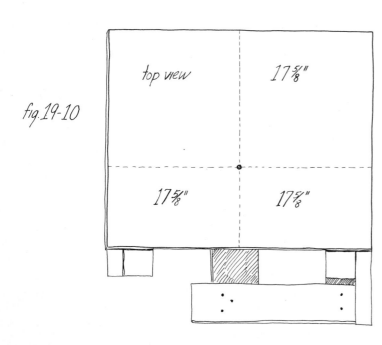

fig. 19-10

top view

17⅝"

17⅝"   17⅝"

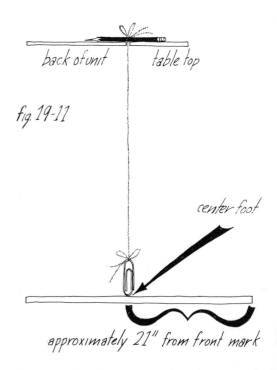

fig. 19-11

back of unit   table top

center foot

approximately 21" from front mark

Now enlarge the hole in the table. Inasmuch as the rod that we're recommending for the axle has a diameter of ¾ inch, plan on drilling this hole a little more than that.

Instead of going any further with the table, this is a good time to focus on the kick wheel, particularly if you want the concrete, which is used to weight it, to set up before you mount it. Naturally, to begin with, you'll have to build a mold. Using the four kick-wheel sides and some 6d nails construct a square frame. You can do this simply by assembling two L forms, each composed of one longer and one shorter piece (with the longer overlapping the end of the shorter), and joining them together to form the square (figure 19-12). Of course, this is only one way, and another may be more familiar to you. Once you've got the sides together, tack on the plywood bottom (also using 6d's).

Drill the axle hole in the table top

Build the kick-wheel mold

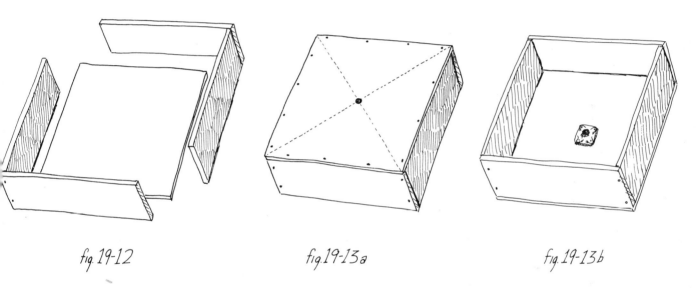

fig. 19-12   fig. 19-13a   fig. 19-13b

Now you'll need your pencil and a ruler. Draw two diagonal lines corner to corner across the plywood, thereby marking the center of the board (figure 19-13). At this point drill a hole having the same diameter as the one that you drilled in the table. Turn the unit over with the plywood down.

Now it's time to prepare the axle for installation. (The axle is the 36-inch-long steel rod.) First you will have to change bits in your drill; this time the one you want should be large enough in diameter to drill a hole that can accommodate a ⅜-inch stabilizer rod. Mount the axle in a vise. Measure in 4 inches from one end. At that point drill a hole. Loosen the vise grip just enough to enable you to rotate the rod about 90 degrees. Measure in 5 inches beyond the first hole and drill another (figure 19-14). Keep in mind that starting a hole in a cylindrical metal shaft can be a little tricky. The main thing is to keep your drill steady on the mark. Sometimes a little nick made with a file or a hacksaw can really make a difference when you're trying to do this.

When the holes are both made, remove your axle from the vise and feed it through the hole in the bottom of the kick-wheel mold so that about 3½ inches are extending through the plywood and the first of the holes that you've just drilled is adjacent to the inside bottom surface of the mold. Feed the two ⅜-inch steel stablizer rods through the axle so that an equal amount extends out both sides (figure 19-15).

Drill the axle hole in the kick-wheel bottom

Drill the stabilizer-rod holes in the axle

Insert the axle into the kick-wheel mold and insert the stabilizer rods into the axle

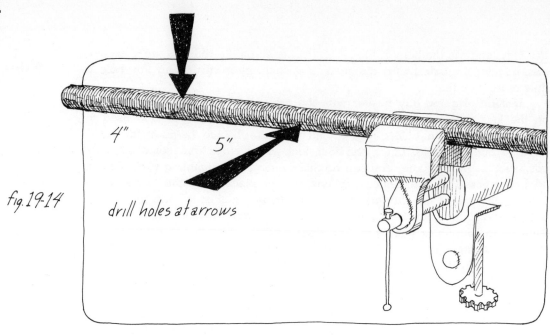

fig. 19-14

4"   5"

drill holes at arrows

**Attach the temporary
stabilizer board**

Place the whole mold-and-axle unit securely upon two sturdy chairs so that the axle can continue to extend through the bottom of the mold. Make certain that the mold is absolutely level; if it isn't, shim up the low corner or side with a piece of scrap wood or even a book. (You can remove this shim before you pour the concrete.) To straighten the axle up and keep it vertical while pouring the concrete, you'll need a temporary means of holding it. This is where the stabilizer board comes in handy. Draw a midline on this board. At 9 inches from one end make a mark on the midline. With the same bit that you used to drill the axle hole in the table top and the mold bottom, drill a hole at this mark. Feed the stabilizer board over the axle and align its ends with the top edges of opposite sides of the mold (figure 19-16). Hold a level against the axle to make certain that it's absolutely vertical. Since the hole is a little too large for the axle, you will have to shim it up with

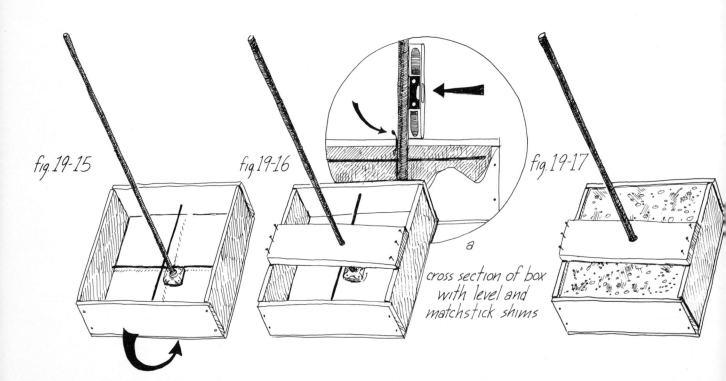

fig. 19-15   fig. 19-16   a   fig. 19-17

cross section of box
with level and
matchstick shims

cardboard or matchsticks or whatever (figure 19-16a). Then tack down the stabilizer board with two 6d nails on each side. But do not drive the nails in all the way. When the stabilizer board is secure, you can remove any shims from underneath the mold.

To prepare the concrete, read the bag! Sakrete comes premixed and ready to use. Just add water in the right proportion and fill the frame. Do this carefully, being certain to distribute the weight evenly. It's a great asset to have a well-balanced kick wheel. When the frame has been entirely filled (figure 19-17), set it aside. It's best to allow about two days for it to set up. During this period wet it down occasionally. This will prevent powdering and will generally strengthen the material.

While you're waiting for the concrete to harden, attach the ball-bearing flange pillow blocks. Locate one on the foot over the spot that you marked with the plumb line, centering it relative to that point as best you can. Remove the table top and mount the other pillow block on its underside, aligning it carefully with the hole for the axle (figure 19-18). Leave the table top off.

Also while you're waiting, you can prepare the two disks—the kick-wheel top and the throwing wheel. Start with the kick-wheel top. This is not very difficult, but, without the aid of an electric saber saw, it may take some time. First, find the center by drawing diagonals corner to corner. At their intersection tack a nail partway into the plywood. Tie a pencil to a string and tie the string to the nail, leaving 15 inches between the nail and the point of the vertically held pencil. Keep the string taut and run the pencil, always held

Fill the mold with concrete

Mount the pillow blocks

Cut out the kick-wheel top and the throwing wheel

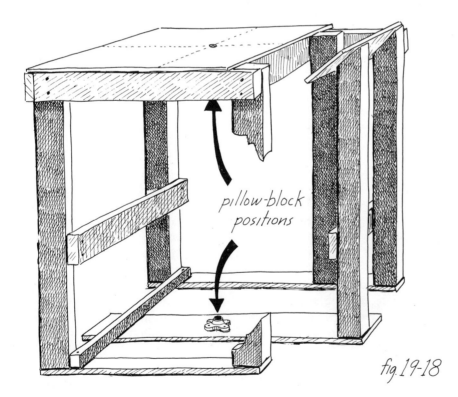

pillow-block positions

fig. 19-18

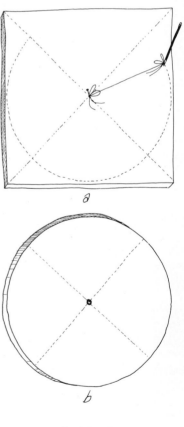

a

b

fig. 19-19

vertically, all around the plywood (figure 19-19). The trail that it will leave should be a circle having a diameter of 30 inches. Cut it out with your saw—an electric saber or jig or a hand-powered coping saw. Repeat the same procedure for the throwing wheel, but here make the distance between the nail and the pencil point a modest 6 inches. Put the completed throwing wheel aside for the time being.

Attach the kick-wheel top to mold

When the cement is dry at last, you can remove the stabilizing board. Drill a hole, large enough to accommodate the axle, through the center of the kick-wheel top. The bit that you used for the holes in the table top and the bottom piece of the kick wheel will be fine here. This hole should be located at the center of the circle. When it's drilled, slip the disk over the axle (figure 19-20a) so that it comes to rest on the frame, over the cement (figure 19-20b). Nail it to the frame with the 4d finishing nails, using about three on each side.

fig. 19-20

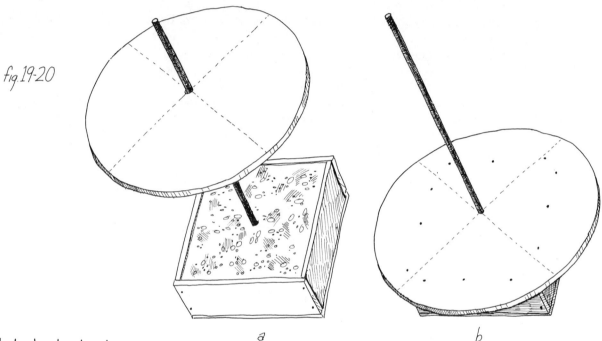

a   b

Install the kick wheel and nail down the table top

With the kick wheel assembled, you had best prepare yourself for some exercise. Your next job is to position it in the frame structure so it will be, in effect, suspended between the bearing on the center foot and the one on the table. Actually, unless you are accustomed to lifting heavy objects, we heartily suggest that you summon someone to help you. Lift the kick wheel over the bearing flange pillow block in the center foot and slowly lower the axle into it. Before it goes all the way through and comes to rest on the wood of the foot itself, hold it steady, reach underneath with your allen wrench, and tighten the allen screws around the axle (figure 19-21). Continue supporting it as you lower the table top into position over the axle. Tighten the allen screws in the table-top bearing pillow block. With the table top correctly aligned, proceed to tack it down with 4d finishing nails, four on each side.

Mount the threaded flange on the throwing wheel

Mount the pegs on the throwing wheel and attach the throwing wheel to the axle

At this point, one thing that will be rather conspicuously missing is the throwing wheel. At the center of this disk attach the threaded flange, taking care to align it well. When you've got this done, drill three holes through the wood, using a ⅜-inch bit. Distribute them unevenly around the flange (figure 19-22). Into these push three ⅜-inch T nuts on the top face of the disk, the side opposite the flange. From the flanged side screw three 1½-inch stove

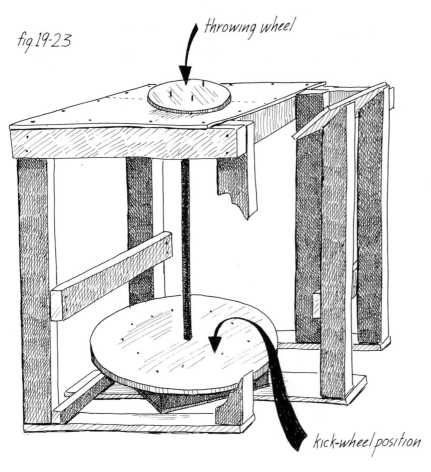

fig. 19-23

throwing wheel

kick-wheel position

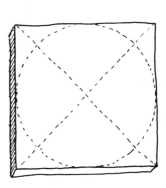

box bottom

axle → ←allen wrench

fig. 19-21

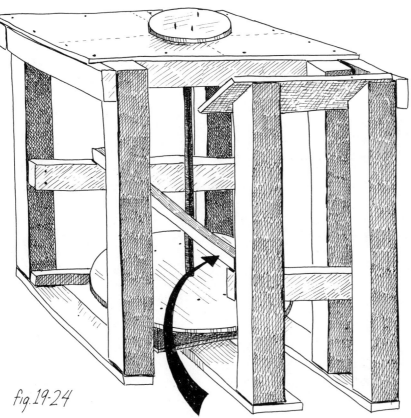

fig. 19-24

fig. 19-22

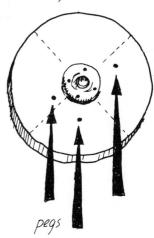

pegs

bolts through the T nuts. When fully tightened, these bolts will stick out about ¾ inch, providing a key for plaster bats (figure 19-23). Then, twist the flange onto the threaded end of the axle until it's snug.

Mount the seat-to-back brace

To add to the overall stability of your unit, there are just a few more braces that we think you should add. One of them doubles as a foot rest, a nice thing to have on a kick wheel. For this you use the seat-to-back brace and four 10d common nails. As its name implies, it runs from the seat brace to the middle-back brace. To mount it, lay it over the seat brace at the left end and over the middle-back brace at the same distance from the right side of the frame (figure 19-24). Carefully nail it in place.

Trim the side braces and attach them

The sizes given for the right- and left-side braces are approximations. In actuality, these must be trimmed down to fit before you mount them. Hold the left-side brace up to its side on the frame as shown in figure 19-25. Mark off the areas to be cut, then remove it, and cut the excess away. Reposition and secure it with 4d's. Repeat with the longer right-side brace.

Mount the table back

All that remains now are the table sides, front, and back. These keep down the mess by catching wet clay in flight. All but the front are 1×6's, the front being a 1×4. Begin by mounting the back piece. Measure down 2 inches from the table at two points along the back. Run a line across the top-back frame piece connecting these points. Hold the table back adjacent to this line and nail it on with three or four 4d finishing nails.

Mount the table sides

The side pieces will overlap the back piece at both ends and should be mounted the same distance down their respective sides. Use the same marking procedure as with the back. When securing these, be sure to overlap and nail into the edges of the back piece (figure 19-26). Again use the 4d's.

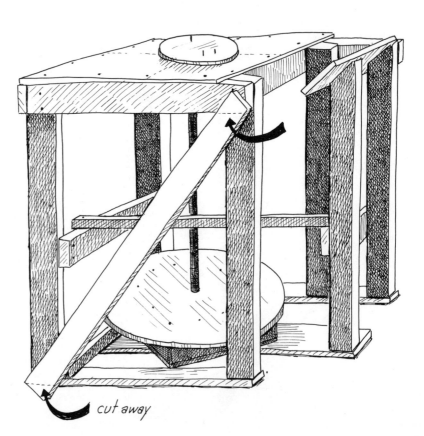

fig. 19-25

cut away

The front piece is put on in a different manner. Unlike the others, it sits right on the table top. Coat the bottom of this piece with waterproof wood adhesive and place it in position (figure 19-26). Drive 4d's through the side pieces into the ends of the front piece.

The bats themselves can be cast right on the throwing wheel (head). To do this, it's necessary to make a mold that will prevent the plaster from running off the edge. The wide flat metal edging used to accomplish this can be affixed with a few staples. In the interest of assuring that you will be able to remove the bats once cast, coat all surfaces, including the key screws, with tincture of green soap. Then pour the plaster. As long as everything is already set up for it, consider making several bats. This way, when you remove the edging, you can just put it away somewhere (at least until you've used up the ones that you've made).

When you've gotten this far, start kicking!

Mount the table front

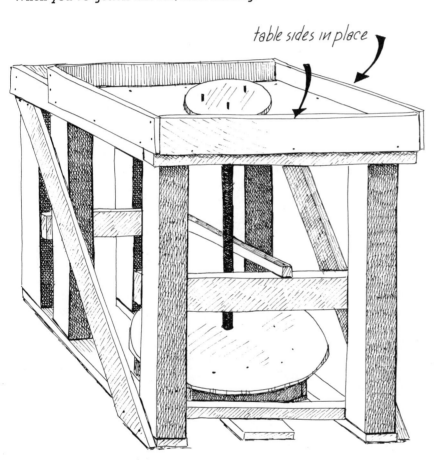

table sides in place

fig. 19-26

20·WEDGING BOARD

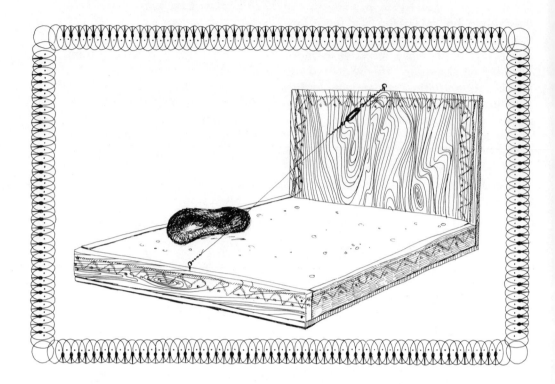

Thoughts of wedging boards take us back to that summer in West Liberty, West Virginia, in 1964. It was on the second floor of a building erected toward the end of the nineteenth century, one of two identical buildings that had been joined by a columned breezeway in the early 1960s. That second floor was the location of the art department of a small state college that had been in those hills since before the Civil War. The room was large and bright with light blazing through huge old double-hung windows that provided an exhilarating view of the rolling West Virginia countryside. This was the pottery department. There all the pottery that was produced in West Liberty that summer was shaped, glazed, and fired. Most of the rich, red clay that we used came from the nearby Ohio River. It was kept in a large clay bin that stood near the center of the room. And behind this sat the wedging board. We'd never seen one before, and the thing that was most impressive about it was the feeling we had while looking at it that the old building had kind of grown up around it. You couldn't help but wonder how many hands had pounded clay against it. It was a beautiful old tool. When you worked the clay, it seemed to press comfortably against its surface. We both remember standing there cutting the red pieces by pressing them against the wire, pounding and kneading them together, and looking out the window and feeling very connected with the earth.

All they had in West Liberty, West Virginia, were the basic tools, nothing very elaborate—a few modeling stands, a small kiln, a clay bin, some modeling tools, glazes, and that wedging board. Working with the clay on the wedging board was somehow reminiscent of playing with dough as a child in mom's kitchen, making snakes and horses while she pounded and rolled the stuff that would become yeast bread or fruit pie.

Years later, when we finally felt the need to have a wedging board in our own studio, we set out to make one. And the one we wanted to build was the one we had used in West Liberty. While the tool that you make may not have a history behind it, if it's well-made and it's handmade, then it has one in front of it. We tried to find one, just like the old West Liberty wedging board, but just couldn't do it—nothing in stock, too slick, not big enough, too big, and on and on. Sometimes building it yourself is the only way.

To begin with, you want your wedging board to be sturdy. Think what it would feel like to be a wedging board, enduring all that pounding, punching, and smashing. Definitely make it strong. The work surface of a wedging board is plaster poured into a frame. The good wedging board also has a backboard and a cutting wire. For stability and strength the backboard should be a part of the basic frame structure, and we suggest using ¾-inch plywood throughout. Half of a 4- by 8-foot sheet will be more than enough. Alternately, if you have access to some shelving board this will make a very fine substitute for the front and side pieces. To assemble the wooden framework, use wood screws and white glue to ensure strength at the joints. This is not to say that using nails would necessarily be inadequate, but screws, for the little extra effort in installing them, provide a greater margin of durability. With the aid of an awl and a screw starter the additional work involved in this procedure is minimal.

This project is a particular joy because it involves plaster. Plaster provides a delightful sensory experience. It sets up fast and gently heats while doing it. Whether clay is in the liquid or the plastic state, plaster absorbs moisture from it. And this is the basis for the relationship between potters and plaster, and it is the reason that we use it here. There are many different kinds of plaster available. Perhaps the best known to potters is U.S. Gypsum's pottery plaster, but in the construction of this tool any good grade of plaster will suffice. In purchasing, try not to buy more than you'll be able to use up in a few weeks unless you have an air-tight place to store it. To mix plaster properly, plan to use about 3 pounds for every quart of water. And always add the plaster to the water, sprinkling it to avoid lumps. Stir it with your hands to drive out the air—about three minutes ought to be enough. You'll know that the plaster is ready to pour when it starts to thicken. When pouring plaster, it's best to slightly overestimate the amount that will be needed so that, as it begins to set up, you can run a straightedge over the top to ensure that the plaster will be evenly distributed. But don't overestimate too much, and pour it right away. If plaster sits a little too long and gets a bit too hard, it's useless. So you've got to move fast. We've unintentionally plaster-lined more buckets than we should probably mention. It's a waste of plaster and a devil to clean up. Fortunately, at least the cleanup problem can be avoided by using a paper bucket. After you've finished the job, just throw it away. Plastic buckets aren't bad in that you can remove hardened plaster by pressing and bending the sides until the plaster cracks out.

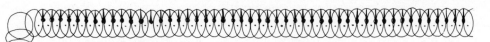

ASSEMBLY

Wood

Quantity	Material	Cut to	Description
1 section	¾-inch plywood	2½ by 25½ inches	front
2 sections	¾-inch plywood	2½ by 18 inches	sides
1 section	¾-inch plywood	15 by 25½ inches	backboard
1 section	¾-inch plywood	19½ by 25½ inches	bottom

Hardware and Other Stuff

Quantity	Material
20	No.8 roundheaded wood screws,[a] 1½ inches long
	pottery plaster
2 sections	wire mesh, 18 by 24 inches
1 length	No.20 rustproof piano wire, 18 inches long
1 length	No.20 rustproof piano wire, 6 inches long
1	small turnbuckle
2	1⅛-inch eye screws
	glue
	water-resistant lacquer

[a] To attach the bottom you may wish to substitute twelve No. 8 flatheaded screws

Attach the front to the sides

The first part of the assembly is to attach the front piece to each of the side pieces to form a large U. Two wood screws and a smear of glue will render each joint secure. Drive the screws at least ¼ inch in from the edges of the front piece, one above the other and with 1½ to 2 inches between them (figure 20-1).

fig 20-1

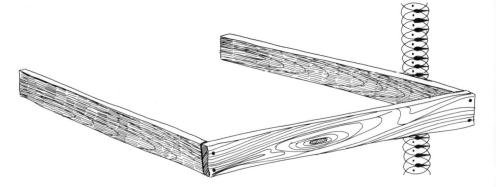

Attach the backboard to the sides

When the U-shaped assembly has been completed, stand the backboard in position against it. At the lower rear of each side of the backboard mark the approximate location of the side pieces. Lay the backboard down, rear side up, and depress two screw holes in each marked area. Begin driving the screws. With all four started, coat the back edges of the side pieces with glue and raise the backboard into position again. Continue driving the screws until the joints are tight (figure 20-2).

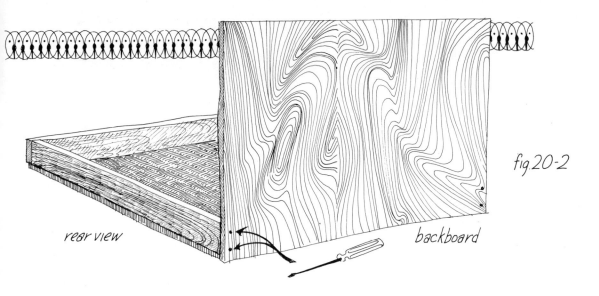

fig. 20-2

rear view   backboard

Now invert the unit on your workbench or table with the backboard hanging over the edge. Position the bottom piece and secure it with glue and twelve wood screws (figure 20-3).

Attach the bottom to the frame

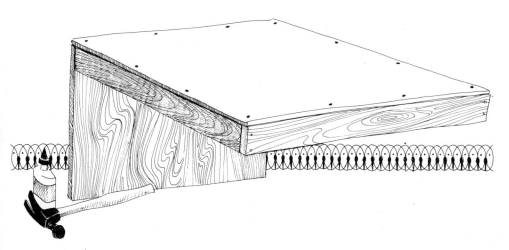

fig. 20-3

Turn the unit over, and you're ready to pour the plaster. We're suggesting that you pour the plaster in three layers, each layer separated by wire mesh. This is a precaution against cracking. Rather than mixing all the plaster that it will take to completely fill the frame at once, prepare only enough for one layer at a time. Pour the first layer of plaster about ¾ inch deep and lay a wire mesh over it. Quickly mix and pour the second layer, again about ¾ inch (figure 20-4). Press the second piece of mesh in place. Follow this up with a third and final layer, this time pouring slightly more than you need. Run a ruler or other straightedge over it to even it off (figure 20-5).

Pour the plaster

For the cutter, No.20 rustproof piano wire is recommended. The cutting wire will literally run up the middle of the wedging board and must withstand a good bit of use. In order for it to cut cleanly through the clay, it has to be very taut. The most commonly used way of keeping it taut is with a

Install the cutting wire

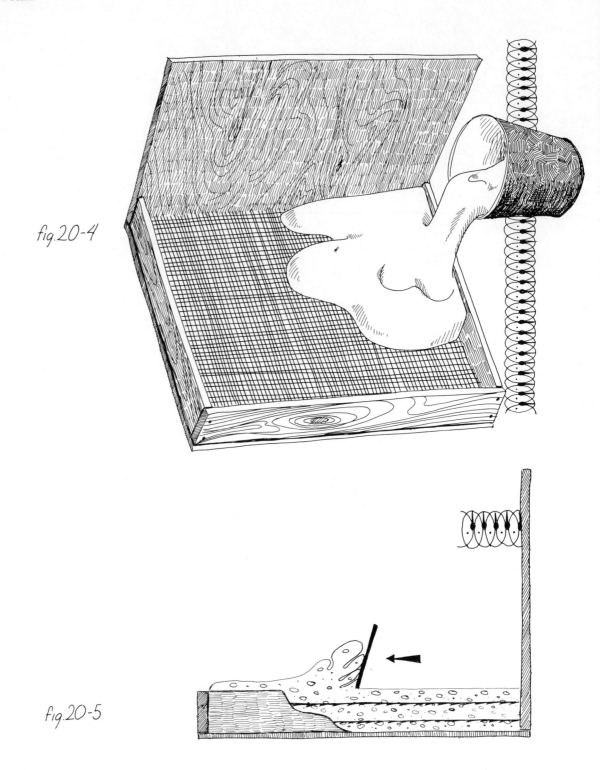

fig. 20-4

fig. 20-5

turnbuckle. This is a clever device made of two eye bolts driven into either end of a sort of rectangular metal frame. When the frame is turned in one direction, the bolts loosen; in the other way they tighten. With this action the wire to which it is attached will do the same (figure 20-6). Drive an eye screw at the center of the top edge of the backboard and another in the same position on the front piece. At the backboard attach a short length of wire, running one end through the eye and twisting it several times around itself.

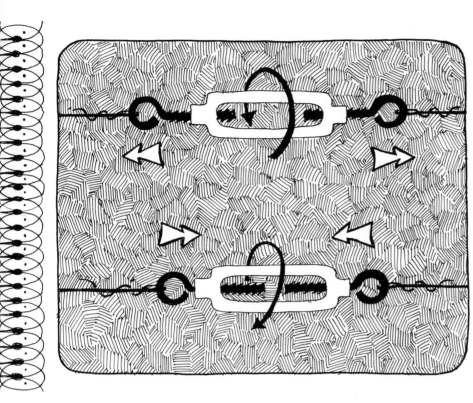

fig. 20-6

You should have about 4 inches left hanging after twisting. Connect the free end to an eye in the turnbuckle, twisting in the same manner. To the other side of the turnbuckle attach a piece of wire long enough to be secured at the turnbuckle and at the eye screw located on the front piece. In tying up this line, try to pull it as tight as you can. Don't worry if you're not in shape. The turnbuckle will do the rest.

When you've got the wire the way you want it, your construction work is done. If you'd like to put a finish on the wood, brush on a water-resistant lacquer. Allow the plaster a few days to really set before subjecting it to heavy use. While you're waiting, you can try woodburning decorative patterns or personal notations on the side pieces. Remember, this is a potential heirloom or, at the very least, a companion.

Apply a coat of finish

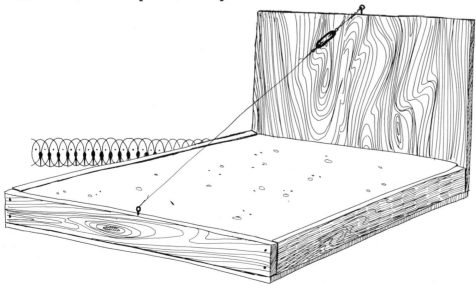

fig. 20-6a

21·ELECTRIC TABLE KILN

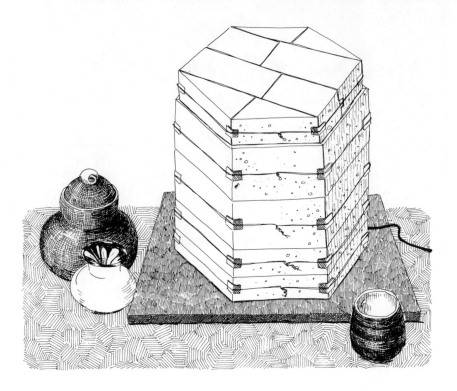

An electric kiln is a very hot place where clays go to harden and glazes go to glaze. It draws its power from the current in your wall, which passes through the circuit breaker or fuse and through the wires that also give power to toasters, radios, refrigerators, and television sets. Most of the time the wires that feed one part of the house don't feed another. Each feeding system is called a circuit, and there are several circuits in all, each doing a different kind of job and each connected to its own fuse or circuit breaker. Just as you can only put so many cars in a tunnel at any one time, or so much water into a hose, each circuit has room for just so many appliances before it gets filled to its capacity and something happens. Usually the circuit breaker snaps open or the fuse burns out, telling you that something has to go. But sometimes this doesn't happen, and when it doesn't, things can get dangerous.

Anyway, an electric kiln does feed off this system, and it has a large appetite. And it doesn't like to share. It usually takes quite a while for a kiln to come up to its working temperature, and all the while it's eating. Needless to say, if the circuit that feeds it isn't equipped to handle it, something very unpleasant might well occur. Therefore, to sum it up, we're recommending that you build this kiln only if you have a 110-volt, 20-amp circuit, and no other electrical devices will be attached to it while it's in use. If you do have such a circuit, you'll find this ½-cubic-foot-capacity kiln a real value, both in terms of the investment you make in time putting it together and money you spend collecting the needed parts. If it's difficult to find suppliers in your area who handle these parts, try writing to any one of the following mail-order suppliers: Sculpture House, Inc., 38 E. 30th St., New York, N.Y. 10016; Stewart Clay Company, 133 Mulberry St., New York, N.Y. 10013; or Dick Blick, P.O. Box 1267, Galesburg, Ill. 61401.

ASSEMBLY

Hardware and Other Stuff

Quantity	Material
29	insulating refractory bricks,[a] 9 by 4½ by 2½ inches
30 sections	tin, cut to approximately 2 by 4 inches [b]
5 lengths	baling wire, 5 feet long [c]
25 pounds	high-temperature cement [d]
2 lengths	.045 (B&S No.16) Kamthal A-1 resistance wire, 54 feet long
1 length	.045 (B&S No.16) Kamthal A-1 resistance wire, 2 feet long
1	⅜-inch rod
3	⅛-inch bolts, 3½ inches long
6	nuts for ⅛-inch bolts
9	washers for ⅛-inch bolts
1 length	No.12 [e] heater cord [f] with heavy-duty male plug [g]
1 piece	slate, at least 18 inches square
1 sheet	large drawing paper

[a] Johns-Manville or Armstrong, rated between N23 and N26.
[b] An ordinary tin can will be sufficient for about three pieces.
[c] Plus one small scrap.
[d] Or one can of furnace cement.
[e] Or No.14.
[f] Type HPD, HS, AFS, or equivalent.
[g] Rated for 20 amps at 125 volts.

The base of the kiln is a hexagonal shape measuring 9 inches on each side and consisting of two layers of brick. Begin by making a pattern for the base on paper. Draw a circle having a 9-inch radius (figure 21-1a). Keeping the setting at 9 inches, place the point of the compass at any location on the circumference and intersect the circle with an arc (figure 21-1b). Continue in that manner all the way around the circle. Connect all the intersections with straight lines (figure 21-1c), generating the hexagon. Cut out the outline (figure 21-1d).

Make the hexagonal pattern

Before starting the brickwork, we'd like to make one recommendation: Cut, fit, and assemble all brickwork dry, prior to the final assembly with cement, to insure proper fit. Now lay out the first course of six base bricks in the formation shown in figure 21-2 and overlay it with the paper pattern. Mark each side brick where the corner of the pattern meets its edge (figure 21-3). Using either a backsaw or hacksaw (or a circular power saw with a masonry blade), cut the bricks as shown in figures 21-4a and b. Use the triangular pieces marked A to complete the hexagon at locations C. Save the rectangular B piece for the secondary course. To lay out the second course of brick, follow the same procedure as for the first course. However, the assembly should be done on top of the first course and rotated 60 degrees, aligned as illustrated in figure 21-5. This will complete the base.

Cut and assemble the two base courses

In building the sides, you'll be using twelve bricks, and each will have to be cut to fit as illustrated in figure 21-6. The same saw that you used on the base will do well here too. Stand all twelve side bricks on edge as they will be in the final assembly and line them up. Find the midline on the top surfaces of all the bricks. At each end of each brick measure down about ½

Cut scarfing in the side bricks

inch from the midline. (The exact amount doesn't matter as long as they are all the same.) Make cut *A* on the midline of each brick down that ½ inch (figure 21-7*a*). Lay each brick down on its side and make cut *B* that same ½ inch down from the top edge and parallel to it until you meet cut *A* (figure 21-7*b*). Take care when sawing not to leave rough edges. Slight unevenness can be smoothed out by rubbing the surfaces against each other.

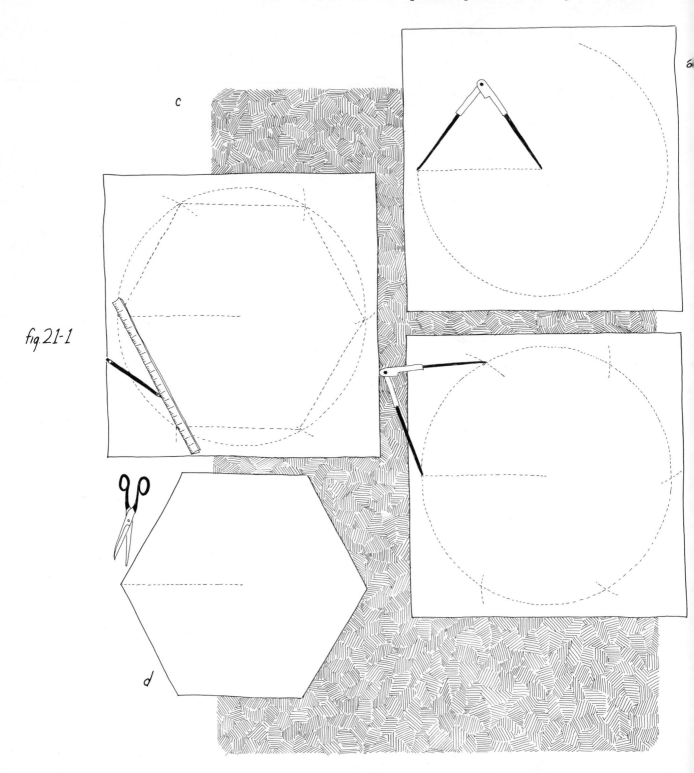

fig. 21-1

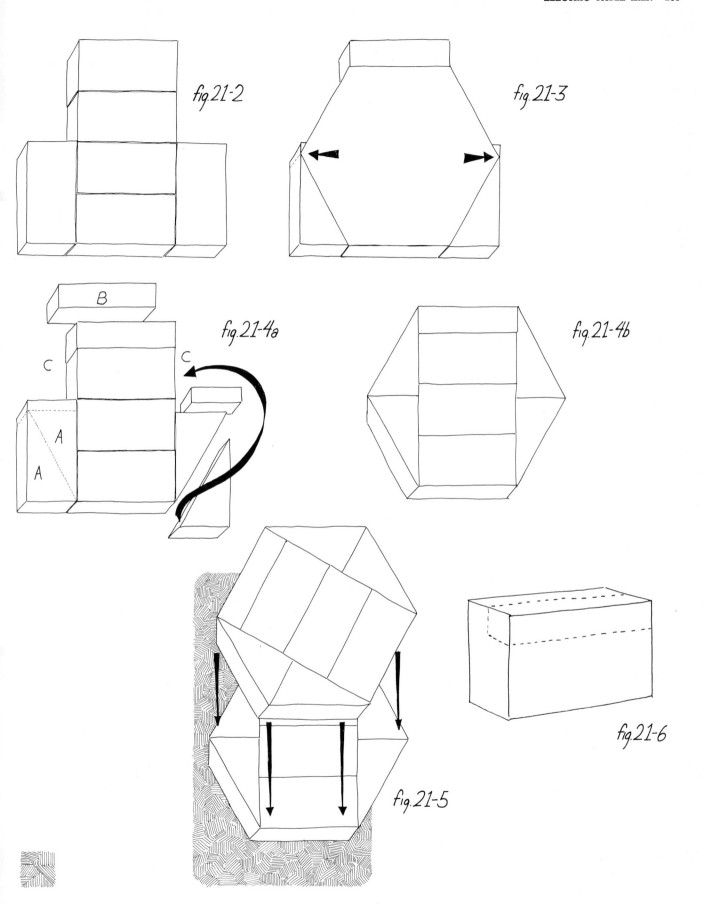

fig. 21-2

fig. 21-3

fig. 21-4a

fig. 21-4b

fig. 21-5

fig. 21-6

B

C

C

A

A

A

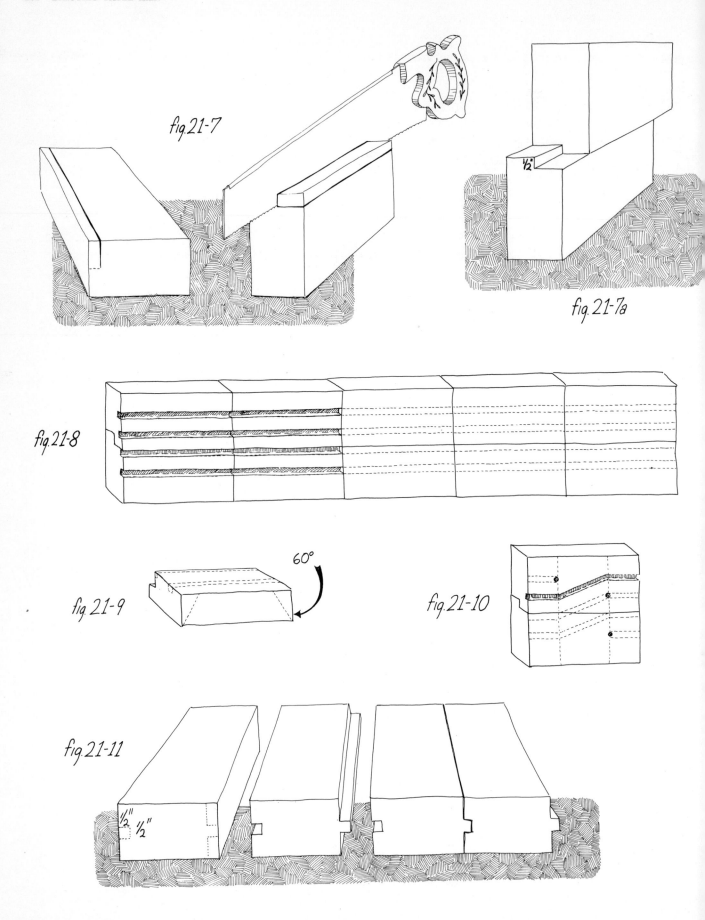

fig. 21-7

fig. 21-7a

fig. 21-8

60°

fig. 21-9

fig. 21-10

fig. 21-11

When all of the bricks are cut, lay them out as shown in figure 21-8 so that you can mark off the location of the grooves that will accommodate the heating elements. Each groove should be ½ inch wide and separated from the next by ¾ inch. The lowest should be 1¾ inches up from the bottom and the highest 1½ inches down from the top.

But don't cut them out yet. First you've got to trim down the corners of the bricks to enable the walls to take proper shape. Mark and cut the ends of the bricks at an angle of 60 degrees (figure 21-9). A miter box here will ensure accuracy.

When all of the trimming is done, cut out the grooves. Make them about ⅝ inch deep. All that this involves, at least in ten of them, is making parallel cuts with the saw and carefully removing the area between them with a chisel. In the remaining two bricks, however, three holes have to be drilled with a ⅛-inch bit in the grooves all the way through the bricks as illustrated (figure 21-10). Note that the channel is routed to allow each heating element to drop one step lower.

You should now have six bricks left. These will make the top cover. For a tight fit and for rigidity, cut a tongue and groove into each of them. Make each groove (and tongue) ½ inch deep (figure 21-11). As a result of this, the perimeter of the top will be smaller than the outside perimeter of the walls. Lay out the bricks in the arrangement illustrated in figure 21-12. Align the remote end of brick 1 with the close end of brick 6 (note the arched arrow).

Mark the grooves for the elements

Miter the ends of the side bricks

Cut the grooves for the elements and drill the holes for the power lines

Cut tongues and grooves into the top bricks

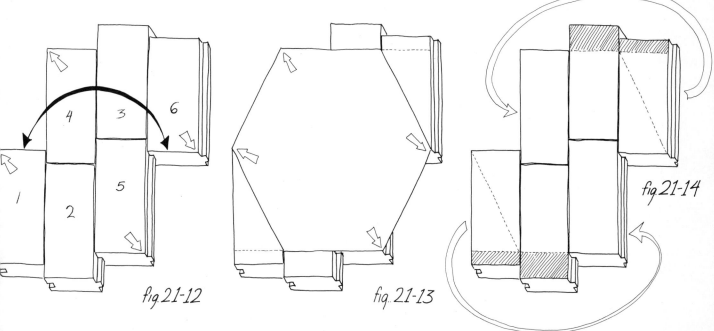

fig. 21-12

fig. 21-13

fig. 21-14

Cut and assemble the top bricks

Place the paper hexagon pattern over this arrangement, keeping in mind that it's a bit too large. Adjust the arrangement so that the close end of brick 3 is aligned with the close side of the hexagon and the remote end of brick 4 is aligned with the remote side of the hexagon. Trim the pattern so that its remote-right corner falls on the joint of bricks 5 and 6, its close-left corner falls on the joint of bricks 1 and 2, and its other four corners fall on the corners of the outside bricks that are indicated by short arrows in figures 21-12 and 21-13. Draw a line around this revised irregular-hexagon pattern and cut the bricks as shown in figure 21-14. Pieces A will fit into spaces C. The completed top piece is shown in figure 21-15.

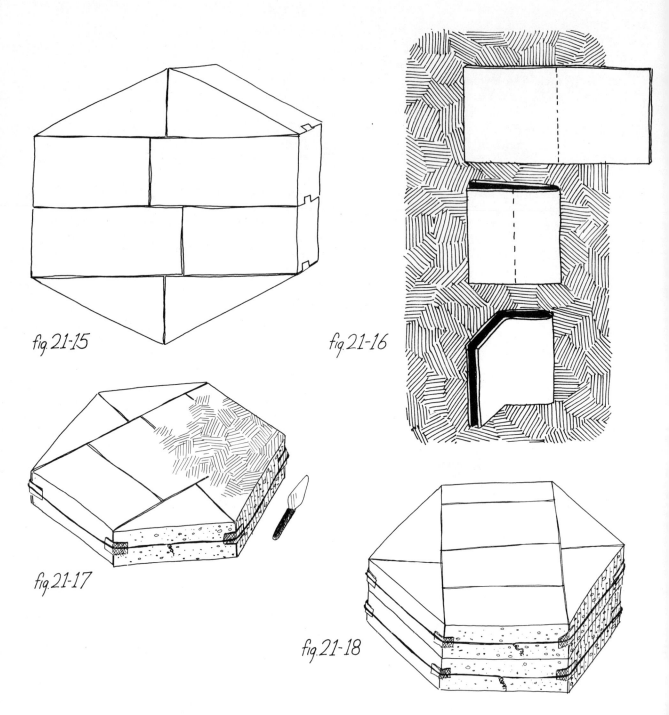

fig. 21-15

fig. 21-16

fig. 21-17

fig. 21-18

Fold the corner protectors

Cement the bricks together
and bind with wire

To complete the preparations, you will have to shape the corner protectors. These are the 2- by 4-inch sections of tin. Fold each piece in half and each half in half again (figure 21-16).

Everything is now prepared for final assembly. Thinly butter with cement all joints of the first course of the base. Assemble it in the same way that you did when it was dry. Place the corner protectors on each corner and bind the whole thing together with baling wire. Twist the wire ends until the assembly is secure (figure 21-17). Butter the top surface of the first course and the joints of the second course. Assemble the second course atop the first. Wire it up with baling wire, and don't forget the corner protectors (figure

21-18). Butter all the contacting surfaces of the first course of the wall (figure 21-19). Put it together and wire it up. Repeat the process for the second course. Then assemble the top. It too gets buttered and wired. Set the whole unit aside and allow it to dry for at least twenty-four hours.

While the kiln structure is drying, the heating elements can be wound. The heater is composed of two elements, each made from resistance wire, which are connected in parallel. Wind one wire around the ⅜-inch-diameter rod (figure 21-20). Leave 2 inches of wire straight at each end. Take care not to scratch or kink the wire; all element bends should be smooth curves. When one element is finished, remove it from the rod and wind the other. Use the 2-foot length of wire to form staples, which will retain the elements once they have been installed in their grooves (figure 21-21).

When the kiln structure is completely dry, place the elements into the grooves. Carefully stretch the coils to allow each to make two loops around the kiln (figure 21-22). Install the bolts in the holes, two washers under each head, from the inside (figure 21-23). Attach the uppermost element lead to the top bolt, between washers (figure 21-24), and tighten another washer and one nut onto the protruding shank (figure 21-25). Attach the two middle element leads to the middle bolt and the lower element lead to the lower bolt in the same way.

Wind the elements

Connect the elements to the bolts

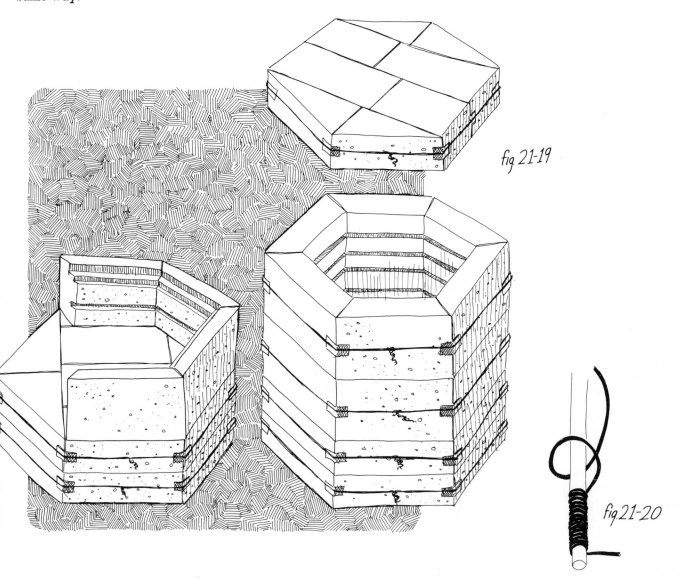

fig. 21-19

fig. 21-20

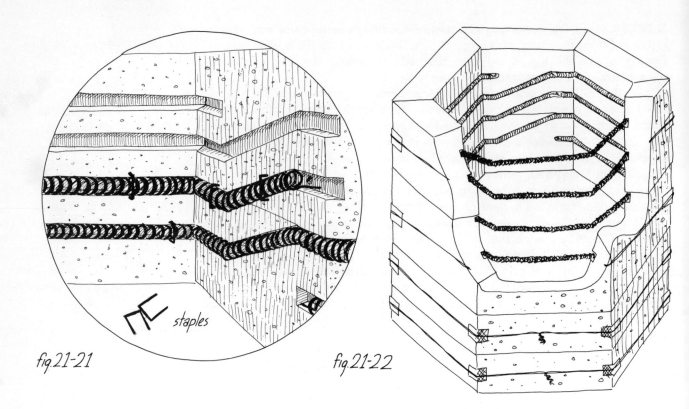

fig. 21-21

staples

fig. 21-22

Connect the heater cord
to the bolts

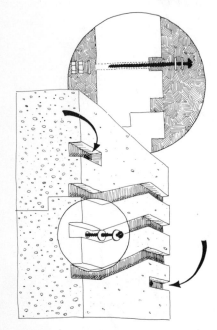

To prepare the heater cord, you'll have to strip it down somewhat un-evenly. While one line is kept rather short, the other should be about 6 inches long (figure 21-26). The shorter line is connected to the middle bolt by exposing a small bit of the metal wire at its end, forming a hook with it, placing the hook over the protruding shank of the bolt so that the wire extends out to the left, and tightening a second nut over it (figure 21-27). The longer one is connected to both bottom and top bolts. It is therefore bared to the metal in two places—on the end and also at a point somewhat lower down (figure 21-28). These areas are, in turn, wrapped around their respective bolts and secured with second nuts (figure 21-29).

fig. 21-24

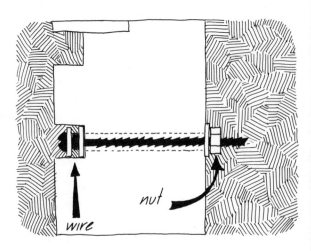

nut

wire

fig. 21-23

fig. 21-25

Strain relief can rather easily be provided for the power cord—and it should be, to help avoid difficulties that can be caused quite accidentally. All that you need to do is to attach a leftover scrap piece of baling wire between the cord and the wire used to bind the second course of the base (figure 21-30).

And finally, to complete the kiln, bore a peephole through one of the walls. Be extra careful not to damage the elements. Carve a stopper for it from a scrap piece of brick. Also, for safety your kiln should be mounted on a piece of slate or other supportive material that is, in turn, elevated over the table surface you're putting it on.

The first time you use your kiln, plug it in and carefully observe it just to be extra sure that the circuit you're in is the one that can handle the load.

Secure the heater cord to the baling wire

Bore a peephole into a wall and carve a stopper for it

Mount the kiln on a slate

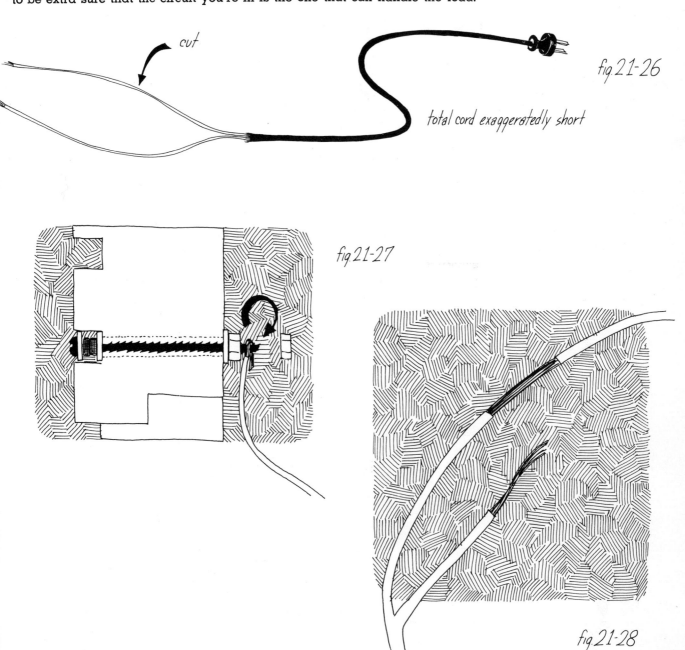

cut

fig. 21-26

total cord exaggeratedly short

fig. 21-27

fig. 21-28

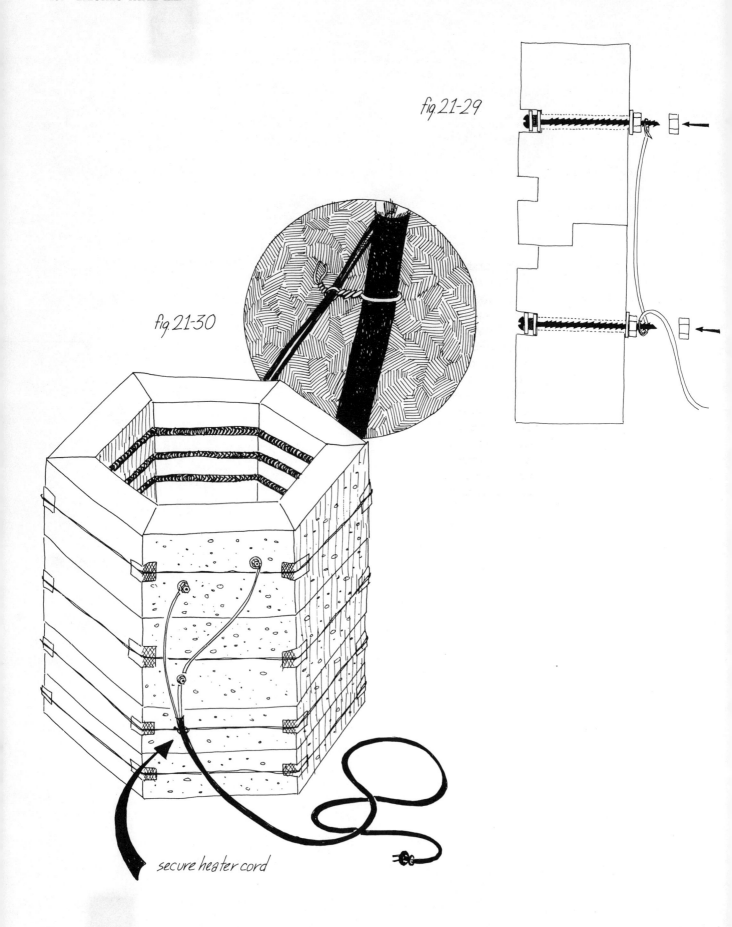

fig. 21-29

fig. 21-30

secure heater cord